JOHN TOLAND
His Methods, Manners, and Mind

This study is the first sympathetic philosophical treatment in English of the complete works of John Toland (1670–1722). Professor Daniel presents Toland as a champion of religious toleration and civil liberty whose writing is important because it brings together many of the ideas, themes, and controversies that dominated the early modern period in Europe. Best known for his call for common-sense thinking in the deist manifesto *Christianity Not Mysterious*, Toland gained notoriety as editor and biographer of Milton, Harrington, and Ludlow; translator and publicist of Giordano Bruno; pamphleteer and spy for Robert Harley; and purveyor of Hermetic and clandestine manuscripts for Prince Eugène of Savoy. A self-proclaimed pantheist, he amused, annoyed, and embarrassed such personal acquaintances as Locke, Swift, Bayle, Leibniz, Shaftesbury, and Sophie Charlotte of Prussia. His works on biblical criticism, philosophical materialism, and the Druids became sources for Diderot and Holbach; and historians of Freemasonry and of English political and diplomatic affairs continue to search for keys to the intrigue that surrounded him.

Drawing on a variety of published and unpublished material representing Toland's broad interests, Professor Daniel reveals a common theme emphasizing man's capacity for independent thought on basic philosophical, religious, and political issues. Roughly chronological, Daniel's treatment describes Toland's progressive refinement of this fundamental aspect of his thought. After examining, in his early works, the process whereby religion becomes mystified, Toland turned to biography, demonstrating that through it one can regain rational control over religion. Prejudices and superstitions, topics of the *Letters to Serena*, are shown to be overcome through corrections implicit in the principles of biographical and historical exegesis. Polemic as philosophic method required Toland to provide a doctrine of esoteric communication. In the course of his later writings this doctrine became grounded in a metaphysics suitable for the Ciceronian religion of the pantheists.

Stephen H. Daniel is a member of the Department of Philosophy at Texas A & M University.

McGill-Queen's Studies in the History of Ideas

JOHN TOLAND
His Methods, Manners, and Mind

Stephen H. Daniel

McGill-Queen's University Press
Kingston and Montreal

© McGill-Queen's University Press 1984
ISBN 0-7735-1007-9
Legal deposit second quarter 1984
Bibliothèque nationale du Québec

Printed in Canada

This book has been published with the help of a grant from the
Canadian Federation for the Humanities, using funds provided by the
Social Sciences and Humanities Research Council of Canada.

Canadian Cataloguing in Publication Data

Daniel, Stephen H. (Stephen Hartley), 1950–
John Toland: his methods, manners and mind
(McGill-Queen's studies in the history of ideas,
ISSN 0711-0995; 7)
Bibliography: p.
Includes index.
ISBN 0-7735-1007-9
1. Toland, John, 1670–1722. I. Title. II. Series.
B1393.Z7D36 1984   192   c83-099228-6

To Breaux

Contents

The only known portrait of Toland, as it appeared in vol. 3 of U. G. Thorschmid's *Versuch einer Vollständige Engländische Freydenker-Bibliothek* (1766) (By courtesy of the Sterling Memorial Library, Yale University)

Preface

FOR ALMOST THREE HUNDRED YEARS John Toland has intrigued, puzzled, and offended students of English literature, political history, theology, and philosophy. Yet just over a decade ago (in his *Utopia and Reform in the Enlightenment*), Franco Venturi expressed amazement that the work of such an "extraordinary man" had not been the object of a modern, general study. Research into specific aspects of Toland's thought has begun to occur with increasing frequency, partially filling the gap Venturi noted. But this book is the first attempt to treat Toland's work as a comprehensive whole deserving attention in its own right. His work defies the boundaries of contemporary specialization—which may explain its neglect—but attention to it is richly rewarding, especially for those seeking a broader and clearer perspective on the dynamic, many-faceted intellectual life of seventeenth- and eighteenth-century Europe.

My book is primarily a presentation of the central themes that unite Toland's writings and activities. I have not limited my treatment of the development of his philosophy to any particular periods of his life, nor have I excluded consideration of those of his works that do not fit neatly into specific categories. One of my major aims has been to show how the division of Toland's writings into religious, political, biographical, philosophical, or historical types fails to respect the integrity of his thought. Often his treatments of topics as disparate as metaphysics, polemic, and biography recur in surprisingly different contexts and separated by many years, revealing a unity of themes that prevail throughout his writings. These themes serve as focal points for my chapters.

A glance at my bibliography will reveal a number of foreign-language studies of specific aspects of Toland's thought. But particularly useful as an "analytic reconstruction" of Toland's work and philosophical relationships is Chiara Giuntini's recent general introduction, *Panteismo e ideologia repubblicana: John Toland (1670–1722)*. My own treatment, completed before I obtained Giuntini's fine study, benefits from her earlier research but focuses more on the methodological characteristics of Toland's writings.

The most recent English-language addition to Toland research is Robert E. Sullivan's *John Toland and the Deist Controversy*. Highlighting Toland's contribution to the deistic movement of the seventeenth and eighteenth centuries, Sullivan relates Toland's attempt to transform Christianity into a reasonable civic religion to the positions adopted by his predecessors and contemporaries. In contrast, my study of Toland is less concerned with these external relations than it is with the interrelations of various parts of his thought. Presented in this way Toland's writings take on a unity that is lost in paraphrasing his remarks so as to set up connections with other thinkers.

In preparing my discussion, I found the research of four authors most helpful. The articles of F. H. Heinemann describe Toland as a polemical philosopher of reason—but reason understood primarily in its eternal, not in its historical, character. A Ph.D. dissertation by Robert R. Evans ("John Toland's Pantheism: A Revolutionary Ideology and Enlightenment Philosophy") organizes Toland's thought around the theme of pantheism as primarily an ideology of political history. Especially good in placing Toland's work within the context of the political developments of his day, Evans's work indicates how political history and philosophizing about the cosmos united Toland's writings. An earlier dissertation, by Eugene I. Dyche ("The Life and Works and Philosophical Relations of John [Janus Junius] Toland [1670–1722]") attempts to show how Toland's interest in such diverse topics as biography, monetary matters, political pamphleteering, textual and biblical exegesis, metaphysics, and theology could be linked by a historical analysis of his role as a unifier of materialism and rationalism. Finally, Margaret C. Jacob's recent works on Toland as a Freemason in the scientific age of Newton highlight the sectarian character of his reaction against the world view of the Newtonian-supported factions of the Church of England.

I have received suggestions and encouragement from a number of individuals. William C. Charron and Linus Thro, S.J., made numerous comments on an early draft of the manuscript; and Giancarlo Carabelli provided me with important bibliographic information during the course of my research. Marie Kessel's careful attention greatly improved the readability and clarity of the text. James R. Groves and David Fate Norton improved the grace and style immeasurably. Beth Cheney and Joy Striplin labored many hours typing the manuscript.

The guiding force behind my work on Toland, however, has been James D. Collins, who first suggested such a book to me and who subsequently provided penetrating and thorough commentaries on early drafts. Finally, I would like to thank my wife, Breaux, for the support that made possible this book and the research behind it. Without her it would not have been written.

Abbreviations

Apology	*An Apology for Mr. Toland.*
BM Add. MS	British Museum Additional Manuscript.
CNM	*Christianity Not Mysterious.*
Collection	*A Collection of Several Pieces of Mr. John Toland.*
Defence	*A Defence of Mr. Toland in a Letter to Himself.*
"Druids"	"A Specimen of the Critical History of the Celtic Religion and Learning: Containing An Account of the Druids," in *A Collection of Several Pieces of Mr. Toland,* vol. 1.
Nazarenus	*Nazarenus: or Jewish, Gentile, and Mahometan Christianity.* Because the page numeration varies in the individual sections, they will be specified: preface, appendix, "Barnabas-Original," and "Irish Manuscript."
ONB MS	Österreichische Nationalbibliothek (Vienna) Manuscript.
Pantheisticon	*Pantheisticon: or, the Form of Celebrating the Socratic Society.* Unless noted otherwise, citations refer to the location in the English translation, followed (in parentheses) by the location in the Latin original.
Portland MSS	*The Manuscripts of the Duke of Portland.*
PRO	Public Record Office, London.
Serena	*Letters to Serena.*

JOHN TOLAND

Introduction

ALTHOUGH MOST MODERN READERS first encounter John Toland in the context of the English deistic movement of the seventeenth and eighteenth centuries, one also finds references to Toland in studies of Milton, the Druids, the origins of Freemasonry, English political and diplomatic history, the Newtonians, the history of biblical criticism, the history of the Jews in England, and even the history of geology. In addition, Toland's name now appears with regularity in studies of John Locke, Jonathan Swift, and the Renaissance philosopher Giordano Bruno. As a personal acquaintance of G. W. Leibniz, Pierre Bayle, Anthony Ashley Cooper (third earl of Shaftesbury), Baron von Hohendorf (the chief lieutenant of Prince Eugène of Savoy), Princess Sophie Charlotte of Prussia, and Robert Harley (first earl of Oxford), Toland attracted the attention of many of the most influential figures of his era.

The topics Toland addressed indicate not only the range of his interests but also the inclination of writers of his age to view such topics as interrelated. One theme uniting much of the discussion of the period is religion, but even within discussions of religion a great deal of seemingly nonreligious discourse took place. Astronomy and geology, politics and social theory, theological doctrine and biblical criticism —all were part of the great debate of the time concerning the true nature of a Christian community.[1] Underlying Whig-Tory disputes, pro- and anti-Newtonian debates, discussions about the naturalization

---

1. John Redwood, *Reason, Ridicule and Religion: The Age of Enlightenment in England, 1660–1750* (Cambridge, Mass.: Harvard University Press, 1976), pp. 10–11.

of foreigners, and arguments about religious toleration was a fear (or, for some, a hope) that human existence might be possible outside of the context of institutionalized religion.

To treat Toland's work from a religious or theological perspective alone, however, would undermine his appeal for many modern students of the cultural and intellectual history of the seventeenth and eighteenth centuries. Scholars have had reason to turn to Toland for information concerning the diplomatic history of England as well as for information concerning the circulation of rare Hermetic tracts and clandestine manuscripts. Very recent bibliographic work on Toland, which has now made it possible to appreciate the complexity and breadth of his writings, has highlighted the need for a comprehensive study of the internal relationships of themes in his writings.

By the end of the seventeenth century a growing interest in the power of human reason gave rise to the sustained deistic critique of revealed religion. The popularity of the new scientific methodology of Newton and his followers; the expectation that the "historical, plain method" of Locke might finally reveal what lay within the scope of human knowledge; and the cautious hope that with a clearer notion of history and how it could be interpreted by reason future political activity could be oriented toward the attainment of peace in an enlightened society—each of these factors contributed to the impact of the English deist movement.

Until the publication of John Toland's *Christianity Not Mysterious* (1696), however, deistic thought had exercised only minimal influence outside philosophy and religion. Following on the heels of the popularly accepted writings of Locke, *Christianity Not Mysterious* appealed to an audience beyond the universities. Its emphasis on the need for rational control over revealed religion, and the scholarship supporting its claims, intrigued laymen and embarrassed clergymen. It occasioned scores of responses from the learned world in Great Britain and elsewhere and brought Toland's book an international notoriety.

In his controversy with Bishop Stillingfleet, Locke had to disassociate himself from Toland publicly. Writers such as Leibniz, Locke, Defoe, and Swift felt compelled to respond in one way or another to Toland's seminal works on biblical criticism, ecclesiastical history, the Jewish and Irish problems in Great Britain, and the philosophic ramifications of the Protestant Succession in England.

As the major deistic thinker of the decades before and after 1700, Toland (like Marin Mersenne or Henry Oldenburg before him) conjoined ideas, movements, and thinkers. He was a key link between the English deistic movement of the early eighteenth century and deism on the Continent later in the century (involving such figures as Diderot and Holbach). With his contacts far beyond the deistic movement, Toland's interests and relationships, travels and experiences, present to us today a portrait in microcosm of early modern Europe.

1. LIFE AND WRITINGS

Almost every article or chapter devoted to Toland begins by retracing the major events of his life; and almost every one of them blends, to some degree or another, genuine information about his life with legend, lie, or exaggeration. Toland's penchant for making enemies contributed to the proliferation of slanderous reports about his origins and activities. Because he did allude, on rare occasions, to some of these rumors when he spoke about his own past, we can discern some of the facts of his life. But since Toland's life indeed included many unusual events, the problem of trying to distinguish the factual from the fictional is doubly difficult.

Probably the bastard son of an Irish cleric and his concubine, Toland was born in Londonderry, Ireland, in 1670. He was christened in the Roman Catholic Church as "Janus Junius"—the bizarre name Toland was later to employ as a pseudonym. However unusual his name, and however it may have provided subsequent interpreters with material for comment, Toland himself was spared a lifetime of attacks on it: when still a small boy at school he was given the name John in order to stop his classmates from making fun of his name every time the roll was called.

A number of stories are told of his youth, some probably apocryphal. One recounts how he was known as "John-of-the-Books" because of his learning. Another describes an encounter between the young boy and a Catholic pastor in which John's ability to debate religious matters prompted the priest to say that he felt that he had been debating the devil himself. It is reported that as a child Toland had already developed an answer for those who ridiculed him as the son of a prostitute: in a not-so-veiled slap at the clergy, he would simply remark that the concubine of a priest should not be confused with a woman of the streets.

According to Toland himself, his ability to reason (developed under the guidance of some acquaintances) was responsible for his break, at sixteen, from Catholicism, "the insupportable Yoke of the most Pompous and Tyrannical *Policy* that ever enslav'd Mankind under the name or shew of *Religion.*"[2] In 1687 he enrolled in the College of Glasgow (later, the University of Glasgow) and studied there until 1690, when he moved for a brief time to the University of Edinburgh to receive his M.A. degree.

Concerning Toland's activities in Glasgow we have only highly suspect reports. On or about the time of his eighteenth birthday he appears to have taken part in demonstrations in favor of the Glorious Revolution. Associating with Presbyterians and political dissidents, Toland directed attacks against the pope and Episcopal clergymen.[3] His association with the Presbyterians continued in Edinburgh and provided further contacts when he moved to London. During his Glasgow stay Toland also may have dabbled in some occult arts (and later would be referred to as a Rosicrucian), but it is unlikely that he had any more than a passing curiosity about such matters.

Why Toland did not receive the degree at Glasgow is a matter of conjecture. Even the principal of the college at Glasgow seemed not to know why Toland went to Edinburgh to obtain the degree.[4] The Edinburgh M.A. degree was commonly granted to Glasgow students who were not prepared to take the oath of allegiance; and Toland's involvement with the Protestant dissenters at the time might explain why he could not take the oath.[5] On the other hand, he might have alienated himself from the college by teaching philosophy in the town of Glasgow (in violation of the rules of the college), thereby drawing students away from the college.[6]

2. *An Apology for Mr. Toland* (London, 1697), p. 16.

3. Edmund Gibson (fellow of Queens College, Oxford) to Arthur Charlett (Master of University College, Oxford), 13 June and 21 June 1694, Rawlinson MS D. 923 and Ballard MS 5, fol. 46, Bodleian Library, Oxford. Also see F. H. Heinemann, "John Toland and the Age of Reason," *Archiv für Philosophie* 4 (1950): 38–40; and Robert Wodrow, *The History of the Sufferings of the Church of Scotland from the Restoration to the Revolution,* 4 vols. (Glasgow: Blackie, 1828–36), 4: 472.

4. James Fall (former principal of the College of Glasgow) to William Dunlop (then current principal of the College of Glasgow), 10 Nov. 1697, MS 9251, fols. 150–51, National Library of Scotland, Edinburgh.

5. See J. G. Simms, "John Toland (1670–1722), a Donegal Heretic," *Irish Historical Studies* 16 (1969): 305.

6. Entry for 1689–90 in the Principal's Memorandum Book for 1684–1702, Archives n. 26630, p. 8, Archives Office, University of Glasgow.

After receiving his M.A. from Edinburgh, Toland used his contacts with the dissenters, especially the Presbyterians in London, to gain acceptance to the University of Leyden to study with Friedrich Spanheim the younger. Under Spanheim, Toland learned the importance of referring to Greek and Hebrew sources in the interpretation of Scriptures and ancient works. The method of ecclesiastical history, developed by Spinoza, Bayle, Richard Simon, and Spanheim, emphasized the need to return to original sources and cast doubt on the reliability of medieval attempts at exegesis (especially by the church fathers). Spanheim served as one of Toland's methodological mentors throughout his life; and though Toland went far beyond the limits of Spanheim's exegetical teachings, he regularly kept with him a copy of Spanheim's opera.

While in Holland Toland became acquainted with some of the major figures in learned circles outside the universities. Particularly at the Rotterdam house of the English merchant Benjamin Furly, Toland joined a circle of men whose names were respected on the Continent and in England. Furly's house was the setting for the informal gatherings of the Lantern, the philosophical-literary society that included such prominent figures as Philip van Limborch and Jean LeClerc (two Dutch Remonstrant theologians) and Pierre Bayle. Among Furly's friends were Locke, Algernon Sidney, Shaftesbury, and Charles Gerard (second earl of Macclesfield). Endorsements from Furly and those in this circle would have been quite influential for an up-and-coming scholar like Toland. And apparently Toland did not miss the opportunity to benefit from such contacts. For by August 1693 he had so impressed those with whom he had come into contact that LeClerc, van Limborch, and Furly wrote to Locke in England, introducing Toland as a "freespirited ingenious man," an "excellent and not unlearned young man, . . . frank, gentlemanly, and not at all of a servile character." Though Locke would later try to disassociate himself from Toland, in 1694 he acknowledged that he had met Toland and found him to be as van Limborch and the others had described him.[7]

---

7. See Furly to Locke, 19 August 1693; van Limborch to Locke, 4 August 1693; and Locke to van Limborch, 13 January 1694, in *The Correspondence of John Locke*, ed. E. S. De Beer (Oxford: Clarendon Press, 1976–), 4: 710, 705, 780. On the Furly connection, see William Hull, *Benjamin Furly and Quakerism in Rotterdam* (Lancaster, Pa.: Lancaster Press, 1941), pp. 77–130; and Heinemann, "Toland and the Age of Reason," pp. 41–42.

Late in 1693 Toland settled in Oxford to work at the Bodleian Library, ostensibly to write an Irish dictionary and a dissertation proving that the Irish had been a colony of the Gauls. His work in the library was to go on for some time, providing him with material that was to be used in publications for the rest of his life. Later, he would remark that his access to rare works and manuscripts in languages (e.g., Celtic) unknown to many researchers gave him an advantage over many other writers.

In Oxford Toland soon became known, as one correspondent put it, as "a man of fine parts, great learning, and little religion."[8] When not working in the library, he spent a great portion of his time discoursing in coffeehouses about religious and political matters. In conservative Oxford this type of behavior made him a highly visible figure. Though word of his scholarly work spread slowly, individuals like Locke became increasingly aware of his presence. Indeed, Locke appears to have written his *Reasonableness of Christianity* at least partially in response to points raised by Toland in a manuscript copy of *Christianity Not Mysterious*.

When Toland published anonymously his most famous work, *Christianity Not Mysterious*, he was but twenty-five years old. In a few short months he became a major figure in the debates on rational religion. A second edition of the work appeared before the end of the same year, and it was on the title page of this edition that Toland's name appeared for the first time. Soon afterward, he traveled to Ireland, only to hear himself and his book attacked from the pulpit. The book was condemned by the Irish Parliament, and Toland had to flee the country in order to avoid being arrested. For at least the next five years he spent a great deal of energy defending his "juvenile thoughts" (as he called them) before finally deciding not to endorse further printings of the work.

Toland's learning and his free-spirited method of inquiry attracted the attention of patrons like Shaftesbury and Harley. His relationship with Shaftesbury developed within the context of a shared interest in antiquity, philosophy, religion, and opposition to superstition. Although both men also agreed in their support of the Revolution of

---

8. Anonymous letter to Toland, 4 May 1694, in *A Collection of Several Pieces of Mr. John Toland*, ed. Pierre Desmaizeaux, 2 vols. (London: J. Peele, 1726), 2: 295.

1688 and of the traditional Whig ideals in general, their friendship gradually cooled as Toland became more dependent upon Harley.

Toland's problematic relationships with Shaftesbury and Harley illustrate not only the conflicts between his private and ideological interests but also the ambiguity of the positions of the political parties in England at the time. After the accession to the throne of William and Mary, Tories and Whigs began to exchange positions, as it were, on the issue of whether the king's authority derived from his selection by God (or heredity) or from his selection by the people. Between 1696 and 1700 this issue was joined through debates about permitting William's standing army to come to England. The Country Party, composed of an unusual coalition of Tories with Jacobite leanings and Whigs with republican leanings, argued against a standing army, preferring that the militia be reformed instead. Toland endorsed such an idea in *The Militia Reform'd* (1698) and thus gained the attention of Harley, the head of the Country Party.

Toland's allegiance to Harley was based on his belief that Harley strongly favored the traditional Whig ideals of the toleration of dissenting religious sects and of the Protestant Succession. With this, Shaftesbury also had no difficulty. But Shaftesbury would have nothing to do with Harley's attempt, as head of the Country coalition, also to accommodate Tory interests in maintaining royal prerogative. Because Toland was financially unable to disassociate himself completely from Harley, and because he expected that Harley would reward his fidelity with a position within the government (especially after 1704, when Harley became secretary of state), Toland tried to ally himself with Harley without endorsing Harley's Tory inclinations. Toland accordingly avoided contact with Harley for several years after William's death. He was unsuccessful, though, in his attempt to convince Shaftesbury of his own faithfulness to the Whigs; and his private interests demanded that he accommodate Harley rather than Shaftesbury.

Commissioned to write biographies of John Milton and James Harrington in 1699 and 1700, Toland developed into one of the foremost Whig writers. His *Anglia Libera* (1701), which strongly supported the Protestant Succession of the House of Hanover, became his ticket to the circles of international diplomacy. In July 1701, at Harley's request, Toland was selected as a secretary to the embassy to Hanover under Lord Macclesfield and had the honor to present the

Act of Settlement and a copy of his book to the Electress Sophia.[9] Electress Sophia, in turn, introduced Toland to the court in Berlin and to her daughter, Sophie Charlotte, queen of Prussia. Amused by his wit and attracted by his good looks and youth, the queen herself liked to walk and converse with Toland for hours at a time.

Here, in numerous discussions in the presence of the queen, Toland met Leibniz and other members of the court. Although Leibniz often expressed doubts about Toland's work and manners, he did respect the younger man's intellectual ability, and even wrote a brief reply (which Toland received with great pleasure) to *Christianity Not Mysterious*. Leibniz's letter to Sophie Charlotte (1702) on the three grades of notions and the natural light, often quoted in anthologies today, was in direct response to a letter to her from Toland about some of Leibniz's positions. The Toland-Leibniz corespondence itself continued for a number of years after 1701.

In 1698, before he left England on the mission to Hanover, Toland came into possession of Queen Elizabeth's original copy of some of Giordano Bruno's dialogues. When he corresponded with Leibniz, Toland encouraged him to read Bruno; but Leibniz remained unimpressed by Bruno's writings (as much as he was unimpressed by Toland's). In later years, Toland sent accounts of Bruno's life, death, and works to correspondents as far away as Vienna. In England and on the Continent, Toland gradually became recognized as a central figure not only in the revival of interest in the Italian thinker but also in the circulation of manuscripts and rare books containing heterodox doctrines.

From 1701 to 1707 Toland traveled to Hanover at least three times. Each time, while passing through Holland, he met individuals with whom he would later correspond and who would spread his ideas. On one of these trips Toland met with Pierre Bayle, and he later submitted material which Bayle incorporated into his *Dictionary*. On another occasion, Toland met Baron von Hohendorf, the chief lieutenant to

---

9. An anonymous engraving in the Ashmolean Museum (Oxford) depicts an individual who might be Toland presenting the Act of Settlement to the electress. The engraving is reproduced in *Poems of Affairs of State*, vol. 6, ed. Frank H. Ellis (New Haven: Yale University Press, 1970), p. 659. For Toland's relations with Harley, see Ellis's edition of Jonathan Swift, *A Discourse on the Contests and Dissentions* (Oxford: Clarendon Press, 1967), pp. 36–42.

Prince Eugène of Savoy, commander of the armies of the Austrian Hapsburgs. After this meeting, Toland was commissioned by Hohendorf to increase Prince Eugène's library of rare and clandestine works. It was in this context, especially, that Toland's interest in Bruno had widespread influence in clandestine circles.

In 1702 Toland returned to England from his second visit to Hanover and Berlin and began to work on the *Letters to Serena* (1704), in which he argued that motion was essential to matter. Not only did the work contain a refutation of Spinoza (in a letter to an anonymous Dutch follower of Spinoza); it also contained an implied refutation of some of Newton's work. Newton's name was used in the letters in various places, ostensibly to give the impression that Toland accepted Newtonian principles. But students of Newton, particularly Samuel Clarke, recognized immediately that Toland was attacking Newtonian physics because of its political implications, namely, that material individuals need motivation and organization from external (monarchical, clerical, spiritual, or divine) sources.

After Harley became Secretary of State in 1704, he employed Toland's talents in several writing projects but continued to put off Toland's requests for a more permanent position in the government. Toland's third trip to Hanover (1707) may have been at Harley's request, perhaps in response to Toland's offers to spy for Harley. Indeed, on this trip Toland made excursions to Vienna and Prague in addition to his stops in Hanover and Berlin. After returning to Holland, Toland learned, in 1708, that Harley had been forced out of office by the Whigs Marlborough and Godolphin. With Harley out of power, Toland was not to make his fortune in England. He thus remained in Holland until receiving word of Harley's return to prominence with the fall of the Whigs in 1710.

During this sojourn in Holland, Toland requested that his friends in England not notify him about political developments so that he could concentrate on biblical criticism. In his research he specifically addressed the question of how the primitive character of Christianity could be distinguished from the accumulated superstitions of centuries of institutionalization. Some of this research he published in Holland, but much of it he circulated in manuscript-form between 1709 and 1718 to friends like Anthony Collins, the English deist and freethinker. Collins, whom Toland very much liked, probably visited Toland in Holland during this time and traveled about the country with him.

When Toland learned of Harley's return to power in the Tory government of 1710, he sent his congratulations to Harley, reminding him that he (Toland) had predicted and wished for such a return. Despite Harley's Tory connections, Toland still believed that Harley was primarily concerned with maintaining the Protestant Succession and with supporting Queen Anne. Early in 1711 Toland returned to England and settled again, with the support of Harley, at Epsom. However, just as Harley was to lose favor with the queen after her brush with death early in 1714, so Toland was to lose favor with Harley after Harley was almost killed in an assassination attempt in March 1711. Enemies of Toland spread the word that the assassin was a correspondent of his; and although Toland repeatedly beseeched Harley to allow him to prove his loyalty in some foreign service, Harley turned a deaf ear to him. During 1712 and 1713 Toland's long-held views concerning religious toleration and civil liberty—which he referred to as his general principles of action—apparently overcame his special interest in serving Harley and providing a comfortable maintenance for himself, because he slackened his efforts to obtain political position through allegiance to Harley.

Particularly upset by the government's negotiation of a commercial treaty with France in the Peace of Utrecht (1713), Toland declared his final break with Harley in his bitter work *The Art of Restoring* (1714). Because Toland had been a close friend and dependent of Harley, his explicit attack confirmed the suspicions of many Englishmen that Harley (now Lord Oxford) had failed to support the ideals of the Protestant Succession. Toland's book went through ten printings in less than a year, providing him with the financial independence to continue his studies for at least the following year. Another political work, *The State Anatomy of Great Britain* (1717), which outlined the general beliefs of the Whig cabinet and which served as the philosophic foundation for a great deal of subsequent legislation, went through nine editions within a year.

By 1718 Toland was ready to publish some of the biblical and textual research he had done nine years earlier in Holland. At the same time, he started contacting potential sponsors for a monumental study of the Druids. The next two years were spent in more textual work and research on the Druids.

As 1720 approached, Toland grew more interested in secretive matters. He began to develop in thematic form an undercurrent found in much of his work and in that of other authors he read, namely, the distinction between esoteric and exoteric doctrines. In works like *Tetradymus* and *Pantheisticon* (both 1720), he declared that his treatment of secret religions and philosophies like those of the Druids was no longer intended for the general reader. Putting this principle into practice, Toland had very few copies of his *Pantheisticon* printed, and these he personally gave to his friends.

During the final years of his life, Toland's support came from such patrons as his Irish countryman Robert Viscount Molesworth. Toland lost what little property he had, though, in the financial collapse of the South Sea Company in 1720. The following year his health began to decline, aggravated by the polluted air of London. Although he moved out of the city to Putney, his condition did not improve appreciably. He died, in March 1722, in such extreme poverty that no grave marker was placed at the spot where he was buried in Putney churchyard. It is said that when asked, immediately before he died, whether he wanted anything, he replied that he wanted only death. And after bidding those about him farewell, he simply said that he was going to sleep—expressing an attitude of his that Voltaire greatly admired.

The epitaph Toland composed for himself emphasizes his learning, his travel, his spirit of free thinking, and finally, his peace with the world. The British Museum manuscript of the epitaph is not in Toland's handwriting. The copyist—perhaps Pierre Desmaizeaux or another of Toland's French refugee friends—apparently filled in the date of death.

> Here Lyeth John Toland.
> Who born near Derry in Ireland
> Studyed young in Scotland and Holland
> Which, growing riper, he did also at Oxford,
> And, having more than once seen Germany
> Spent his Age of Manhood in, and about London.
> He was an assertor of Liberty
> A lover of all sorts of Learning
> A speaker of Truth
> But no mans follower, or dependant,
> Nor could frowns, or fortune bend him
> To decline from the ways he had chosen
> His spirit is join'd with its aithereal father
> From whom it originally proceeded,
> His body yielding likewise to nature

Is laid again in the Lap of its Mother.
But he's frequently to rise himself again,
Yet never to be the same Toland more.
  Born ye 30 of Novemb. 1670
  Dy'd the 11th of March 1722.
If you would know more of him
Search his Writings.[10]

Toland seems to have been aware, at the end, that his chosen individuality would probably preclude his being the object of study for more than a few.

2. SOURCES, POLICIES, AND FORMAT

A recurring problem for Toland scholars is that of distinguishing his authentic works from the spurious ones attributed to him. Because many of his major works were published anonymously, researchers have had to depend on techniques of indirect identification, sometimes no more reliable than a note scribbled in a copy of some work, attributing the book to Toland. Estimates of the number of his works have been as low as thirty and as high as one hundred. Until very recently, even a relatively reliable bibliography of Toland's works was simply not available to Toland scholars. This problem, perhaps as much as any other, may have prevented scholars from offering an overview of Toland's thought.

In 1975, however, a work of major bibliographic importance for Toland studies was published, in Italy, by Giancarlo Carabelli.[11] More than four hundred pages in length, Carabelli's study incorporates material from every previous attempt at a bibliography, includes detailed comments on all works previously attributed to Toland, and contains annotations on hundreds of items published before 1974. Since the publication of his bibliography, Carabelli has continued the project, updating and correcting the original list. His second and most recent list of errata and addenda, including works published as late as 1978, comprises some 150 pages.[12]

10. BM Add. MS 4295, fol. 76. Note the spelling of "dependant." The copyist incorrectly identified Toland's year of birth as 1674. My change of that date to 1670 is intended to preclude any confusion in referring back to the epitaph.

11. *Tolandiana: materiali bibliografici per lo studio dell'opera e della fortune di John Toland* (Firenze: La Nuova Italia, 1975).

12. *Tolandiana . . . Errata, addenda e indici* (Ferrara: Universita de Ferrara, 1978).

In trying to determine authenticity, I have used Carabelli's suggestions but have not been limited by them. For example, I have also employed stylistic analysis. The style and tone of a work for which there are no external and reliable means of determining authenticity must correspond to that of works known to be by Toland. One is justified in excluding works that do not so correspond, I believe, even though some may have been used by other writers on Toland. However, along with Carabelli I have accepted as authentic certain questionable works, for example, *Two Essays Sent in a Letter from Oxford* (1695). *Two Essays* is of moderate importance for Toland's early statements, and I have treated it as such. On the other hand, I have excluded some titles that Carabelli accepts (e.g., *Limitations for the Next Foreign Successor*, 1701). As an example of how I have reached my judgment about a work like the *Limitations*, I note the following. The work sounds too anti-German and anti-Scottish for Toland. It places too much concentration on the interlocutor's objections to the author and contains too few references to the author himself. The noticeable presence of the author is a staple commodity in any of Toland's known works. Nevertheless, I often agree with Carabelli in rejecting a work as Toland's (e.g., *A Letter from an Arabian Physician*, 1706) for internal reasons similar to those given above. The titles I have judged spurious do not appear at all in my account. For the most part these doubtful works are small pamphlets containing little of philosophic substance.

Toland wrote a number of works under the direction of Harley or Shaftesbury. Items such as *Reasons against a Standing Army* (originally published in 1699; edited and republished in 1717) were written by Shaftesbury and revised by Toland. Other works (e.g., *The Memorial of the State of England*, 1705) were written by Toland at the direction of Harley. In cases where Toland is the actual author, even when he is writing for a patron, I have considered the work as authentically Toland's, because his manner and style so infect the message that it becomes his own. In cases where he is editing, translating, or reprinting another author's work, I have considered only the prefaces or introductions as his.

There is, at present, no edition of the collected works of Toland. Some sixty-five published titles and manuscript collections in at least five libraries have served as sources for my work.[13] This material has

13. Bodleian (Oxford), British Museum, Lambeth Palace, Public Record Office (London), National Austrian Library (Vienna).

been supplemented by published transcriptions of Toland manuscripts from other libraries.

Although I have not limited myself to Toland's major works, the following titles often appear in my treatment: *Christianity Not Mysterious, Clito* (1700), *Letters to Serena, Nazarenus* (1718), *Pantheisticon, Tetradymus,* and *A Collection of Several Pieces of Mr. John Toland* (1726). Similarly, the manuscript collections at the British Museum and the Bodleian Library act as essential starting points for many of my ideas. In order to obtain as broad a picture as possible of Toland's thought, manners, and methods—in terms of Toland the polemicist, letter writer, debator, and speaker—I have turned often to his contemporaries for information about how he lived what he wrote.

In some cases, it is rather difficult to say exactly when Toland wrote specific works and whether he revised them and kept them for years without publishing them. With the exception of a few instances (e.g., the 1709 Vienna manuscript of *Nazarenus,* published in 1718, or the 1707 "Livius Vindicatus" prototype of *Adeisidaemon,* published in 1709), we do not have early drafts of Toland's works. To depend heavily on the dates of publication would be as unhelpful as to ignore them totally. Development does occur in Toland's thinking about questions; however, it is a development noticeable in terms of the themes which interact with one another. His treatments of these themes mature in time, often responding to the political, religious, and social events surrounding his life. My aim has been to avoid the rigidity of previous studies that have been limited to discussing only those of Toland's works with political or religious sounding titles or that have slavishly followed the order of publication of his major works.

Often my treatment of Toland is devoted to quoting him directly rather than paraphrasing him. One reason for this stems from Toland's insistence that the "indifferent historian" must allow the author with whom he deals to speak for himself. After completing his "Life of Milton" (1699), in which long quotations of Milton appeared, Toland noted that no one had charged him with misrepresenting Milton; rather, he was accused of making Milton's opinions too clear, by quoting particular passages.[14] The Toland scholar thus has his guide in his subject himself. And although Toland claimed that he adhered religiously to this "peculiar method or Rule" of respecting the thought,

14. *Amyntor; or a Defence of Milton's Life* (London: Booksellers of London and Westminster, 1699), pp. 3–5.

manner, and style of the authors he treated, he always indicated by further comment his own view of his subject's meaning. In this as well, I have tried to follow Toland.

Furthermore, by the time Toland wrote his epitaph, he must have already been aware of the difficulty encountered in the search for his writings. Many of the works I have used are very difficult to obtain outside Britain. Here again, I have followed the example of my subject:

Besides the citations of authors, indispensably requisite in proving matters of fact newly advanc'd, or in deciding of antient doubts and controversies (not to speak of such as come in by way of ornament, or that a writer modestly prefers to his own expressions) I have sometimes occasion to touch upon passages, which, tho' I cou'd easily abridge, or needed but barely hint with relation to the purpose for which I produce them: yet being in themselves either very curious and instructive, or lying in books that come into few people's hands, I chuse to give them in my *History* intire. This method I have learnt from my best masters among the antients, who practis'd it with much success; tho, like them, I use it very sparingly.[15]

In general, my quotations serve to portray Toland according to the manner of his time and in the way in which his writing can be recognized (particularly in contractions) as affected by the spoken word. Dialogue, debate, polemic—in sum, the modes of speaking— serve a major function in Toland's philosophizing. To fail to respect the way in which speech affected his writing would lessen the intriguing, curious, and instructive character of his thought. Much of the joy of my treatment of Toland will derive from these quotations.

The order and structure of the following chapters are intended to support the major contention of this book, namely, that Toland's varied interests and treatments of often seemingly unrelated topics can be understood as parts of a unifying pattern. The identification of such a unifying pattern can serve to correct the impression, too often given in studies of Toland's life and works, that his interests were determined either by the moods or wishes of his patrons or by those topics that were controversial at the time he wrote. Roughly chronological, the chapter themes present the movement of Toland's thought as unifying and developmental.

My treatment concentrates on Toland's methodology as the key for

15. "A Specimen of the Critical History of the Celtic Religion and Learning: Containing An Account of the Druids," in *Collection*, 1: 120.

understanding the unity of his thinking and writing. By Toland's methodology I mean the way in which his work is united by a common pattern of thought emphasizing the capacities of the individual to think for himself on philosophic, religious, and political issues. Conceptual, content-oriented features of Toland's philosophy often only make thematically explicit his insistence on the personal nature of thoughtful communication. His writings are correspondence, and his message resonates with the awareness of himself and his reader as principals (and principles) of philosophic discourse.

At the same time, I do not want to argue that a case can be made for thinking that this overarching concern for methodology can be treated as a central thesis supported by the chapters as steps in an argument. One of the reasons why I choose to refer to the methodological emphasis on the individual as the major contention of the book is that I suspect that the variety of Toland's concerns and writings will simply not support the strong claim that his work presents a unified whole. My approach has been to highlight features in his methodology so as to provide a heuristic device that can be used to understand his thought and that can be supported by substantial textual evidence.

This book is not intended simply as a summary of Toland's life and works. If it were, I would have placed much greater emphasis on describing Toland's individual writings, political associations, and clandestine activities (tasks that other researchers, particularly Giuntini, have undertaken). My focus on methodology reveals the pattern of thought that characterizes Toland's way of philosophizing. As such, much of my treatment pays careful attention to Toland's own prefaces, introductions, or commentaries on the process of his reflective activity.

Chapter 1 discusses Toland's claim, put forth most noticeably in the deist manifesto, *Christianity Not Mysterious*, that the mystification of religion alienates the individual and challenges the ability of the common man to think for himself. Toland's attack on the attempts of clergymen to gain and maintain power centers on the description of how laymen are excluded from having a voice in theological matters. Philosophical and theological positions that anticipated Toland's arguments are discussed in this chapter, as well as some of the numerous replies to Toland's claim that Christianity contains no valid mysteries.

Chapter 2, which recognizes the importance of Toland's biographies of James Harrington and John Milton, focuses on his argument that all individuals in society (especially authors) have some authority in religious and political matters insofar as they are novel sources of reason and revelation. Here I describe how Toland incorporated biography into philosophy. Biography and the recognition of the importance of novelty in authors are treated as essential elements in Toland's understanding of the development of reason and in his analysis of human and divine forms of revelation. Together, chapters 1 and 2 present Toland's discussion of (*a*) why individuals have lost confidence in their ability to make decisions for themselves and (*b*) how biography discloses the sources of knowledge and the means of exercising control over it.

Exegesis is the concern of the third and fourth chapters. Toland's *Letters to Serena* epitomizes his indictment of educational practices that support prejudices and superstitions and that generate conflicts among men. He argues that the craftlike character of education is revealed through exegetical studies not only of written communication but of all forms of human interaction. This investigation of Toland's treatment of the negative impact of education (in its broadest sense) is addressed in chapter 3.

The concentration on Toland's work in biblical and historical exegesis, in chapter 4, provides a positive balance to chapter 3 insofar as it reveals how travel and conversation can explain and correct the process of provincial education. Toland's investigation of the canon of the New Testament shows how a new authority is granted to all interpreters of the written and spoken word by the exegete who unites scholarship and literary grace. Toland's treatment of this new authority is central in chapter 4.

In chapter 5 the emphasis shifts back to Toland's demand that the reflective thinker engage in polemic. Toland's activities in Oxford, London, and Hanover give expression to a particular theme in his writings: the task of the author, in coffeehouse confrontation and in retirement, is to serve as a guide to others who attempt to put into practice the insights of reflective thinking. This chapter, more than any of the others, includes accounts of those who knew Toland and emphasizes the embodiment in his polemical forms of writing and speaking of those specifically philosophic themes found in his works.

Again, however, the positive and optimistic tone of one chapter is balanced by the next, for chapter 6 discloses the dangers surrounding the project of polemical self-discovery and revelation. Toland's theory of religious and philosophic toleration grew out of his political dealings with Harley, Shaftesbury, and other members of Whig and Tory factions. But his political activities in England and abroad taught him that civil government did not appear to be intended for, or capable of, the toleration necessary for large-scale polemic. His doctrine of esoteric communication as part of his philosophic response to this intolerance, then, is addressed in this chapter.

Chapter 7 discusses the metaphysics that underlies and necessitates the polemical struggles of individuals asserting their own identities. Epistemological themes implicit in the writigs of Giordano Bruno were reintroduced by Toland in his debates with Leibniz and the Newtonians. Toland's application of such themes to matters of geology, political rule, and the relationship of God and nature is covered here.

Toland's turn to the God-theme prompts a return, in chapter 8, to the broad question of religion and to Toland's specific treatment of the individuals he was the first to call "pantheists." This chapter describes how pantheistic religious practices and beliefs fit within Toland's thought as a whole. Toland's contacts with certain English and Continental clubs and societies are presented in such a way that doubts are raised about the often-made claim that his pantheists were precursors of Freemasons.

The conclusion of my book reveals how the structure and movement of Toland's thought embodied, as he himself hinted, the Ciceronian ideal of the most accomplished man. It is suggested that these characteristics of Toland's thought might be expressive of elements found in other seventeenth- and eighteenth-century thinkers with similar inclinations.

To present Toland's philosophy in the way I have outlined is not to consider it as completely novel or to propose Toland as a pivotal thinker of the period. It is intended to show that he was as comprehensive in his interests as any of his contemporaries, and was able to weave intricate political, religious, and philosophic themes together in ways previously neither noticed nor appreciated.

I

The Response to Priestcraft

JOHN TOLAND'S WRITINGS could be described as a continual effort to overcome the prejudices or superstitions of the unlearned, the "vulgar." Although Toland frequently noted the ease with which the vulgar can be misled into adopting superstitious beliefs, he never lost faith in intelligence as basically reliable. The ordinary man's credulity, Toland proposed, is based upon his belief that things are what they seem and what a man says can be accepted at face value for what he means. Admittedly, men often differ in their opinions and sometimes need to be corrected. But, for Toland, this does not undermine the procedure of beginning an inquiry with confidence in the ability of an individual to arrive at some position that satisfies that individual's interests or purposes.

This initial confidence in the ordinary man's ability to think for himself received its most damaging challenge, Toland thought, in the attempts of some to make religion mystifying. That which had begun as the straightforward endeavor to deal with other men in the context of a religious world had become convoluted through sectarian emphases on superstitious customs based on doctrines that were in principle, it was argued, too mysterious to be comprehended by any man. This challenge extended beyond religion, implying that the individual, even in conjunction with other men, lacked the ability to resolve satisfactorily fundamental questions affecting his life (e.g., questions concerning the role and character of religion or government). To restore a proper respect for man's cognitive abilities Toland sought to clarify the connection between the reasonableness of a belief and its authority. Men should believe only what they understand, he argued, only what is meaningful to them. He thus placed the authority of *any* belief, not in its intrinsic intelligibility or in the source of the doctrine, but in the believer himself.

The first section of this chapter considers Toland's description of the suffocating effects of the mystification of religion. His reasons for holding that the common man cannot be excluded from the process of developing meaning or general philosophizing are taken up in the second section. In the third I deal with Toland's suggestion that the mystification of religion might be avoided by expanding the notion of authority to include both the revealer and the individual to whom the revelation is made. This section thus acts as a general preparation for the issues dealt with in chapter 2.

1. THE MYSTIFICATION OF RELIGION

Much of Toland's activity during his early studies in Scotland, Holland and Oxford (roughly, 1687–95) concerned his shifts from one religious perspective to another. Born an Irish Catholic, accepted as a fervent Presbyterian in Scotland, allied closely with a number of sects dissenting from the established Church of England, then recognized as a Low Churchman in the Church of England, he enjoyed a life epitomizing the vitality and turmoil, the excitement and conflict, that characterized the sectarian disputes of the 1690s. Presbyterians, Independents, Nonconformists, Latitudinarians, Arminians, Socinians, High Churchmen, Low Churchmen—all claimed fundamental insights into the true nature of Christianity. And Toland lent an ear to each.

That Toland early in his life found a fascination with this vibrant diversity can be seen in his first known publication, a letter in Jean LeClerc's *Bibliothèque universelle et historique.*[1] In this letter Toland shifted the focus of the sectarian problem from the particular arguments dividing the factions to the historical issues that led to the development of these various sects. He noted that religious groups appeared divided by fundamental differences about the reasonableness and human accessibility of the Scriptures and religious dogmas. For example, Calvinists preferred a literal interpretation of the Scriptures without appealing to the critique of reason. Arminians argued that inscrutable decrees are to be rejected as unreasonable to

---

1. Toland to LeClerc, commenting on Daniel Williams's *Gospel Truth Stated and Vindicated*, in *Bibliothèque Universelle et Historique* 23 (1692): 504–9.

man because they are unbecoming to God. Scholastics reasoned that dogmas cannot contradict reason, because they share the same divine source. Socinians proposed that reason defines the contradictory and eliminates any meaning for suprarational truths. These and other differences contributed to the atmosphere of perplexity and to what Toland was later to refer to as the "universal disposition of this age bent upon a rational religion."[2] For Toland, this universal disposition was toward a religion that made some sense. And he recognized early that disputes among the sects did not contribute to the clarification and sensibleness of religion.

The labeling and name-calling associated with the disturbances of the sects, Toland observed, had taken the place of the divisive arguments themselves. He noted a spirit of contrivance implicit in the identification of oneself and others according to a particular sect:

It is no small artifice to give nicknames in Religion, and to bestow an odious or a creditable title, according to the words in present fashion: for what's the bug-bear of one age is the honour of another. . . . and the only thing to which most are constant, is, that if a man's not found within the pale of some certain Sect, he's looked upon by all as an outlying deer, which it's lawful for every one to kill. But notwithstanding my fore-knowledge of this matter, yet, as I shall not ambitiously assume the name of any party, neither shall I be concern'd what name they'll please to impose upon me.[3]

Belonging to a sect, assuming a religious designation by which one could be identified—in short, implicitly giving up control of the meanings of religious terms to the passing fashion—characterized all the sectarian disputes. One who declined to pledge his allegiance to any sect in effect refused to limit his beliefs in such a way that he lost control of what he meant when stating his beliefs. Toland maintained that the artifices constructed in the mutual designations of sects fixed their members within a system of meanings eventually interpretable only by the religious leaders themselves.

2. See Robert R. Evans, "John Toland's Pantheism: A Revolutionary Ideology and Enlightenment Philosophy" (Ph.D. diss., Brandeis University, 1965), pp. 4–23; and Eugene I. Dyche, "The Life and Works and Philosophical Relations of John (Janus Junius) Toland (1670–1722)" (Ph.D. diss., University of Southern California, 1944), pp. 85–99.

3. "The Primitive Constitution of the Christian Church" (undated, though probably 1704), in *Collection*, 2: 129.

The challenge to the religious sensibility of individuals lay not so much in the disputes among the various sects, for Toland, as in the practice of deferring to the fashionable (in any sect). If men agreed to base their ability to determine sensibleness on a solitary system of manners and customs, then sectarian disputes could not develop. Some men, in fact, have not surrendered their ability to determine what makes sense. Instead, they have become enslaved by their own manners and customs, losing their sense of being the original authors of those customs. This has resulted, Toland believed, in their alienation from themselves in sectarian religion. In choosing the artifice of the sect, they have forfeited their ability to determine meanings. In the course of time, many of those practices and beliefs that become doctrines of the sect grow beyond the control of the individual. His identity defined by the mysterious (i.e., hidden from him) customs of his sect or culture, the individual then foolishly struggles against men of different sects or cultures for reasons ultimately unknown to him: "So great is the aversion which diversity of manners in general begets among men, and especially contrary rites or doctrines of Religion, that, farr from mutual love and good offices, as creatures of the same species, they foolishly despise and hate one another for their civil customs, but cruelly persecute and murder one another on the score of their religious ones."[4] Disagreement among members of differing sects, manners, and customs depended, as Toland viewed it, upon their foolish failure to see how they had given up their concern for others in their species. They had done so by allowing themselves, and forcing others, to give up their own authority in religious and civil matters — which authority, they had become convinced, was irretrievable.

Toland did not say that customs and manners were inherently evil or caused disputes. Attitudes toward sects and toward individuals in them could generate hatred and persecution. But such negative results occurred only as long as individuals failed to recognize their natural ability to withhold commitment to a sectarian position that lacked common sense.

But why do men allow others to do their thinking for them, particularly in light of the damaging effect of such acquiescence?

---

4. *Reasons for Naturalizing the Jews in Great Britain and Ireland, On the same foot with all other nations. Containing also, A Defence of the Jews against All vulgar Prejudices in all Countries* (London: J. Roberts, 1714), p. 21.

Ironically, Toland pointed out, the mutual confidence men place in one another's testimony and the self-confidence individuals have in the appropriateness of their own choices set up the conditions for error and unhappiness:

Tho such as call their Religion under Examination do often differ in their Notions about It, yet in all Contrys of the World the greatest Part of the People give themselves up to the Public Leading in divine Things, as well as in other Matters; and this they do whether the generally receiv'd Opinions happen to be true or erroneous. It were to be earnestly wisht, no Doubt, that every Religion were free from Error, and had sincerely receiv'd the Truth; but . . . Men deny themselves this Happiness by indulging their Vices, minding nothing but their Business, or for Want of Consideration.[5]

Many place too much confidence in their judgments within their professional fields (indulging their vices) and not enough in their abilities in other areas, for example, in their religion. When religion is encompassed within their concern, they prefer to commit themselves uncritically to possible error rather than attain the happiness of a critical examination and full appreciation of their religion.

Making religion one's business, though, does not mean making a business of one's religion. This crucial point was the means by which Toland distinguished those who retain understanding and control of their religious notions from those who make religion a craft or trade. Religion and theology become crafts or trades when they are thought to contain mysteries accessible only to those who have made a profession (a business) of religion and theology.

At times Toland wrote as though it is the individual who is primarily at fault for having surrendered his ability to remain in control of what he believes (in terms of understanding what he believes). If it is natural for men to change their religious beliefs to accommodate themselves to current customs, he argued, it is also their nature to be the source of what those religious beliefs mean. From the time of Christ, for example, men had altered what Christianity was "as their interest or the necessity of their affairs requir'd, to all the opinions and customs any where in vogue. . . . The time serving and fickleness of many

5. *Anglia Libera; or the Limitation and Succession of the Crown of England explain'd and asserted* (London: Bernard Lintott, 1701), pp. 94–95.

Christians are too manifest to be deny'd. This is the nature of man."[6] When acting in accord with their own interests or in response to the necessities of social living, men have acted naturally, that is, in accord with their nature. When entrusting their ability to interpret religious doctrines to religious "leaders"—thinking that such a move was in their own interest or in response to social necessity—they again acted naturally. But such an action was time-serving and fickle because it contradicted the fundamental basis for the action. There was something essentially contradictory about clearly choosing to confuse or mystify oneself. One cannot "naturally" choose to deny his nature.

This realization prompted Toland to indicate that the unnatural source of man's attempted religious self-alienation lies in the practice of thinking that religion is the particular domain of the theologically adept. This practice, referred to by Toland as "priestcraft," was the very reverse of religion—as contrasted with superstition, which was only religion misunderstood.[7] Priestcraft reversed the order of true religious authority, substituting religious tradesmen and professional theologians for the individual. This reversal involved an internal contradiction, namely, the *choice* no longer to be able to choose what one means when he says "I believe." Those who supported priestcraft thus did so dishonestly.

Toland used this concept of a contradictory choice to distinguish between wicked priests and those ministers of the gospel he referred to as "an Order of Men not only useful and necessary, but likewise reputable and venerable."[8] Toland was quite explicit about his intention not to cast aspersions on the priesthood itself. In fact, among Toland's manuscripts is evidence that, about 1705, he partially completed a work entitled "Priesthood without Priestcraft," which ran to at least fifty-nine folio pages. The complete title of this projected work indicates Toland's belief that the priestcraft problem extended

---

6. *Nazarenus: or Jewish, Gentile, and Mahometan Christianity. Containing The History of the Antient Gospel of Barnabas . . . also The Original Plan of Christianity . . . with the Relation of an Irish Manuscript of the Four Gospels* (London: J. Brown, 1718), "Barnabas-Original," p. 77.
  7. "Druids," p. 9.
  8. "A Word to the Honest Priests," in *An Appeal to Honest People Against Wicked Priests: or, The very Heathen Laity's Declarations for Civil Disobedience and Liberty of Conscience, contrary to the Rebellious and Persecuting Principles of some of the Old Christian Clergy; with an Application to the Corrupt Part of the Priests of this Present Time, publish'd on Occasion of Dr. Sacheverell's last Sermon* (London: Booksellers of London and Westminster [1713]), p. i.

beyond the limits of religion: "Priesthood without Priestcraft: or Superstition distinguish'd from Religion, Dominion from Order, and Bigotry from Reason; in the most principle Controversies about Church-Government, which at present divide and deform Christianity."[9] In his Toland bibliography, Carabelli notes that a title like this appears in the list of manuscripts owned by Anthony Collins. Carabelli also notes that at least part of the work seems to be found in Toland's "Primitive Constitution of the Christian Church."[10]

Why the work was not published might be explained by a comparison of the subtitle's identification of priestcraft-as-superstition with the "Account-of-the-Druids" remark that priestcraft and superstition are different in type. Toland seems to have maintained that true religion might be able to allow for priesthood and some superstitions but that it would not allow for priestcraft. Leibniz asked Toland to clarify his distinction between true religion and superstition, arguing that failure to do so would risk enveloping religion in the downfall of superstition.[11] Even though Toland's reply did not address the question, other remarks by him do indicate how a distinction might be developed. *Priestcraft* proposes that the individual *should* believe things proposed to him by religious leaders, even if he does not understand them; *superstition* is the result of an individual's thinking he *can* believe things he does not understand; and *true religion* entails the individual's thinking that he *should* believe only those things he *does* understand.

Toland's oft-repeated favorable remarks about individual ministers and prelates certainly do not portray him as thoroughly anticlerical, as he has sometimes been described. He directed his objections against those who saw the priesthood and the pronouncements of the clergy as the means by which God reveals himself to man. As far as Toland was concerned, there is no "divine right" to be God's spokesmen:

I do not admit the Church it self to be a Society under a certain form of Government and Officers; or that there is in the world at present, and that there has continu'd for 1704 years past, any constant System and Discipline maintain'd by such a Society, deserving the title of the Catholick Church, to

9. BM Add. MS 4295, fol. 66.

10. *Tolandiana*, p. 119.

11. Leibniz to Toland, 30 April 1709. For the Toland-Leibniz correspondence, see Carabelli, "John Toland e G. W. Leibniz: Otto Lettere," *Rivista critica di storia della filosofia* 29 (1974): 412–31.

which all particular Churches ought to conform or submit, and with which all private persons are oblig'd to hold communion. Much less do I believe that there was instituted in the Church a peculiar Order of Priests (tho' Christian Priests I do allow) no Priests, I say, whose office it is to instruct the People alone, and successively to appoint those of their own function, whether by the hands of one presiding Bishop, or of several equal Presbyters, Pastors, Ministers, or Priests of any degree or denomination.[12]

The institutional presence of the clergy always presents a threat to the well-being of men, Toland believed, in that a clerical hierarchy easily lends itself to the manipulation of those who seek to wield authority over the laity.

Popery was thought by Toland to be the extreme case of this type of threat. He repeatedly returned to this threat as a challenge to the common layman: "Popery in reality is nothing else, but the Clergy's assuming a Right to think for the Laity."[13] He seldom referred to popery other than in terms of the authority of clergy over laity. Following the example of Milton, he rarely placed popery in the context of a religion (Roman Catholicism) but preferred always to treat it as a "tyrannical Faction oppressing all others."[14] It was the institution-alized, politicized character of *any* sect, expressed in the tendency to destroy all other sects and individualized thinking within the sect itself.

Popery could take on the guise of a religion, admittedly. But Toland regarded it "not so much a Religion, as a Politic Faction wherof the Members, whersoever they are, own the Pope for their Superior, to the prejudice of the Allegiance due to their Natural Soverains. Besides, that they never tolerate others where they have the mastery; and that their Doctrine of Dispensations, or keeping no Faith with such as they count Heretics, renders 'em worse than Atheists, and the declar'd Enemies of all Mankind besides those of their own Communion."[15] Because it embodied a political threat to the peace and stability of a

---

12. "The Primitive Constitution of the Christian Church," in *Collection*, 2: 122.

13. *Appeal to Honest People*, p. 38.

14. "The Life of John Milton," in *A Complete Collection of the Historical, Political, and Miscellaneous Works of John Milton* (Amsterdam, 1698), 1:45; reprinted in *The Early Lives of Milton*, ed. Helen Darbishire (London: Constable, 1932).

15. "Life of Milton," p. 36. Also see Toland's "Life of James Harrington," in *The Oceana of James Harrington, and his other works; som wherof are now first publish'd from his own manuscripts. The whole collected methodiz'd and review'd, with an exact account of his life prefix'd by John Toland* (London: Booksellers of London and Westminster, 1700), p. iii.

"nation" (the "natural" birthplace of the individual) and undermined the fundamental credibility among men, Popery served as the doctrine of authority implicit in Roman Catholicism devoid of its religious content. Toland's appeal to the example of the Catholics focused attention on an identifiable group that embodied most clearly, especially to his English readers, the effect of institutionalized priestcraft:

I hope I need not spend many words to perswade *Englishmen* that Popery in general is an extract of whatever is Ridiculous, Knavish, or Impious in all Religions; that it is Priestcraft arriv'd at the highest Perfection; that it contains peculiar absurdities never known in any other perswasion; and that it is the most insolent imposition that ever was made on the Credulity of Mankind. I might here truly represent the mischievous influence of this abominable Superstition on the Morals and Understandings of its Professors; how it subjects 'em to all manner of Tyranny and Oppression; drains their Purses, as well as deprives them of their Reason; how most of its Doctrines are calculated for the advantage of the Priests; what authority these exercise over the Laity; their Idolatry, Hippocrisy, Licentiousness, and Cruelty.[16]

Toland addressed this tirade not against Catholicism as a religion but against a system of thought that undermined the individual's right to reason about and be responsible for his own life—in the moral, intellectual, and even financial spheres. The moral oppression of reason within popery was calculated to enhance the position of those who were entrusted with the business of religion. Aware that churchmen in England and elsewhere might try to limit popery to Catholicism, freethinkers such as Toland were not easily misled by linguistic convention. For if popery meant nothing but the clergy's assumption of a right to think for the laity, then "there may very well be such a thing as Protestant Popery."[17]

The more respect paid to the offices of the clergy, the more the officers would support their power bases and positions of authority using the rubrics of religion and virtue:

I take it for granted, as a thing of publick notoriety, that but too many of the Clergy of England have no regard for any thing but profit and power; that the

---

16. *The Art of Governing by Partys: particularly, in Religion, in Politicks, in Parliament, on the Bench, and in the Ministry* (London: Bernard Lintott, 1701), pp. 145–46.
17. "A Memorial for the Earl of [Oxford], 17 Dec. 1711," in *Collection*, 2: 230.

more you enrich or advance them, the more haughty and mischievous they will be: not valuing any sort of Religion or Virtue, further than it merely serves their interest. . . . [They] hamper the Government [and] disturb the Peace of the People by their intrigues and importunities with relation to the first; or their imposing upon and gaining the money of the last, by wheedling, and especially by practising upon sick people.[18]

Toland warned his correspondents in the government and his readers in general that the power-and-profit activities of the clergy were far from politically harmless. The superstitious and mysterious doctrines supported by many clergymen could undermine the foundation of a country's political structure, in very much the same way that the wiles and "mysteries" of a woman could cloud the thinking of a man. Indeed, Toland noted, the analogy between the disruptive influence of a priest and the unsettling effect of a woman is particularly apt. In a wry, suggestive remark about the political impact of priestly and also womanly mystery, Toland declared that "no revolution happens in the world without a *Woman* or a *Priest* at the bottom of it."[19] He believed that power based on the incomprehensible threatens the stability of the state just as much as that of the individual.

In extending the meaning of popery to include a characteristic found perhaps in many sects, and in observing that popery is not specifically religious in nature, Toland implied that priestcraft could be practiced by anyone who shrouded the doctrines of his profession in mystery. The layman is excluded from the mysteries of the professionals not just in religion but in all fields—medicine, politics, philosophy, and so on. Professionals, unable to justify their doctrines to the layman or even to themselves (when they are honest with themselves), take refuge in the mysterious. More often than not, they bring in God as an explanation, "which is not to explain things, but to cover their own Negligence or Short-sightedness."[20] The appeal to the mysterious activity of God usually serves only to point out the ineptitude of the individual who employs such an appeal. Although this type of appeal may have the appearance of religious zeal or deference, it ultimately conflates religious revelation and rational description, undermining

18. "A Memorial to a Present Minister of State," in *Collection*, 2: 239–40.
19. *Reasons for Naturalizing the Jews*, p. 36.
20. *Letters to Serena*, ed. Günter Gawlick (Stuttgart–Bad Cannstatt: Friedrich Frommann, 1964), p. 158.

confidence in both.[21] When theologians attempt to reconcile religious revelation with personal reason, they often only contribute further to the mystification of revelation. The attempt to explain revelation rationally simply removes it from the clear grasp of reason. When natural philosophers try to reconcile descriptions of nature with belief in God, they usually only raise problems (for example, about determinism) which are then resolved only by appeal to the mysterious.

The "professional" use of mystery was a theme Toland returned to again and again. Although much of his attention to the topic was directed (as in *Christianity Not Mysterious*) against theologians and members of the clergy, he argued that it was necessary to consider all professionals as capable of falling easily into the mode of the mysterious. Physicians were "men, who, the greatest part of them, ruin Nature by Art; and who, by endeavouring to be always very cunning for others, by making every thing a mystery, are frequently too cunning for themselves."[22] Just as the priesthood could function without the burden of the mystery-shrouded practices of priestcraft, so medicine could be considered apart from, and perhaps even purged of, false professionalism.

Toland applied the mystique of the professional to the political domain as well. Particularly after 1714, and his break with Harley, he focused on the methods by which the Tory coalition in power under Harley sought to prevent clarification of the purposes and functions of government. He complained that Harley's government employed the brightest minds in the kingdom to work on minor matters like genealogies. Precisely those individuals who might have been able to demystify the processes of government engaged instead in "fruitless disputes about words and syllables, or . . . endless disquisitions about things, which, if possible to be discover'd, yet are of no advantage to themselves or the World."[23] According to Toland, scholarship that eschewed attempts to resolve mysteries of personal, social, political, or religious importance thereby contributed to the "grand mystery"—the delusion that mere scholarly attention bestowed meaning on things otherwise considered meaningless for all practical purposes.

21. See André Leroy, *La Critique et la religion chez David Hume* (Paris: Félix Alcan, 1930), p. 99.

22. "Physic without Physicians," in *Collection*, 2: 275–86.

23. *The Grand Mystery Laid Open: Namely, By dividing of the Protestants to weaken the Hanover Succession to extirpate the Protestant Religion* (London: J. Roberts, 1714), p. 21.

The scholarly techniques employed in rendering meaningless claims meaningful were most obvious and most destructive in religious scholarship. As early as 1695 Toland began what would become a lifetime of cautious approvals, repeated qualifications, and bitter invectives regarding the theological use of fable, allegory, and metaphor. He conceded that they are required for conveying certain religious ideas, but he deplored attempts to justify their extensive use by denigrating the religious layman's intelligence. These same techniques, he cautioned, are also used to reinforce the general hypothesis that the common man either cannot understand plain language or refuses to believe and act on propositions not delivered under the convoluted form of fable, allegory, or metaphor.

Toland's thought about the appropriate use of such interpretive techniques appears to have developed and changed during the twenty-five years following 1695. Three points, however, remained constant: the common man has been underestimated as an interpreter of Scripture; theologians and biblical scholars have duped others (and perhaps even themselves) into thinking that it was necessary to read into the Scriptures various interpretations that contradict common sense; and the assumptions allowing for such readings threaten the common-sense credulity of the ordinary man.

Early in his writing career, Toland argued that fables (or, in modern terms, myths) had become the popular form of teaching religious or moral doctrines because the *fable form* appealed as much to the teacher as to his listener. The fables, myths, stories, and legends of the Greeks, Egyptians, and Hebrews provided Christian monks with models for developing their own variations and applications of what Toland called the "art of Lying": "The bare, naked, or simple way of Instructing by Precept, being found jejune and nauseous, a mixture of *Fable* was therefore thought necessary to sweeten and allure the minds of men, naturally Superstitious and Credulous."[24] *To whom* such instruction was found jejune and nauseous—instructor or pupil—was left sufficiently ambiguous to allow Toland the opportunity to show the benefits and drawbacks of the use of fables.

24. *Two Essays Sent in a Letter from Oxford to a Nobleman in London. The First Concerning some errors about the Creation, General Flood, and the Peopling of the World. In Two Parts. The Second concerning the Rise, Progress, and Destruction of Fables and Romances* (London: R. Baldwin, 1695), pp. 29–31. Also see Toland's *A Short Essay upon Lying* (London: A. Moore, 1720), pp. 8–11.

Years later Toland returned to much the same theme: the explanation often given (by theologians and churchmen, of course) for why the original ideas of Christianity are no better known than the symbols and allegories surrounding them is that heathens would have despised the simplicity of such ideas. They had to be complicated to be appreciated.[25] Fables, allegories, and metaphors were thus necessary in scriptural writing and interpretation because the teachings of religion, made complex to please the heathens, had come to be viewed as unfathomable without great insight or prolonged study. Such a belief appalled Toland and prompted him to give careful attention to the function of fables, allegories, and metaphors in all manner of writing.

Toland did not object to those fables acknowledged by their authors to be exhortative and not descriptive. In his translation of *The Fables of Aesop*, he joined Anthony Collins (to whom the translation was dedicated) in the endorsement of fables as a nonreligious inspiration to virtue, praising Aesop as an author whose every syllable tends "to the discrediting of Vice, the encouraging of Vertue, and [is] exactly adapted to the whole practice of Life, to all Sorts and Conditions of Men."[26] Not only did the fable have a moral that individuals could choose to apply to their own practice of life; but the fable also had merit in its straightforward claim to authority simply as a story. This last point reflects Toland's emphasis on the self-asserting authority implicit in fable making and fable reading as explicitly constitutive rather than explanatory activities. Animal tales such as those of Aesop told a story but did not claim to *explain* something about the world. The fable was not intended to clarify some mysterious or difficult doctrine; it was a coteaching tool for the learned by which meanings and concepts were mutually established and learned within some philosophic, communal, or communicative setting.

Although Toland did not make extensive use of the fable form, he

---

25. *Tetradymus. Containing I. Hodegus; or the Pillar of Cloud and Fire, that Guided the Isrealites in the Wilderness, not Miraculous. II. Clidophorus; or of the Exoteric and Esoteric Philosophy. III. Hypatia; or the history of a most beautiful ... Lady, who was torn to pieces by the Clergy of Alexandria. ... IV. Magoneutes; being a defense of Nazarenus* (London: J. Brotherton and W. Meadows, 1720), "Clidophorus," p. 79.

26. *The Fables of Aesop*, preface, first page (unnumbered). See my "Political and Philosophical Uses of Fables in Eighteenth-Century England," *The Eighteenth Century: Theory and Interpretation* 23 (1982): 163.

recognized its philosophic importance.[27] Philosophy itself, for Toland, was a constitutive, cooperative, and thus fabular enterprise. Among his manuscripts is a letter written from one animal to another, in which it is said that their masters (who are identified as philosophers) "frequently confabulate."[28] Philosophers were co–fable makers, co–story makers, cohistorians. Fables were the building blocks of crucial human meanings, not the toys of children (as late as 1720, Toland was still not ready to encourage the use of fables and allegories in the education of the young and the common man in general).[29] The fable not only was a useful writing form for the philosopher; it also contained characteristics emphasizing the creative, constitutive nature of philosophizing itself.

However, the common practice of using fables and myths to conceal religious doctrines or to make religion more palatable merely confirmed Toland's contention that the doctrines themselves were not straightforward and intelligible. Priestcraft had to fall back upon fables to conceal unintelligible and foolish doctrines. Beginning with the claim that fables were necessary to explain religious doctrines to the vulgar, priestcraft then claimed that the vulgar were unqualified to interpret the fables. This type of circularity prompted Toland to remark, in a rare use of verse:

> RELIGION's safe, with PRIESTCRAFT is the War,
> All Friends to Priestcraft, Foes of Mankind are.
> Their impious Fanes and Altars I'll o'erthrow,
> And the whole Farce of their feign'd Saintship show;
> Their pious Tricks disclose; their murd'ring Zeal,
> And all their awful Mysterys reveal;
> Their lying Prophets, and their jugling Thieves
> Discredit quite; their foolish Books (as Leaves
> From Trees in Autumn fall) I'll scatter wide,
> And show those Fables which they fain wou'd hide.[30]

27. In this regard, as well as in others, Toland had close affinities with Bernard Mandeville, author of *The Fable of the Bees*. Indeed, Toland belongs to the ranks of such writers as Mandeville, Swift, Descartes, Vico, and Bacon, who find that fables and myths have important philosophic applications.

28. BM Add. MS 4465, fol. 54.

29. "Clidophorus," *Tetradymus*, p. 87.

30. *Clito: A Poem on the Force of Eloquence* (London: Booksellers of London and Westminster, 1700), p. 16

To portray a fable as a fable, to reveal the mysterious, to disclose the trickster—these were the tasks of the defender of common-sense credulity, according to Toland.

In all things but religion, some apology might be given for the use of fables, allegories, and metaphors. But about religion, Toland stood firm: religion is the one case "wherein I think all Fables to be intolerable, and that no Allegories ought to be admitted, but onely in expressing the DIVINE NATURE and ATTRIBUTES. To say that Fables will quicken our diligence, is the same plea with that for Mysteries; as if time lay heavily on our hands, and that we had no other occupation but Criticism."[31] Allegories, but not fables, can be used to express the divine nature and attributes, because the nature of things is better conveyed by allegories than by fables. Allegories only cover the truth; fables confound and overwhelm it.[32] Fables, like priestcraft, contradict the principle upon which they are supposedly based. Fables and priestcraft exhort and control but do not *describe*; allegories and superstition conceal and distort. It is a "much easier task," Toland noted, "to write of things plainly and directly, than in a perplext circuit of words under the veil of allegory and fable."[33] Even so, symbols and metaphors—what Toland called the "language of custom and not of reason"—are apt and useful for conceiving of and explaining the divine nature and attributes.[34]

Religious fables, according to Toland, were in principle mysterious and not open to any final human resolution. The common, or "vulgar," man did not have access to, or control over, the meanings behind fable-encrusted religious doctrines. As for the learned man, there was no need to make an intelligible doctrine unintelligible by placing it within the context of a fable. "Where is the necessity, what is the end, of teaching the Vulgar any thing they cannot understand or practise? and as for the Learned, tis a jest to talk of exercising their diligence; when time can never fail them in imploying their industry about what is intelligible and usefull: for all those studies are vain, superfluous, nay ridiculous; that relate to matters in themselves incomprehensible, or of

31. "Clidophorus," *Tetradymus*, p. 87.
32. Ibid., p. 85.
33. *Tetradymus*, preface, pp. v–vi.
34. "The Primitive Constitution of the Christian Church," *Collection*, 2: 197; and "Clidophorus," *Tetradymus*, p. 88.

no manner of concern to human life."[35] Religious fables, like mysteries, did not promote diligence in the daily occupations of life, for men live according only to what they understand and can act upon.

Toland despised allegorical or analogical interpretations of the Bible, "especially us'd in a book we hold to be sacred, and which least needs them of all others."[36] Allegorical interpretations of the Scriptures were fit only "to puzzle the curious, to amaze the indifferent, and to distract the ignorant."[37] Using the comparative exegetical techniques employed by his teachers Spanheim and LeClerc, Toland argued that the books of the Bible deserve an intelligible explication no less than Herodotus or Livy and deserve to be treated according to the same standards of plausibility and credibility. To see exactly how allegorical interpretations of the Bible threatened common-sense credulity, Toland asked his readers to think of the effect of using these same techniques in trying to understand the writings of a classical author or historian. In effect, he cautioned, no source of information could be accepted at face value as expressing truth if the tortuous techniques of some types of biblical criticism were used in everyday life. In dealing with one another, men accept only what makes sense to them; it should not be any different, Toland suggested, in religion.

From Toland's point of view, then, the mystification of religion, promoted through popery and priestcraft, had resulted in the layman's loss of confidence in his ability to think for himself. This meant that he had yielded his authority to make judgments in theological and religious matters to professional moral and religious watchdogs. "As authority in matters of judgement, necessarily causes laziness and stupidity: so from ignorance thus establish'd under the management of Priests, whose interest leads them to continue it, no less naturally procede loose morals and savage customs."[38] As men become lax in making their own decisions about religious and moral matters they lose their ability to evaluate rationally their own customs. Their implicit confidence in one another degenerates into an uncritical acceptance of the judgment of authorities.

After the publication of *Christianity Not Mysterious*, Toland repeat-

---

35. "Clidophorus," *Tetradymus*, p. 81.
36. "Hodegus," *Tetradymus*, p. 11.
37. *Nazarenus*, preface, p. viii. See Chiara Giuntini, *Panteismo e ideologia repubblicana: John Toland (1670–1722)* (Bologna: Il Mulino, 1979), pp. 27–30, 112.
38. "Irish Manuscript," *Nazarenus*, p. 17.

edly ran up against examples of individuals who had ceded their ability to judge for themselves to religious authorities. Referring to himself in the third person, he wrote:

When Mr. Toland us'd to be traduc'd in Ireland for *Deism* with many other Opinions, and his Friends demanded of his Accusers where they made those Discoveries in his Writings, the ready Answer always was, that truly they had never read the Book, and by the Grace of God never would; but that they receiv'd their Information from such as were proper Judges of the thing. O how inseparable is *Popery* from *Ignorance*! And what is the source of all *Popery* but *Implicit Belief* whereever it is found?[39]

Toland's warning was this: intellectual, moral, and religious laziness and stupidity result when the individual fails to maintain the strong habit of making critical decisions. Once the individual is hoodwinked into thinking that he can no longer make proper judgments in matters affecting his life he has lost control of decision making based upon common sense and upon what he understands.

2. THE NATURAL ABILITY TO PHILOSOPHIZE

Interest in the expansion of religious authority to include the common man was neither new nor unique to Toland. Throughout the seventeenth century authors in England repeatedly returned to the theme of the role of individual and communal reason in the evaluation of Scripture-based religion. Herbert of Cherbury (1583–1648) had warned against placing too much confidence in the authority of priests and preachers; and he argued that mysteries and prophecies inconsistent with or unencompassed by the "common notions" of mankind were to be rejected.

Members of the Great Tew Circle—a group of scholars and poets who met at the house of Lucius Cary, Viscount Falkland (1610–43) at Great Tew, seventeen miles from Oxford—proclaimed that the *individual's* mind was the final court in which matters of religion were to be tried. Among this group were to be found such men as John Hales (1584–1656), who argued that the seat of authority in religion was to be

---

39. *Apology*, p. 19.

found ultimately in reason and conscience, that revelation must be interpreted by the enlightened mind of man, and that no other person or group could do an individual's thinking for him. William Chillingworth (1602–44), another member of the Great Tew Circle, noted that men attained salvation from God, not by grasping some particular truth, but in truly striving to live the life they thought God intended for them.[40]

In the 1640s Falkland's library at Great Tew and the Bodleian Library at Oxford contained numerous Socinian works and attracted a number of thinkers who incorporated the Socinian emphasis on toleration, reason, and Scripture into their works. Socinian thinkers like John Bidle (1616–62) and John Fry (1609–57) went so far as to claim that beliefs either *contrary to* or *above* rational understanding could not be part of true Christian religion.[41] But such claims conflicted with the teachings of Faustus Socinus (1539–1604), who had allowed for truths in Christianity *beyond* reason.

Socinus, however, had sown the seeds for the development of ideas like those of Bidle and Fry by proposing the following argument. Certain divine truths are above reason and human capacity as long as divine revelation does not manifest them; when they are revealed, however, they cease to be above reason. If it is wrong, Socinus reasoned, to deny something because we cannot comprehend it, then it is fitting that we can deny something (such as the doctrine of the Trinity) that is contradictory. That is, if we must accept a doctrine we do not comprehend, and if the reason for this acceptance of a suprarational doctrine is that it transcends reason, then the very distinction between doctrines in accord with reason and those beyond implies the assumed validity of the principle of noncontradiction as encompassed by reason. Otherwise, those things that are beyond reason are beyond the principle of noncontradiction and are unintelligible. The very principle that allows for meaningful distinctions between rational, irrational, and suprarational doctrines is convoluted in the discussion of suprarational doctrines. To say that the Christian

40. For more on the Great Tew Circle, Hales, and Chillingworth, see Herbert J. McLachlan, *Socinianism in Seventeenth Century England* (Oxford: Oxford University Press, 1951), pp. 63–83.
41. Ibid., pp. 186, 245.

religion is *true* is to claim that it must be rationally accessible; otherwise, claims to the truth of its doctrines are meaningless.[42]

The Socinian influence, so strong in the Oxford area at midcentury, persisted fifty years later when Toland went to do research at the Bodleian. Through the efforts of Bidle's Socinian converts, such as the London merchant and philanthropist Thomas Firmin (1632–97), Socinian ideas spread to London, to Cambridge, and eventually throughout England. Firmin, like Furly across the Channel, developed friendships and exchanged Socinian ideas with prominent writers like Locke and Archbishop John Tillotson. It was Firmin who encouraged Stephen Nye (1648?–1719) to compile *A Brief History of the Unitarians, commonly called Socinians* (1687), in which the Socinian emphasis on the abilities of the individual reasoner was further highlighted.

In the fifty or so years between the activity of the Great Tew Circle and Toland's research at the Bodleian, the Socinian support for toleration had become of widespread interest to religious thinkers, in large measure because of the increased presence of groups that dissented from the established Church of England. Reliable figures on the size of such groups are not available for the period before the Glorious Revolution; but by 1714, nearly one out of every ten inhabitants of England and Wales was a Dissenter, with the number as high as one in five in London and one in three in large towns like Norwich, Bristol, Birmingham, and Exeter.[43]

Socinian doctrines came under more critical scrutiny as the Socinian attitude toward toleration was perceived as a proper response to the growth of dissenting groups. Within the Church of England itself, such toleration took the form of Latitudinarianism and attracted such adherents as Locke and Newton. When Toland formally turned his attention to the central tenets of Socinianism, in 1705, he relegated the

---

42. A line of thought very similar to Socinus's characterized Toland's later discussion of mysteries in *Christianity Not Mysterious* and certainly had its effect on the writings of Bidle and Fry. On the relationship between Toland and Socinianism, see Massimo Firpo, "Il rapporto tra socinianismo e primo deismo inglese negli studi di uno storico polacco," *Critica storica* 10 (1973): 275–80; and Zbigniew Ogonowski, "Le 'Christianisme sans mystères' selon John Toland et les sociniens," *Archiwum Historii Filozofii i Myśli Społecznej* 12 (1966): 205–23.

43. Geoffrey Holmes, *Religion and Party in Late Stuart England*, Historical Association General Series Pamphlet no. 86 (London: The Historical Association, 1975), p. 14.

religious doctrines to a secondary status, elevating to prominence the concept of toleration.

When Toland arrived at Oxford, however, the air was charged with Socinian religious beliefs. The background for the disputes over the nature of the Trinity had been set in Socinian writings of the previous fifty years. With the new (though still restrained) liberties in publishing afforded by the Revolution, discussion of Socinian ideas concerning the interpretation and authority of Scripture gradually became widespread. In general, the Socinians had chosen to fight their theological battles on the question of the relation of reason and religious doctrines—particularly suprarational doctrines—rather than on the issue of the Trinity. Though Locke and Bishop Stillingfleet would later devote hundreds of pages to the Trinitarian disputes, they were several years away (in time and in interest) from what the Socinians saw as the fundamental issue in the dispute, namely, the general question of the role of human reason in religion. It was within that setting that Toland came upon the public scene.

In his first major work, *Christianity Not Mysterious*, Toland's avowed aim was to show that if Christianity contained doctrines contrary to or beyond reason, it would be meaningless and unbelievable. He thus established, at the beginning of his publishing career, a fundamental theme: that which is asserted as meaningful must be shown to be reasonable. Statements that are beyond reason not only are unreasonable but also are unbelievable, because they are meaningless.

Toland was aware that in limiting the believable to that which human reason can understand, he was challenging a widely held belief, namely, that many of the doctrines of Christianity are mysteries beyond the compass of human understanding. As early as 1694 he had been warned that any attempt to depict Christianity as devoid of mystery was ill advised and would certainly occasion censure from religious leaders.[44] Previous tracts disputing various religious claims had evoked rebuttals, attacks, and harangues even among the doctors of theology and ministers of the Church. Toland's work would have been but one more piece in the ongoing debate had he only acknowledged that some of the doctrines of Christianity were believable and reasonable in themselves though still beyond the rational understanding of men. Instead, he posited human understanding as the

44. Anonymous correspondent to Toland, 30 May 1694, in *Collection*, 2: 312.

criterion of meaning and belief: the individual can believe only what he understands; otherwise, he would not know what it is that he believes.

The argument of *Christianity Not Mysterious* can be summarized thus: Reason is the only basis of certitude; certitude does not lie in authority. This should be apparent, particularly in view of the conflicting claims of "authorities." Knowledge has its basis in clear and distinct ideas, and reason is that faculty by which we attain certainty through comparing the dubious or obscure with the evidently known. Revelation is a means by which we receive information; but the information imparted by revelation does not carry its own grounds of persuasion—unless, of course, we know beforehand that this information is, in reality, divine in origin. But as with any revelation, human or divine, we must await evidence to justify our belief that this information has, in fact, the origin claimed for it. In the case of divine revelation, all we have to work with in determining its origin is the revelation itself.

Nothing in Christianity, Toland continued, is contrary to reason, because we cannot form an idea of such a thing. For the same reason, nothing in Christianity is above reason. Revelation is accepted as divine only because it bears the marks of divine wisdom and sound reason. Any revelation exceeding the grasp of human reason would simply be unintelligible. By Christian "mysteries," either we mean (*a*) intelligible doctrines veiled in the figures and symbols of heathen or Jewish practices and made intelligible to the common man in the New Testament, or we mean (*b*) intelligible doctrines convoluted by the clergy so that they might exercise some power over laymen, or we mean (*c*) things inconceivable in themselves. Mysteries are not things that are simply inadequately known, for that is the case in all that we know (even concerning a blade of grass). In the New Testament we have the explanation of previously hidden doctrines, and we have the assurance that Christianity is directed to all men and therefore must contain doctrines essentially easy to grasp. Those "mysteries" that still survive must be the contrivances by which men try to persuade each other to adopt certain beliefs without having to provide evidence for those beliefs.

In some ways, Toland's line of argument appears to be in accord with the Socinian view that because Christian revelation is from God and is therefore true, it must be rational and accessible. But the similarity is deceptive. Toland's approach differed from the Socinians' in that he recommended that the Scriptures be tested for reasonableness *before* being accepted as divine revelations.

Toland began his argument with the implied premises that (*a*) true religion is reasonable, that (*b*) true Christianity is reasonable, and that (*c*) Christian religion is founded on revelation. The final premise is the problematic one: (*d*) only those revelations that are reasonable could possibly qualify as the bases for true Christianity, because revelations contradicting or exceeding reason would not be regulated by the rational distinction of truth and falsity. To say that a revelation is true or false is to say that it is rationally accessible. Any revelation (including Christian revelations) that is not rationally accessible, then, cannot be true. Toland concludes that *if* Christian revelation is reasonable, it is true.[45] He thus forces the Christian apologist into the predicament of having to say either that Christian revelation is not reasonable or that it is not true. The Socinians' very premises Toland cast into the form of a hypothetical doubt.

In effect, Toland's argument assumes that intelligibility and meaning are not first *constituted* by infinite reason and only later *discovered* by finite reason. If one adopts the view that some religious doctrines are intelligible in themselves, or are intelligible to infinite reason but are inaccessible to finite reason (in that they are mysteries), then finite reason must blindly submit to infinite reason. Insofar as finite reason would not have access to such mysteries, it could understand neither them nor the infinite reason that comprehends them. Reason could not be recognized as finite without some infinite reason to which it could be contrasted. But if such an infinite reason could not be understood, then the finite character of finite reason would also be unintelligible.

In short, if the meanings of infinite reason and that which infinite reason comprehends are inaccessible to finite reason, then the very concepts of an infinite reason and of doctrines accessible only to infinite reason are meaningless to finite reasoners. Human reasoners, then, must reject as meaningless the dichotomy of infinite reason and finite reason.

Even before the publication of *Christianity Not Mysterious*, Toland's concern for a reinterpretation of reason's ability to understand Christian mysteries began to generate responses outside the realm of religious debate. Recent evidence from Locke's manuscripts indicates

45. Firpo, "Il rapporte," pp. 275–76. See also Gerard Reedy, S.J., "Socinians, John Toland, and the Anglican Rationalists," *Harvard Theological Review* 70 (1977): 285–304; and Alfredo Sabetti, *John Toland, un irregolare della società e della cultura Inglese tra seicento e settecento* (Naples: Liguori, 1976), p. 158.

that contrary to the widespread belief that Toland's *Christianity Not Mysterious* was a reply to Locke's *Reasonableness of Christianity* (1695), the latter was actually a response to the manuscript notes of Toland's work.[46] Having seen Toland's manuscript a full two years before its publication, Locke recognized the work as a threat to his own attempt to limit claims about the capabilities of human reason. He thus was careful to show that his emphasis on human understanding did not eliminate the need for faith as an aid to reason in religious matters. Toland, of course, had argued that human reason places limits on matters properly called religious. In effect, it is Toland's reduction of faith to a form of knowledge that distinguishes his position from Locke's.[47]

When *Christianity Not Mysterious* was finally published, the resulting outcry startled even Toland. True, he had questioned the mysteriousness of Christianity; but that in itself does not explain the book's impact. To appreciate its effect not only on Locke and Leibniz but on laymen and students as well, we must understand that Toland intentionally addressed a broad audience, demonstrating in his very mode of writing that reason was not the possession of the learned alone:

I have endeavour'd to speak very intelligibly, and am not without Hope that my Assertions do carry their own Light along with them. I have in many places made explanatory Repetitions of difficult Words, by synonymous Terms of more general and known Use. This Labour, I grant, is of no Benefit to Philosophers, but is of considerable Advantage to the Vulgar, which I'm far from neglecting, like those who in every Preface tell us they neither court nor care for them. I wonder how any can speak at this rate, especially those whose very Business it is to serve the Vulgar, and spare them the Labour of long and painful Study, which their ordinary Occupations will not allow them.[48]

46. See John C. Biddle, "Locke's Critique of Innate Principles and Toland's Deism," *Journal of the History of Ideas* 37 (1976): 418–20; and Margaret C. Jacob, *The Newtonians and the English Revolution, 1689–1720* (Ithaca, N.Y.: Cornell University Press, 1976), p. 214.

47. See Giuntini, *Panteismo*, p. 88.

48. *Christianity Not Mysterious: or, a Treatise Shewing that there is nothing in the Gospel Contrary to Reason, nor above it: and that no Christian Doctrine can be properly call'd A Mystery*, ed. Günter Gawlick (Stuttgart–Bad Cannstatt: Friedrich Frommann, 1964), pp. xviii–xix.

The philosopher, Toland argued, should intend that his labor be intelligible to the generality of men, the ordinary, the vulgar. Otherwise, philosophy becomes a business, or occupation, of specialists oblivious of their duty to serve men with ordinary occupations. To grant to the learned a capacity for independent thought while denying it to the vulgar is unjustified, Toland maintained. For just as the learned rely on experience and universal principles when judging of matters outside their professions, so can the vulgar:

Nor can any from this Office of the Clergy infer, that the Vulgar are implicitly to receive their Arbitrary Dictates, no more than I am to make over my Reason to him I employ to read, transcribe, or collect for me. The Learned will not, contrary to the Experience of their own Taste, take the Brewer's or the Baker's Word for the Goodness of Bread or Drink, tho ignorant of their Craft. And why may not the Vulgar likewise be Judges of the true Sense of Things, tho they understand nothing of the Tongues from whence they are translated for their Use? Truth is always and every where the same; And an unintelligible or absurd Proposition is to be never the more respected for being antient or strange, for being originally written in Latin, Greek, or Hebrew. Besides, a Divinity only intelligible to such as live by it, is, in humane Language, a Trade.[49]

Toland did not object to the arbitrariness per se of the clergy's dictates: the arbitrations or judgments of the vulgar were just as dependent upon personal experiences. The idea, however, that truth (specifically, religious truth) should be understood as the special domain of a particular craft or trade, he found offensive.

Toland believed that no one should presume to reason for another. One reasons for himself—dictating, asserting his judgments of the "true sense" of things, that is, the sense in which those things are meaningful to him. He cannot relinquish his ability to reason, because no one else properly speaks for him. Particular reason is essentially assertive. Meaning is constituted in use and repetition. Insofar as one asserts that which is intelligible to him, he *reasons* individually.

In *Christianity Not Mysterious* Toland appealed to ordinary men for support in his attack on the unintelligible or absurd elements in religion. More importantly, in his deliberate use of a particular literary style, he encouraged his readers to rely on their own assertions for determining intelligibility. Toland's republicanism expressed in political form his aim of enfranchising the vulgar with the power of their

49. Ibid., pp. xix–xxi.

own reason, the power to question the prominence of religious ministers and magistrates in discussions about religion. It was primarily for this reason that Toland's book provoked more than fifty replies in print, was attacked by clergymen from their pulpits, and was condemned and burned by the lower house of the Irish Parliament.

From the very beginning, Toland was aware of the need to regard his endeavor to speak intelligibly as part of a communal endeavor. Although he often used the first person in speaking about his own assertions and often affirmed the individual's capacity for independent thought, he recognized the social character of the light of nature: men enlighten each other—at least they hope to—by means of their assertions. Essential to this mutual enlightenment was the endeavor to instill and to support in others confidence in the benefit of shared assertions. Toland remarked in 1698 that "a Man would be in a miserable state of Darkness and Ignorance, were it not for the Light that others afford him: and therefore they are obliged to increase as much as they can each others Knowledg, especially in Religion, which they can no otherwise do, than by communicating to one another what they think is the Truth, and the Reason by which they endeavour to prove it."[50] In this way Toland invited ordinary men to engage in joint probative reasoning toward truth as well as in the assertion of what they meant. Immediately after the above passage he noted that men are encouraged to help one another by the light of nature and by the written word. His reference to the light of nature in this context underscored the mutual enlightening effect of communication: *Our* light of nature complements and fulfills *my* light of nature.

The light metaphor was one Toland returned to often, always conscious of the distinction of this-light-as-personal-reason and this-light-as-communal-reason. In one of his late works, *Pantheisticon*, he referred to the distinction in terms of the difference between *lux* and *lumen*: "Ratio est vera & prima Lex; Lux, lumenque vitae." Reason is the true and first law, the light and illumination of life.[51] Light-as-source (in the individual) is joined with light-as-transmitted (in the

50. *A Letter to a Member of Parliament, Shewing that a restraint On the Press is inconsistent with the Protestant Religion* (London: J. Darby, 1698), pp. 6–7. For Toland's explicit views on the social means for improving meanings and probative reasonings, see below, chaps. 5 and 6.

51. *Pantheisticon: or, the Form of Celebrating the Socratic Society* (London: Sam Peterson, 1751), p. 73 (p. 57).

community). It was Toland's hope that his assertions (as sources) enlightened—"carried their own light to"—his readers. There was no guarantee that light-as-source would illuminate anything: this was where the communicator-reasoner would fall back on hope.

Toland's broad invitation to a communal endeavor to determine truth admitted not only of the need but also of the right to communicate what men think is the truth. "Men have the same right to communicate their thoughts," he wrote, "as to think themselves; and where the one is denied, the other is seldom used, or to little purpose."[52] By pointing up the relationship between every man's thought ("truths") and every man's endeavor to communicate those thoughts to others, Toland linked thought to communication. This highlighted communication's reflexive effect on thought. As long as the common man maintained his authority to speak, and thereby his right to think, he would be implicitly asserting his own contribution to the establishment of truth.

None of this is meant to imply that Toland assumed that ordinary people did or would agree on the terms they used, the ideas they had, or the particular reasons for the positions they held. Indeed, he conceded, in *Christianity Not Mysterious*, that some men who desire to make a name for themselves question the very meaning of the words they use—as if the meanings themselves could be correct or incorrect:

It appears to me very odd, that Men should need Definitions and Explanations of that whereby they define and explain all other things: or that they cannot agree about what they all pretend, in some measure at least, to possess; and is the only Privilege they claim over Brutes and Inanimates. But we find by Experience, that the word *Reason* is become as equivocal and ambiguous as any other; though all that are not tickl'd with the Vanity of Singularity, or Itch of Dispute, are at bottom agreed about the Thing.[53]

Surely, Toland recognized, men may disagree on what they mean by particular words: "As Men have different Capacities, Apprehensions, and Opportunities, so they cannot possibly but have *different Notions* of things."[54] Each person's use of a particular word probably is shaded in a way that distinguishes that meaning or notion from all others.

But Toland was more concerned with the question of whether some

---

52. *Letter to a Member of Parliament*, p. 8.
53. *CNM*, p. 8.
54. *The Memorial of the State of England* (London: Booksellers of London and Westminster, 1705), p. 44.

notions for which the same term is used are *better* (progressively improvable) or more justified than others. He objected to the implication that there was some *best* meaning of a term, grounded in something other than how men (the learned as well as the vulgar) chose to use the term. In determining the correct use of a term men should not expect a justification of the definition itself. Initial notions or working definitions can be modified in light of general usage, not of a closer approximation to some "real" meaning, corresponding to a reality that transcends everyday usage.

The involvement of the common man in the philosophic enterprise meant, for Toland, the recognition of a relatively widespread community of language users. Such language users know roughly (i.e., sufficiently for their everyday purposes) what they mean when conversing with one another. Within such a community, Toland reasoned, an individual should feel confident in sharing communal determinations of meanings.

This is not to say that private, individual assertions bestow meaning or provide the standard upon which questions of meaning could be answered. Toland respected his self-imposed limitation in this regard: "I shall never make an agreement with my own notions, to be the measure of other men's abilities."[55] The challenge was to explain how meaning is established by individual assertions whereas truth is limited to a communally determined meaning. Toland's position encourages the individual to share in the constitution of meaning without going so far as to say that the individual determines truth in a purely private way.

For example, once we understand the truths of religion as having meaning because they are our shared dictates, we break free of the idea that religious truths are somehow "out there," discernible only by those who have made it their profession to study religion or theology. The immediate danger in this liberation lies in going to the other extreme, in thinking that religious truths are meaningful in terms of private notions. Toland quickly thwarted such a move. "Religion is not to be modell'd according to our Fancies, nor to be judg'd of as it relates to our private Designs; else there would be full as many Creeds as Persons: but how little soever our Notions agree, and let our worldly Conveniences be what they will, Religion is always the same."[56] Unlike some of

---

55. "Hodegus," *Tetradymus*, p. 55.
56. *CNM*, p. xiii. See Giuntini, *Panteismo*, p. 265.

the seventeenth-century deists (e.g., Herbert of Cherbury and Charles Blount) and contemporaries such as Shaftesbury and Matthew Tindal, Toland did not believe that religion is an instinctive tendency in man. It is by means of religion, however, that individuals from all cultures continue to respond sympathetically to the ancient doctrine that men participate directly and immediately in the material, infinite, and eternal life of the universe. This sense of a relationship to the divine is universal and thus places restraints on private notions of religion.

The everyday confidence men have in one another needs to be tempered, Toland believed, by the recognition that individuals and even large groups can be mistaken. In his *Letters to Serena* he noted that the entire letter on idolatry and the reasons for heathenism "is a memorable Proof and Instance to what an astonishing degree of Extravagance human Nature is capable of arriving."[57] But acknowledging the authority of the vulgar's assertions did not lead him to idealize the insights or pronouncements of the common man: nothing about human nature is necessarily moderate. This qualification—that the pronouncements of the common man were not necessarily to be preferred over those of the "professionals"—developed only gradually in Toland's writings. His confidence in the ability of the vulgar to recognize their own right to make judgments in religious matters was deeply shaken by the widespread negative response, even among the lay population, to his *Christianity Not Mysterious*. The popularizing tone of the statements like "Religion is always the same," in *Christianity Not Mysterious*, was replaced eight years later, in the *Letters to Serena*, by more cynical statements like "in all times Superstition is the same." "If any shou'd wonder how Men cou'd leave the direct and easy Path of Reason to wander in such inextricable Mazes, let him but consider how in very many and considerable Regions the plain Institution of JESUS CHRIST cou'd degenerate into the most absurd Doctrins, unintelligible Jargon, ridiculous Practices, and inexplicable Mysterys: and how almost in every corner of the world Religion and Truth cou'd be chang'd into Superstition and Priestcraft."[58] Both religion and superstition could result from Toland's call to the vulgar to recognize that the ordinary, day-to-day activity of reasoning in divine matters is the same direct and easy process by which they reason about mundane affairs.

57. *Serena*, p. 129.
58. Ibid.

Toland wanted to tap man's natural curiosity without allowing it to give way to superstition. Even judicious assertions were to be regulated by the suspension of judgment until reasonable explanations were discovered. By this he meant, even as late as 1718, that the natural inclination to explain things in terms of their causes must be tempered by patience. "Men are by nature curious enough to know the causes of things, but they are not patient enough in their search; and so will rather assign any cause, tho ever so absurd; than suspend their judgements, till they discover the true cause."[59] In emphasizing the common man's capacity for independent thought, Toland risked that some would become enamored with this authority, forming judgments —particularly in religion—from information they would consider insufficient in their ordinary occupations. As long as the brewer or baker made religious judgments with the same patient, almost skeptical restraint employed in their professions, they would avoid the excesses philosophers and theologians had noted in their claims that the common man was theologically incompetent. Toland suspected that such claims overlook the basis of our respect for the common man when he reasons on matters outside his trade. A universal assumption must operate when men deal with one another—namely, a shared sense of a common disposition—which needs to be clarified and corrected when transformed into something unreasonable and superstitious.

Although Toland's concern was to focus attention on this universal disposition toward common sense, his procedure was to go beyond the "short and easy method" of using common sense as the only yardstick in his research and writings. Early in his career, even before the publication of *Christianity Not Mysterious*, he had argued that the common-sensical, reasonable way of explaining everyday life was precisely the method men of his age would like to think was justified in questions of religion. In 1695 he wrote that "the universal disposition of this Age is bent upon a Rational Religion."[60] He viewed the characteristic inclination of his time as directed toward making religion understandable. For Toland, the movement toward enlightenment was not so much toward understanding everything; it was toward (*a*) understanding what the generality of men knew already and (*b*) evaluating knowledge claims in terms of what could be communicated (made common) to all.

59. "Druids," pp. 116–17.
60. *Two Essays Sent in a Letter*, p. i.

At that same early point in his life Toland was involved in critical, exegetical work on classical and scriptural writings. By means of such work he hoped to show how this universal disposition among his contemporaries toward a short and easy method of addressing religion itself could be justified historically. His desire for a comprehensive, historical investigation of the origin of Christianity reveals his awareness that the short and easy method of common sense was not self-justifying.[61] The methodic approach of the common man had to be justified by the historian and scholar in ways that themselves were not short and easy. It was hoped that a justification would inspire the ordinary man to have faith in his own common-sense pronouncements in all matters, including religion.

In Toland's view, the task of the philosopher was to devote himself to an enterprise whose goal was the widespread communication of the results of serious contemplation and impartial inquiry. It is not surprising that one of the few places where Toland spoke about "what we truly call Philosophy, and not any peculiar system of the Schools," was a short work outlining a means of publishing the results of philosophic inquiry—"A Project of a Journal Intended to be Published Weekly." The philosopher, he noted there, had "addicted himself to a serious contemplation of the works of God and Nature, to a diligent examination of times and places, and to an impartial enquiry into men and opinions."[62] Contemplation, examination, and inquiry—all were often inaccessible to the vulgar because their ordinary occupations did not allow them the opportunity for this "labour of long and painful Study." Toland's philosophic investigations indicated to him that the vulgar were justified in their common-sense beliefs about how the world was meaningful to them. But he realized that to fulfill his task as a reflective thinker he had to convey his findings in ways that not only asserted the common man's capacity for independent thought but also intelligibly appealed to a common audience.

61. For an account of how this characteristic of Toland distinguishes him from other Deistic writers and explains, in some part, his effect on nineteenth-century German biblical scholarship, see David Patrick, "Two English Forerunners of the Tübingen School: Thomas Morgan and John Toland," *Theological Review* (London) 14 (1877): 593–601.

62. In *Collection*, 2: 211–12.

3. AUTHORITY BEYOND MYSTERY

As he recognized that men often do not have time to evaluate the "mysterious" aspects of religion and government and that fables, allegories, and metaphor could be effective in educating men in the practical demands of life Toland gradually became aware of the need to direct his argument toward a less-than-universal audience. That all men have the *ability* to make common-sense judgments did not necessarily entail that all would appreciate being told so. Many considered it untrue that they might believe (or think they believe) something that made no sense to them.

Toland thus began to address the need to distinguish between various common forms of sense—political, practical, and so on. All men, whatever their profession, assume that they understand what they talk about. The politician need not understand the art of baking to determine whether some bread is good, nor the baker the workings of government to judge a government incompetent. At least the major figures in any good government, Toland noted, ought to be "rightly informed, and have due notions, not only of what's true in speculation, but likewise of what's useful in practice, or beneficial to the society. And if they begin with the last, they may be sure to discover the first."[63] The practical usefulness and benefit of particular information and ideas hint at speculative truths—in politics, in baking, even in religion.

Toland did not explicitly claim that speculative propositions were true *because* they were useful or beneficial. The point of his pragmatic method—which starts with use and benefit, then works back to speculative truth—was to show that the very meaning of speculative claims is determined and limited by what one practically understands. The pragmatic criteria for truth remain the same in religion. "Nothing that serves to lessen the quiet, peace, union, and happiness of men, can be true Religion; since one of its main ends (and perhaps the chiefest in this world) is to retain 'em the more effectually in their several duties."[64] Just as true religion guided men in their duties, so the result of priestcraft was loose morals and savage customs.[65]

Underlying this emphasis on the social character of man's duties,

---

63. "The Primitive Constitution of the Christian Church," in *Collection*, 2: 121.
64. Ibid.
65. See above, n. 38.

peace, union, and happiness is the worldly character of the meaning of religious claims in general. The determination of the truth or falsity of a religious claim presumes the meaningfulness of the claim. Mysteries, insofar as they claim something that cannot be understood in a common-sense, practical way, cannot be true or false; they are humanly meaningless. They cannot be "common to" (shared by) men without appeal to some authority beyond the individual believer. But in relinquishing his authority to limit truth to what seems reasonable to him one relinquishes his capacity for independent thought. Because of this, Toland argued, each man should recognize his essential role in contributing to the communal authority of statements regarding communal ("practical") matters while not yielding to anyone his authority in speculative matters.

Toland approached the classic conflict between reason and authority as one between that which makes sense to the individual and that which is proposed as sensible because it seems sensible to others. Reason, he maintained, is its own authority. When the individual reasons for himself he limits his beliefs to what he understands rather than to what he is told he would understand had he a greater ability to reason. For Toland, the individual's reason "author-ized" facts; it answered the skeptic and provided a critique of the authority of others. "I will never allow that I am actually mistaken, because I possibly may be so: which is the silly sophism of the Sceptics, on the one hand; and, on the other, of such as wou'd dogmatically subject REASON to AUTHORITY."[66] The middle road between skepticism and dogmatic authoritarianism had characteristics of both positions: the individual's authority determined the *factual*, the meaningful; and pragmatic, communal criteria determined the *truth* of such facts.

A religion that encourages appreciation of its reasonableness but does not allow the individual to use that same criterion (of making sense) to evaluate the doctrine of the religion is essentially hypocritical. Allowed to think for himself in adopting a religion, the individual is then prevented from evaluating the authority of that religion: "You may reason yourself (for example) into what Religion you please; but, pray, what Religion will permit you to reason your self out of it?"[67] The

66. *Tetradymus*, preface, p. xvii.
67. *Serena*, p. 13.

contrast of reason and authority undermines, at the very start, claims for the authority of reason.

In short, Toland argued that if the individual reasons, then the individual himself has authority. He is an *author* of new facts. To give up one's control of what makes sense to him is to give up control of his reason and his power to provide new facts for consideration by others.

Scholars cite authors in order to provide the authority for newly advanced factual claims; it is "indispensably requisite in proving matters of fact newly advanc'd."[68] Something that is "authored"—and thus made a new matter of fact—may later be determined by communal criteria to be false, but as a fact, it will not die. Facts are tenacious; "facts are obstinate things."[69] To give up one's authority is to give up one's stake in individual existence. To be an author is to affirm one's existence through one's ability to contribute to that which is *factual*. "Such is the Nature of a Matter of Fact that though it may be conceiv'd possible enough, yet he only can with Assurance assert its Existence who is himself the Author, or by some *Means of Information* comes first to the certain Knowledg of it."[70] A matter of fact exists only through its assertion by an author or by those who endorse ("author-ize") the fact as their own as well. Others can conceive of only the *possibility* of a matter of fact.

After the furor surrounding *Christianity Not Mysterious*, Toland tempered his endorsement of this optimistic and positive description of the authority of individuals. The question of *important* facts and *true* facts started to dominate more of his thinking. He began to argue that the opinions of any author or reader, church father or English baker, were of little worth (or should have been considered as such) without the support of good reasons. In his *Letters to Serena* he wrote: "As our Opinion ought to go for nothing without good Reasons, so we admit of no Right from Possession, or no Privilege by Prescription in Philo-sophy, how much soever we allow it in national Laws or Customs. Authority is to decide matters of Fact, but not to determine the Truths of Nature."[71] Perhaps Toland was prompted by Leibniz to make his

68. "Druids," p. 167.
69. "Mangoneutes," *Tetradymus*, p. 160.
70. *CNM*, p. 40.
71. P. 164.

position on this matter clearer than he had done prior to the *Letters to Serena*. In 1702 Leibniz had written to the Electress Sophia concerning Toland: "Instead of amusing himself with philosophy, which is hardly his business, it would be better that he stick to researching facts. But I am afraid that what he wants to pass for historical description is only a novel."[72] Actually, Toland did suggest that facts are novel, that story telling (his story, history) is constitutive and fact making as much as fact researching. Leibniz's insight into Toland's project was even more to the point than Leibniz realized. For Toland, "fact" and "fiction" had very similar meanings in regard to the individual; "fact" and "truth" were very close apropos of a community. If opinions are deemed worthwhile insofar as they are supported by good reasons, then reasons themselves are determined as good insofar as they make sense to the learned and vulgar alike.

In religion, and particularly in Christianity, the determination of truth depended, Toland argued, upon the authority of those addressed rather than upon the authority of those to whom appeals were made. He emphasized that "Christ did not institute one Religion for the learned, and another for the vulgar."[73] Indeed, the plain and convincing instructions of Christ—understood by the poor, who were not supposed to understand "philosophical systems"—had their authority in virtue of their simplicity and common intelligibility. To appeal to authority, then, meant to appeal to the reader or the listener, not to some text or other author.

Toland viewed the reformation ideal of respecting the authority of the layman as extending beyond the simple belief that each individual should interpret the Scriptures for himself. All men were invited to become authorities and to speak out about the religion that had become accessible to them regardless of their professional expertise in divinity. Some of the Protestant clergy, like their "popish" counterparts, would have preferred keeping the vulgar ignorant about religious matters. They therefore were uneasy with the prospect that

any of the Laity wou'd ever write on points of Divinity or Ecclesiastical history: wheras by the original right of Nature, and the main principle of the

---

72. 9 Sept. 1702, *Die Werke von Leibniz*, ed. Onno Klopp (Hanover: Klindworth, 1873–77), ser. 1, 8: 363.

73. "Primitive Constitution," in *Collection*, 2: 131. Also see *CNM*, p. xxi.

Reformation, tis the privilege of every man, whether by word or by writing, to inform others, or to seek information from them; and this in all places, the Pulpits and other public Chairs onely excepted, which no man may lawfully fill, but they to whom the supreme power has assign'd them. To confine writing on the subjects mention'd to any set of men, wou'd be the certain way in a short time to have neither true doctrine nor true history; as is the case in fact, where and whenever this practice has been sottishly authoriz'd or even indulg'd. Ignorance becoming thus triumphant begets Credulity, as Credulity unavoidably occasions Lyes; and Lyes have recourse to Force for their support against Reason, which left free wou'd soon expose them to contemt, and then quite explode them.[74]

This privilege to speak out on matters of religion depended upon taking seriously the Reformation concentration on the individual. As an "original right of Nature" it was also a demand of man as a social, communicating being. Because doctrines were understood as true in social contexts, and because history was the result of contributions by all men, limiting such contributions to a particular set of men would lead to error since it excludes a part of nature from the source of meaning.

Because the clergy had a vested interest in maintaining their privilege and power within a relatively fixed interpretation of Scripture, their threat to the open exchange of ideas on religious topics had to be met, Toland argued, by lay management of the press. "'Tis evident that almost all the Errors and wrong Notions in Religion have had their rise and chief Support from [the Clergy]. So that upon the whole, if the Press should be trusted with any, it ought to be with Lay-men, who have no Powers, Prerogatives, or Privileges to gain by perverting of Scripture, since they pretend to none but what they receive from the Society."[75] This, of course, did not mean that laymen were more qualified in religious matters than the clergy: "*Lay-men* are as improper judges of Religion as the *Priests*."[76] With a universal freedom of speech, though, men would be able to test the authority of their own convictions against the criterion of what convinced them: "Since Religion is calculated for reasonable Creatures, 'tis Conviction and not Authority that should bear weight with them."[77]

74. "Mangoneutes," *Tetradymus*, p. 142.
75. *Letter to a Member of Parliament*, p. 23.
76. *A Defence of Mr. Toland in a Letter to Himself* (London: E. Whitlock, 1697), p. 13.
77. *CNM*, p. xv.

Conviction—believing only what is evident—has both an individual and a communal character. Men often think they can believe that which they do not understand, that is, they think they can assent to something without its being evident to them. This is not properly called "believing." Rather, it is being caught up in a superstitious conviction (which is only improperly called "belief").

Whatever is evidently repugnant to the individual's clear and distinct ideas, or whatever is evidently repugnant to our commonly shared meanings or "notions," is contrary to reason.[78] That is, anything that contradicts how we intend our ideas to be understood is contrary to reason. The way to approach the description of reason, Toland suggested, is to stress the need for men to limit themselves, individually and collectively, to what is evident. He pointed out that God has

endu'd us with the Power *of suspending our Judgments about whatever is uncertain, and of never assenting but to clear Perceptions.* He is so far from putting us upon any Necessity of erring, that as he has thus privileg'd us on the one hand with a Faculty of guarding our selves against Prepossession or Precipitation, by *placing our Liberty only in what is indifferent, or dubious and obscure;* so he provides on the other hand, that we should discern and embrace the Truth, *by taking it out of our Power to dissent from an evident Proposition.*[79]

It is not a sign of obstinacy to suspend judgment about the uncertain and unsatisfying. Toland himself remarked on several occasions that he could be persuaded by cogent arguments to change his views. But clerical attacks and physical abuse from street crowds could not force a retreat from the beliefs he maintained and for which he felt he had satisfactory reasons.[80]

According to Toland, we *cannot* dissent from an evident proposition —one that is satisfying, understandable, and coherent with other beliefs we hold true:

It is impossible for us to err as long as we take *Evidence* for our Guide; and we never mistake, but when we wander from it by abusing our *Liberty,* in denying that of any thing which belongs to it, or attributing to it what we do not see in its Idea. This is the primary and universal Origin of all our *Errors.* . . . [God

78. Ibid., p. 23.
79. Ibid., p. 20.
80. *Amyntor,* p. 59.

himself] has put us under a Law of bowing before the Light and Majesty of *Evidence*. And truly if we might doubt of any thing that is clear, or be deceiv'd by distinct Conceptions, there could be nothing certain: Neither Conscience, nor God himself, should be regarded: No Society or Government could subsist. . . . If Things be deliver'd in Words not understood by the Hearer, nor demonstrated to agree with other Truths already very clear, or now so made to him, he cannot conceive 'em. Likewise if the Order of Nature and due Simplicity be not observ'd, he cannot see them evidently true or false; and so suspends his Judgment (if no Affection sways him) where another, it may be, receives perfect Satisfaction.[81]

Evidence serves not only as the guide for the determination of speculative truths but also as the justification for promoting the moral precepts without which society and government could not subsist. The speculative doctrines of Christianity, for example, are offered to "the light of internal persuasion"; its moral precepts are left to "the care of external laws."[82] Evidence to the individual, in terms of the conviction of his own conscience, is distinct from that to a group or society. And though the determination of what is evident in matters of "common practice" must sometimes admit only probability, a much more strict ("perfect") satisfaction is required of what is evident to the individual.

The cascading effect of Toland's use of the terminology of evidence, truth, meaning, and reason prompted some of his contemporaries to observe that he had confused some of these topics. Richard Willis, in his *Reflexions* on *Christianity Not Mysterious* (1697), noted that Toland's definition of *evidence* was really a proper definition of *truth*.[83] One may think something truly, Willis argued, but not have evidence for what one thinks. However, Toland had been very cautious when he defined evidence as the conformity of our ideas with their objects *or with the things we think upon*. Something is meaningful *as evidence* insofar as it can be incorporated into those things we can think. We do not truly think of anything for which we do not have evidence. A proposition cannot be true unless it is incorporated into a set of beliefs that are evident to us.

John Norris also disagreed with Toland's notion of truth. In *An*

81. *CNM*, pp. 19–22.
82. "Primitive Constitution," in *Collection*, 2: 136.
83. *Reflexions upon Mr. Toland's Book, Called Christianity Not Mysterious*, 2nd ed. (London: M. Wotton, 1701), p. 5. The first edition of Willis's book was no. 3 of the *Occasional Paper* (1697).

Account of Reason and Faith (1697), Norris remarked that faith concerns the *truth* of a proposition, not its *meaning*—the connection of ideas, not the ideas themselves.[84] But Toland had not argued that belief or faith is the basis for our education in meanings. Meanings are not open to belief or disbelief. If they were, then in learning a meaning one would not *understand* what he is to believe. On the other hand, a proposition cannot be true unless it is meaningful. We have to know that a proposition is meaningful *before* we can judge its truth. The very meaning of the term "truth" is determined in the context of meanings that are interdependently *evident*. To claim that a proposition might be true, even though it is not meaningful to us, is to portray the notion of truth as outside the general understanding of all meanings.

To put Toland's position in more contemporary terms, the concept of truth is meaningful only in the context of its coherence with other meanings. Even if we say, along with Norris, that our belief refers to the correspondence of the proposition with objective reality, we still must *understand* the reality itself before we can believe in its correspondence with the proposition. And the only way this can be done involves recognizing propositions and objects as evident.

Although Toland distinguished individual from communal types of evidence, his point in emphasizing the necessity of strict adherence to evidence was to encourage the individual to believe in his own authority when making decisions. Particularly in regard to religion, the individual's right to claim certainty must be upheld in order to answer the skeptic's charges about conflicting appeals to revelations or interpretations by "authorities." If the individual depends wholly on the authority of others in religious matters, he extinguishes that light within himself by which other men could benefit and by which he adjudicates conflicts in authority. To accept religious mysteries as beyond human reason, or to believe that religious authorities have more insight than the vulgar, is to underestimate individual and collective human abilities:

There are a thousand things in our Power to know, of which, through Prejudice or Neglect, we may be, and frequently remain ignorant all our Life; and innumerable Difficulties may be made by imagining *Mysteries* where there are none, or by conceiving too discouraging and unjust an Opinion of our own

84. (London: S. Manship, 1697), p. 77.

Abilities: whereas, by a Parity of Reason, we may hope to outdo all that outdid others before us, as Posterity may exceed both. *'Tis no presumption* therefore *for us to endeavour setting things in a better light*.[85]

Reason is the special domain of neither the ancients nor the theologians. The equal dispersion, or "parity," of reason serves to restrain the claims of the skeptic and dogmatist alike. For skepticism and religious dogmatism result in fundamentally the same thing—the denial of man's ability to attain certain knowledge in religion.

In asserting the right of the individual to think for himself, Toland certainly did not attempt to destroy religion. Mystery religions (including a Christianity that contained mysteries beyond man's understanding) destroy themselves because they generate internal skepticism. Had Toland wished to destroy religion by recognizing the ability of the individual to see beyond proposed "mysteries" (as some of his detractors charged), he would have made it more rather than less mysterious.

There is a question, however, about the extent to which concentration on the individual can be pushed in regard to *revealed* religions, especially in cases where revelations are proposed as transcending the grasp of human reason. For an answer we must turn to Toland's treatment of the meaningfulness of reason and revelation, particularly as it becomes expressed in the historically novel individual.

---

85. *CNM*, pp. 63–64. Also see *Vindicius Liberius: or M. Toland's Defence of himself Against the late Lower House of Convocation, and Others* (London: Bernard Lintott, 1702), pp. 18–19.

II

Reason in Biography

UNLIKE MANY OTHER PHILOSOPHERS, Toland devoted a sizable amount of his time and energy to biographical work. Although he also produced historical works on movements or peoples (e.g., the Druids) and often remarked the need for a complete history of England, he preferred to focus on the *individual* in history. Whether in a biography of Milton or Harrington, in brief accounts of the major figures of the House of Hanover, or in introductions to collected memoirs of such prominent figures as Lord Holles of Ifield (1599–1680), and Lieutenant General Edmund Ludlow (1617–92), Toland's treatments always portrayed the individual as the center around which events occurred.

Toland regarded authors as special individuals. Revealing themselves in their writings, they helped each reader to recognize the novelty of his own life. Each individual's life revealed something about all other lives and something found in no other life. His biographical works allude to those special revelations but do not pursue the thematic importance of the individual expressed elsewhere in his writings.

Biography served Toland as an oblique reference to the uniqueness and particular importance of his own writings. In addition, biography had a further significance for Toland's insistence that every individual think for himself. Insofar as the individual reasons for himself and is not prejudiced by outside opinions, he distinguishes himself from all others. The reflexive impact of biography on the biographer is revelatory in itself. In writing about another's life, the biographer transcends that life; and in recognizing this transcendence, he also acknowledges the continuous impulse to transcend what he himself is at any moment.

This chapter starts with a consideration of Toland's treatment of the author as a source of revelation and moves (in section 2) to his discussion of the author's role in public communication, that is, communal revelation. When public communication fails to adapt to what individuals see as reasonable, prejudices result; section 3 is concerned with how this occurs in Toland's treatment of reason and its revelatory acts. Section four describes the ways in which the self can transcend itself (according to Toland) and takes up Toland's application of the concept of transcendence to himself as prophet and physician.

1. THE PROBLEM OF NOVEL AUTHORS

Much of Toland's explicitly biographical work occurred in the years 1698–1700. During this period following the turmoil created by *Christianity Not Mysterious*, Toland wrote biographies of John Milton and of James Harrington, author of *The Commonwealth of Oceana*. In 1699 he edited the memoirs of Lord Holles and General Ludlow, both of whom had become heroes of the radical Whigs because of their struggles against the repressive governments of Charles I and Oliver Cromwell. In addition, Toland's *Amyntor* (1699), which answered critics of his "Life of Milton," appeared during this time and served as an indication of how quickly and seriously Toland responded to attacks against what was called his "peculiar method" of biography.

In the case of his "Life of Milton," Toland's peculiar method was to let Milton's words speak for themselves. As an "indifferent Historian," Toland noted that this method was for him a "Rule religiously adhered to."[1] He realized that his peculiar method of presenting what he regarded as the true Milton was not that followed by most historians, who trod the "common road" and described the actions or sentiments of their subjects through paraphrase or summary. In anticipation of the objection that he was putting his own sentiments in the mouth of Milton, Toland decided upon direct quotation as "the best and only good way of writing the History of such a man.... For what, I pray is the principal Part of a Learned Man's Life, but the exact History of his Books and Opinions, to inform the World about the occasion of his

---

1. *Amyntor*, pp. 3–5. On Toland's 1698–99 connections with the radical Whigs and with the republican thought of Milton, Algernon Sidney, and Harrington, see Sabetti, *John Toland*, pp. 115–32; Giuntini, *Panteismo*, pp. 166–98; and Margaret C. Jacob, *The Radical Enlightenment: Pantheists, Freemasons, and Republicans* (London: George Allen and Unwin, 1981), pp. 60, 118, 151.

writing, what it contain'd, how he perform'd it, and with what Consequences or Success?"[2]

Admittedly, this method of exact history is not available to the biographer of a man of action. But the words of a man of letters have been preserved and thus become the central point of reference for his biographer. The author *lives* in his words, and his *life* should be largely an account of his writings. Had the ancients followed this rule of direct quotation more thoroughly, Toland noted, modern critics would not face the difficulty of trying to decide whether an author has been properly understood by historians.[3]

In his epitaph Toland returned to this theme of letting the author's words speak for themselves. To those who followed him and wanted to know more of him, Toland suggested a search of his writings. He saw himself continuing to live on through each reader, frequently to rise again, yet never to remain the same.[4] For him, life consisted in being "the author," the source, the originator. In this regard, Leibniz was rather perceptive (and not purely ironical) when he wrote that Toland "loves to make the grand discourse, in a word, he wants to be an author."[5] The learned man's life, Toland believed, *is* in his communication. He lives specifically in his writings, which continue to exist after he dies. Any biography that does no more than summarize or paraphrase an author's writings implicitly fails to respect the life in the author's very words.

This is not to say that Toland, as an editor, hesitated in placing his own mark on compilations of the writings of Milton, Harrington, and Ludlow. In his biography of Milton, which prefaced an edition of Milton's works, Toland complained that he was unable to persuade the publisher to leave out some of the political essays that were of interest only to Milton's contemporaries. Toland was more successful when he edited Harrington's works, in that he was able to select which works were to be included. He had access to some of Harrington's manuscripts as well and presumably exercised editorial discretion in preparing them for publication.[6]

There is also a strong likelihood that it was Toland who extensively

2. Ibid., p. 6.
3. Ibid., pp. 6–7.
4. BM Add. MS 4295, fol. 76.
5. Leibniz to Electress Sophia, 9 Sept. 1702, *Werke*, ser. 1, 8: 362.
6. "Life of Harrington," p. x.

revised the manuscript of Ludlow's memoirs. The published *Memoirs* differs greatly in style and tone from the manuscript.[7] This could indicate that Toland, with his early fervor for the Country Party and with his antipathy for the prospect of a standing army, was not above modifying Ludlow's text to present him as a country gentleman with classical (even republican) interests. Toland's treatment of these memoirs reveals his conviction that it was important to republish selected works and to adapt manuscripts and previously unpublished material to the stylistic needs and practical concerns of his contemporaries. He later justified his publication of some letters by Shaftesbury on similar grounds, namely, that the letters would benefit his contemporaries. Toland refrained from editorial intrusions, however, when *re*publishing.

For Toland, biography highlighted its subject as the starting point, the author and originator of novelty in the world. When delivering a novel message, each speaker or writer is, for him, "the author." Putting this view to practice, Toland chose silence when he had nothing new to say. In a letter to Shaftesbury, for example, he indicated his disdain for writing pieces that were not lasting and novel: "Gentlemen's Letters of Ceremony, and Schollar's Letters of Trifles, are things I never rellisht; and therefore you must not look on my Respect or Gratitude to be less, tho I never write, having in Reality nothing worth while to communicate."[8] The ceremonies of gentlemen and the trifling concerns of scholars are of little worth because they lack novelty. Every true *author* feels that he contributes a new perspective, a discovery, or a better understanding of religion, law, or history. For this reason, Toland relished the stance of the author, specifying that the worth of such a stance was dependent upon its novelty.

Toland agreed with his critics that his ideas were not of the sort commonly approved. But to say something out of the ordinary, he believed, is precisely the means by which the author avoids speaking in a trifling manner: "And indeed He trifles extremely with the World, who is not convinc'd, that, at least, he makes Things clearer than they were; if He explodes no vulgar Errors, detects no dangerous Fallacies,

---

7. See Blair Worden, "Edmund Ludlow: The Puritan and the Whig," *Times Literary Supplement*, 7 Jan. 1977, p. 15; and Jacob, *Radical Enlightenment*, p. 69.

8. Undated (but after 22 Oct. 1705), Shaftesbury Papers, 30/24/21, fol. 237, Public Record Office, London; quoted in Heinemann, "Toland and Age of Reason," p. 51.

nor adds any stronger Light or Proof to what was generally receiv'd before. Those and such like are the real or pretended Motives of all Authors, of *Divines* as well as others; and they actually advance new *Notions, Expositions,* and *Hypotheses* in their Books every Day."[9] The author is one whose motive is to advance new notions and hypotheses; in this sense, every author is a *novelist.*

For thinkers of the seventeenth and eighteenth centuries, the writer of "the novel" presented special challenges. In his *Essay concerning Human Understanding,* Locke alluded to the fact that the traditional academic mentality had great difficulties understanding and accepting the explanations of the "upstart novelists" of the era.[10] Such difficulties were no doubt caused in part by the identification of innovation or novelty as pure fabrication. Toland restrains the inclination to absorb novelty into less true-to-life romances.

To be the author of novelty means at least two things. First, the novel author has some *new insight* and communicates it to his readers. Second, he is the *storyteller,* the fiction writer, the dreamer, the originator of new words or scenes. As far as Toland was concerned, the true author brings together both characteristics in his writing.

The first characteristic underscored the importance of the individual as the indispensable source of insight. Toland went so far as to say that each man has a *duty* to other men and particularly to his own country to recognize his individual importance in contributing to the whole: "Every Man is bound to assist his Country by his Advice, as well as by his Purse, or the use of his Arm; and as the Collective body of the Government is made up of many individuals, so whatever is propos'd for the Honor, Profit, or Safety of the whole, must still originally proceed from som one Man, whether in Parliament, Council, Cabinet, or after the manner I presume to do at present."[11] Even though those who discoursed best on these matters of importance were seldom recognized as the authors of novel ideas when they were put into law, they should have been respected, Toland suggested, for their ability to provide arguments and to prepare audiences to receive such arguments.[12] In publishing his ideas, Toland made public those novel and

---

9. *Vindicius Liberius,* pp. 16–17.

10. Ed. Peter H. Nidditch (Oxford: Clarendon Press, 1975), p. 714 (4.20.11).

11. *Art of Governing by Partys,* p. 2.

12. *The Second Part of the State Anatomy of Great Britain* (London: John Philips et al., 1717), p. 2.

individual notions born, he said, of his "fertil Brain." Those who are not authors (e.g., government officials who support inquiry) can play the role of the midwife, "able and ready to assist Nature in her Pangs, and to help into the World those heroic Births and surprizing Discoveries, which would bring Mankind to a clearer knowledg of themselves and other things."[13] The fertile mind of the author is nature's firstborn. The trials of the author are the trials of nature in the process of giving birth to the surprising discoveries of the men who come to know themselves.

Because writing or speaking are processes whereby nature reveals itself to men through the author, they demand the respect accorded to any life. Here Toland's respect for these "births of nature" acquires a religious aspect. And those who share this religious attitude toward the author's words belong to the "Church of the First-Born," in which Toland identified himself as a divine.[14]

As a spokesman for nature, the author is often compelled by nature to address the crowds of men who have failed to recognize their own authority. By means of the author, Toland declared, nature maintains and promotes its own fertility:

> But when the Crowd I'm chosen to persuade
> By long Orations for the purpose made;
> Or by what reaches more with more success,
> The labor'd Compositions of the Press:
> Then shall my fertil Brain new Terms produce,
> Or old Expressions bring again in use,
> Make all Ideas with their Signs agree,
> And sooner Things than Words shall wanting be.[15]

Leibniz correctly identified Toland as one who loved to make the "grand discourse," in the literal locutory sense as well as in the sense of

13. Footnote comment in Toland's translation of *The Ordinances, Statutes, and Privileges of the Royal Academy, Erected by His Majesty the King of Prussia* (London: John Darby, 1705), p. 16.

14. *The Destiny of Rome: or, the Probability of the Speedy and Final Destruction of the Pope. Concluded partly, from natural reasons, and political Observations; and partly, on Occasion of the famous Prophesy of St. Malachy, Archibishop of Armagh, in the XIIIth Century. . . . In a Letter to a Divine of the Church of England, From a Divine of the Church of the First-Born* (London: J. Roberts, 1718), title page.

15. *Clito*, p. 6.

a written discourse or commemoration such as was becoming popular in the academies of science. However, Toland recognized the need to control the generation of new terms and the use of the old: "though none ought to be slaves to any set of words, yet great judgment is to be employ'd in creating anew, or reviving an old word."[16] To lose authority is to become enslaved to another; but to be an author is to bear the weighty responsibility for the very life that characterizes nature and language.

To treat words as signs of things or ideas and to make words agree with those things or ideas were first in Toland's list of objectives in the poem *Clito*. His initial task was "to rightly name everything about nature." Because *Clito* was recognized as the intended scheme of Toland's studies,[17] *Clito* was the *key*, Toland was *Clidophorus* (the "key-bearer"), and the theme of *naming* was central for Toland. However, he viewed naming as a communal activity: in order that a name be accepted, the crowd must be *persuaded* to accept it. Novelty (or *singularité*, as Leibniz called it), if unpersuasive, was futile. This was where history made its judgment of novelty. In this regard, it is probably not accidental that Toland recalled the muse of history, *Clio*, in naming his work *Clito*.

The second characteristic of the author as novelist is his storytelling and dreaming. Those around Toland reported that he had an ability to capture his listeners in the course of telling a story.[18] But many of them did not recognize that he used the techniques and assumptions of the novelist and storyteller when he wrote philosophically.

For instance, the novelist does not claim to give a description of any actual event or state of affairs. Pure description would not introduce novelty into the world nor give men clearer knowledge of themselves. To gain insight into new truths, the individual must engage in some imaginative thinking, for "we know that it's hard to find a thing, where no body dreams of looking for it."[19] The dreamer, like the novelist, constructs his own notions and creates a whole world in which nothing is

16. "Druids," p. 68.

17. William Hewet, publisher's note to *Clito*, pp. iii–iv.

18. For example, see Electress Sophia to von Bothmer, 5 Aug. 1702, and to von Schutz, 22 Aug. 1702, *Briefe der Königin Sophie Charlotte von Preussen und der Kurfürstin Sophie von Hannover an Hannoversche Diplomaten*, ed. Richard Doebner, vol. 79 (Leipzig: S. Hirzel, 1805), pp. 220 and 163 respectively.

19. *Serena*, pp. 171–72.

probable and everything is known with certainty. Because it is of his own construction, there is nothing hypothetical about it for him. To admit hypotheses into the world of one's philosophy would be like doubting whether a fictional character *really* appeared as described in a novel.

The novelist proposes his work as a declaration of certainty, precisely because his treatment of reality is prescriptive rather than descriptive. Toland was quite explicit in his claim that in his philosophy there were no hypotheses: "*since PROBABILITY is not KNOWLEDG, I banish all Hypotheses from my Philosophy*; because if I admit never so many, yet *my Knowledg is not a jot increas'd.*"[20] Like Newton, Toland did not wish to frame hypotheses, but for reasons totally different from Newton's and with radically different implications. Unlike Newton, Toland was not describing a state of affairs in his philosophy. As far as Toland was concerned, knowledge is increased in the context of a coherent system of beliefs. To ask a novelist whether he is certain that one of his characters appears as described is to misunderstand his intent. So too, one does not understand Toland's intent if he must ask how Toland knows with certainty rather than with probability.

This feature in Toland's method of writing did not, of course, go long unnoticed. After the appearance of the second edition of *Christianity Not Mysterious*, critics complained that Toland's method was much too dogmatic and failed to convince others. Bold assertions, one critic noted, never make anything plainer than it was before.[21] But that type of objection missed Toland's point that an author's statements are hypotheses for his audience only, never for himself. In other words, Toland's philosophy was a description of the world-as-real-for-him; and in this there were no hypothetical elements.

The criticism of his method in *Christianity Not Mysterious* made Toland aware of the need for a further, more explicit example of what his method entailed. In *A Defence of Mr. Toland in a Letter to Himself* (1697), he spoke to the author of *Christianity Not Mysterious* in the second person—a device indicating that he already felt a need to distance himself from his past work. He did not deny his connection with the earlier work; rather, he indicated how readers should treat any author. In demonstrating how an author discusses his writing from

20. *CNM*, 2nd ed. addition, p. 180.
21. Willis, *Reflexions*, p. 11.

the viewpoint of his readers, Toland allowed his biographical description of the author of *Christianity Not Mysterious* (as seen in the work itself) to serve as autobiography.

Just as the words of an author serve as hypotheses for others—propositions to be tested—so his past works become hypotheses for him in the future. As an example of this principle, Toland remarked at the beginning of the *Defence* that he knew the Mr. Toland of *Christianity Not Mysterious* only by his writings and character (i.e., only through information available to the public).[22] That such information be available to the public was of utmost necessity if an author's novelty, insight, or discovery was to benefit mankind. The author had to "go public" so that others could evaluate his contribution and so that he could gain the distance necessary for the development of further novelty.

Toland generally believed that the public is seldom interested in the debates of private men. But questions of extraordinary weight affecting the tranquillity of many deserved public exposure, even when they occurred in the context of private communications.[23] This, Toland recognized, sets up a tension between the public's right to know and the individual's right to privacy. The question came up particularly in determining the authorship of anonymous works. The prevailing custom of his day—which he was criticized for not adopting—was to interpret the content of a book in light of what was known about the author's behavior and character.[24] But Toland considered such an inquiry superfluous and, at times, even prejudicial to an objective reading of a work.[25]

The identification of authors—and this included Toland's identification of himself as the author of particular works—had a mixed value. Identifying its author gave *authority* to a work. It became a fact for the

22. P. 1.

23. See *Amyntor*, p. i; and the preface of Toland's edition of the *Memoirs of Denzil, Lord Holles* (London: Tim. Goodwin, 1699). On how Toland uses this argument to justify publishing Shaftesbury's correspondence, see below, chap. 6.

24. See Thomas Mangey, *Remarks upon Nazarenus* (London: William & John Innys, 1718), p. 17.

25. *A Philippick Oration to Incite the English against the French*, an English translation of Matthaus Schiner's *Oratio Philippica ad excitandos contra Galliam Britannos* (London: Egbert Sanger and John Chantry, 1707), pp. xxxi–xxxii. Also see *Memorial of the State of England*, p. 2.

consideration of others, beyond which the author himself could move as long as his association with a past work did not serve as a label preventing his development in subsequent writings. Toland's inclusion of his name to the second edition of *Christianity Not Mysterious* was due to his desire not simply to bask in the notoriety of the book but also to limit his own claims of authority over the work to the time of its first publication (1696). To author-ize a book and to identify oneself as the person responsible for it means to become accountable for it. To assume publicly such a responsibility is to affirm one's commitment to what one has written.

Anonymity, on the other hand, could serve as a shield from behind which an irresponsible author makes claims for which he has little or no justification:

A nameless Writer may throw out at Random whatever comes in his Way without any Regard to Truth or the Merits of the Cause: yet he is conceal'd from the Hands of Justice and the Resentments of his Adversary, which in Matters of Fact takes away his Credit with all Men of Justice or Honor; since no Body is secure from the Accusation of any Guilt, when the Reputation of his Accuser is no more to be known, than his Person is accountable. Tis som Comfort if you have not a generous Adversary, to meet with a considerable one.[26]

Of course, anonymity may be the only alternative open to an author whose ideas are controversial.[27] Toland sometimes chose the politically prudent method of not revealing his authorship or of using a variety of fictitious names, abbreviations, and pseudonyms when signing his works.[28] Political prudence was not the only reason for remaining anonymous or for writing about oneself in the second or third person:

---

26. *Vindicius Liberius*, p. 116. Also see "Life of Harrington," p. xxxvi.

27. See *CNM*, pp. iv–v.

28. Toland's signatures include the following: "L.P.," *Two Essays Sent in a Letter from Oxford*; "Adeisidaemon," *A Lady's Religion* and *Clito*; "J. Londat," *A Letter Against Popery*; "Britto-Batavus," *The Description of Epsom*; "Patricola," *State Anatomy of Great Britain* and *Second Part of the State Anatomy of Great Britain*; "Z.Z.," *Letters from Shaftesbury to Molesworth*; "Hierophilus," *An Appeal to Honest People Against Wicked Priests*; "X.Z.," *The Destiny of Rome*; "Pantheus," MS of Toland's French version of *Nazarenus* sent to von Hohendorf in Vienna; "Philogathus," letter to Barnum Goode, commenting on Toland's use of a pseudonym in the *Pantheisticon* (BM Add. MS 4295, fol. 40); "Janus Junius Eoganensius," *Pantheisticon*.

To prevent any future Antagonist from encreasing the bulk or price of his elaborate lucubrations, by a curious and very important Disquisition, whether this *Preface* be written by myself or a friend (as the author of the late *Remarks* [Richard Fiddes] against me has been at those pains, because I thought fit to speak in the third person) I shall now, to gratify such studious enquirers, bespeak my Readers in the first person: assuring them it was out of pure Variety, authoriz'd by frequent custom, I did otherwise in the Preface of the other part [*The State Anatomy of Great Britain*]; but not as to any the least apprehension I cou'd have, either with relation to the affairs whereof I treated, or the persons which I had occasion to mention. I desire the same may be understood, of my not putting my name to this book, no more than that: for did the *Remarker* or his *fellow-servent* know anything of the several reasons, besides caution, that writers may have sometimes not to express their Names, they might have sav'd themselves the labour of telling mine. It was sufficiently publish'd, and by my own friends too, before their libels appear'd. Nor had I been a whit more shy, were I certain beforehand of being attack'd by a thousand answers: for as Error and Falshood may as well be confuted by one man, as by one thousand; so Reason and Truth have no more to fear from one thousand, than from one man.[29]

The use of pseudonyms allowed Toland to move beyond certain works that he did not wish to be tied to. But because of the brazen use of his own name in the second edition of *Christianity Not Mysterious*, he found it difficult to convince others that the faults and mistakes of his youth gave way to "another person" as he got older.[30]

The incidents following publication of *Christianity Not Mysterious* impressed upon Toland the need for discretion and for making clear his continual development. Especially after his initial contacts with members of the court of Hanover, Toland spread the word that problems with *Christianity Not Mysterious* might have been due to his young age at the time or his "little Knowledge of the World": "I was but five and twenty Years old when I wrote, which ought to be Excuse enough for any unadvis'd Expressions."[31] Indeed, he not only recognized that expressions might have been ill-advised; he doubted the wisdom of his publication of the work at all at a time when his notions

---

29. *Second Part of State Anatomy*, p. i.

30. See, for example, Toland to Harley, 28 Aug. 1705, in the Harley manuscript collection, published by the Historical Manuscripts Commission in *The Manuscripts of His Grace, the Duke of Portland* (London: Her Majesty's Stationery Office, 1893–1907), 4: 236.

31. *Vindicius Liberius*, pp. 23, 82.

were not thoroughly settled. He communicated this message to Electress Sophia;[32] and it later provided the theme for a letter from Elisha Smith, a clergyman and acquaintance of Toland, to the editor of Livy's works, Thomas Hearnes: "I think myself obliged to vindicate him [Toland] from the publication of his first Book *Christianity Not Mysterious*; he is very sensible of it and has confessed to me that those were only his Juvenile Thots at 25 and waits only for an opportunity to convince the world how much they have mistaken him from that Book."[33] As Smith's letter indicates, Toland's activities were still encumbered, as late as 1706, by the world's inability to distinguish him from his book.

Toland's use of pseudonyms and anonymity allowed him to propose ideas he was doubtful about or did not fully understand. Pseudonyms and anonymity, in general, served as an invitation to others to take up and pursue the line of investigation outlined by any author who was still feeling his way toward resolution of a problem. Toland hesitated to identify authors of anonymous works in part, at least, because he knew that anonymity was sometimes used to keep the author's personality out of the development of his ideas. To identify the author of an intentionally anonymous work changed the character of the work itself.

For an example of Toland's application of this line of thought to his own work, we can compare *Christianity Not Mysterious* with his *Defence of Mr. Toland*. The former had been originally proposed as the first of a three part work. But Toland never got around to publishing the last two parts. Commentators have proposed numerous reasons for his failure to write them. The one reason that is overlooked, and that the *Defence* seems to point to, is that Toland never intended to write those parts himself, as an individual. Only a community of investigators —perhaps including Toland as a future researcher—could fulfill the design foreshadowed in *Christianity Not Mysterious*.

The explanation of how Christianity contains no mysteries was only begun in Toland's book. As he noted in his *Defence* (directing himself toward the author of *Christianity Not Mysterious*):

The World has no reason to cry out against you yet . . . for you are not yet come to the proof of your *New Divinity* in that part of your discourse which is already

32. Electress Sophia to von Schutz, 27 Jan. 1702, and Sophia to von Bothmer, 24 June 1702, *Briefe*, 79: 150, 219.
33. Rawlinson MS C. 146, fol. 47, Bodleian Library, Oxford.

printed: you have only prepared the way and Skirmisht a little with some flying suggestions in order to lead on the main arguments with more force in the second part, which are to be backed and maintained by a strong reserve in the third. This is your design, and it is yet only a design; but you give us such mighty promises and assurances of bringing this design about, that there's no body can justly doubt but you are firmly perswaded of your own sufficiency to effect it; which is all you undertook to prove in your Book besides what is before mentioned. And therefore, having made good every thing you took upon you to do as farr as you are gone, I must needs say, 'tis a prejudging the cause to condemn you before the other parts you have promised are put out: whereupon I will suspend my judgment of your work till I have it altogether, and will live in expectation of seeing all the supposed *Mysteries* of the *Christian Religion* unlockt. . . . Oh what a glorious Scene will here be, and how happy should I think myself if I should live to see the day when the *Revelations* shall be as easy to be understood as any History of past matters of fact.[34]

In this passage Toland noted that the readers of *Christianity Not Mysterious* were persuaded that the task of unlocking the Christian mysteries was one Toland claimed he should be able to accomplish. But the question raised here was, *should* they necessarily think that? He could have been calling for a communal endeavor, which his *Defence* (written in the intimate second person, rather than in the unparticipative and distanced third) served to promote. If others saw someone defending Toland, even if it was Toland himself, they might be more inclined to join the endeavor.

Toland's final remark in the *Defence*, indicating relish at the thought of being able to understand the biblical book Revelation, provides further support for this interpretation of why parts two and three were never written. Revelation is precisely the book of the Bible that the Toland of *Christianity Not Mysterious* said he did *not* wish to treat other than in a very indirect way. Revelation refers to the mysteries of the future that apply to all men, which are different from the individualized message of the gospel that could be interpreted by the individual Protestant. But a community of investigators was necessary to decipher the mysteries of mankind.

Also noteworthy is Toland's anticipation of the time when Revelation would be "as easy to be understood as any History of past matters of fact." Here again he drew a connection between what is understood

34. Pp. 5–6.

as meaningful and what is history: in history, meaning is constituted for the individual, the community, and mankind in general.

One further comment about the above passage: Toland proposes the suspension of judgment, developed by Descartes, Bayle, and the skeptics, as a technique that must be incorporated into communal investigations. Such investigations cannot be limited by the prejudices of personalities without jeopardizing the very development of meaning and reason in history. The world has "no reason" to prejudge Toland's plan, because careful and patient communal investigations constitute the reasonable. Patience and concern for the temporal aspect of human inquiry thus become philosophical requirements. The adverse reaction to *Christianity Not Mysterious* served as a prime example of the hasty judgment that results from lack of an essential characteristic of communal reasoning—patience.

Withholding his name is not the only means through which an author achieves distance from his work. By manipulating his style an author can obscure his own views about his subject matter—a tactic about which Toland had mixed feelings. He proposed that for the purpose of teaching, the simplest style is the best. The plainest authors, who write as they speak "without the Disguise of pompous Elegance," have always been considered the best of authors by all good judges.[35] Toward this end Toland often noted that he endeavored to avoid the "witty conceits and harmonious flourishes" that contributed to obscurity in writing; for "every man, who clearly conceives any subject, may as clearly express it."[36] Obscure writing can, then, be an indication of some confusion or inadequacy in the author's understanding of his subject.

To balance these observations about obscure writing Toland returned to the theme of writing to provoke further thinking in others. In his *Defence*, Toland acknowledged the thought-provoking obscurity of the author of *Christianity Not Mysterious*: "I could not help observing this fault my self, tho' I was willing to lay it upon my own Understanding, till I found myself oblig'd by the general consent of others to put it to your Account."[37] The Toland of the *Defence* claimed that at first he was unsure whether *Christianity Not Mysterious* was truly obscure or

35. *CNM*, p. 51.
36. *Nazarenus*, preface, p. xii.
37. P. 9.

whether he simply did not understand it but that, supported by a consensus of readers, he later came to believe that the book indeed was obscure. Then he noted that it really does not matter that the style of *Christianity Not Mysterious* is obscure if it results in brightening the dark parts of the Christian religion: "'Tis of Importance to have our Religion clear, but not your Book."[38] The book, Toland seems to have concluded, would succeed in its purpose if readers began to think that the mysteries of religion were humanly resolvable.

2. THE EXPERIENCE OF REASON IN THE PUBLIC AUTHOR

By means of the extraordinary approach adopted in the *Defence*, Toland argued that when an author writes something of communal importance, it is resolvable only through a communal endeavor. That means that what the author writes is (in some manner or degree) inevitably obscure to his readers; otherwise, it is not novel. The difficulty resides neither in the author nor in the reader, for it is an essential characteristic of novel writing that it be obscure. It was not important to make *Christianity Not Mysterious* less obscure; indeed, that might jeopardize its value in provoking new insights in others. What was important was that readers did now allow this necessary obscurity to stand in the way of their participation in the overall project of obtaining enlightenment about religion. Once this was recognized, the goal of *Christianity Not Mysterious* could be attained. In this way, the book would have achieved its end (to explain Christian mysteries) because of its provocative obscurity. The *Defence* was Toland's attempt to lessen the confusion about the overall project in which *others* have the major role—the project outlined in *Christianity Not Mysterious*. He did this by pointing out that the project had been misunderstood insofar as readers thought that he planned to write the second and third parts of his "New Divinity" by himself.

The obscurity necessary to novelty is generally unintended by an author, but it cannot be avoided. When he was able to write in a plain style about the "mysterys of philosophy," Toland set up a tension between the simplicity he hoped would appeal to a wide audience and the novelty he knew would generate objections because of its obscurity. Although it would have been easier for him to discuss such matters in

38. P. 10.

the jargon of the learned, he knew that such a tactic would leave fewer readers as judges.[39] The author, he believed, should be concerned with as broad an appeal as possible, because the more novel his ideas, the broader the spectrum of coinvestigators would have to be.

The "common easie Notions" of familiar authors, Toland acknowledged, seemed to be used in his writings in odd ways. Notions like reason and evidence, which appeared to be taken from Locke, became obscure and perplexing in Toland and made it difficult if not impossible for him to "play his game" with so ill a hand.[40] But as long as Locke dealt out terms that could not be improved upon by other authors, knowledge could not be said to progress and reason could not be understood as developmental. A general consensus on the meanings of particular notions could inhibit linguistic development just as much as could an individual's prejudices.

Although referred to by Toland as the greatest philosopher after Cicero, Locke was not only a source of new concepts and linguistic conventions for Toland but also a hurdle beyond which he had to move in order to further the development of language. While he used some of Locke's terminology, Toland made it clear that his own usages were, for certain purposes, truer than Locke's.[41] When correspondents wrote to Locke about Toland, they made a point of noting Toland's candid, free-spirited method of scholarship.[42] Toland intended not to be tied down to Locke or to the ancients. And he expressly recognized the difficulties he faced as an author of novelty:

How fond are we all apt to be of what we learn'd in our Youth, as the Sight or Remembrance of the Places where we past that agreeable Time, does strangely affect us! A Mother is more charm'd with the lisping half-form'd Words of her pratling Infant, than with the best Language and most solid Discourses. That any Upstart, but of Yesterday, should pretend to overthrow what cost the Ancients so much Time and Breath to establish, and themselves so great Pains and Charges to learn, is of hard Digestion to some.[43]

Readers felt at home with familiar authors and found it hard to accept,

39. *Serena*, preface, para. 14.
40. *Defence*, p. 9.
41. See, for example, *A Short Essay upon Lying* (London: A. Moore, 1720), pp. 3, 17.
42. For example, see Benjamin Furly to Locke, 19 Aug. 1693, *Correspondence of Locke*, 4: 710. Also see Molyneux to Locke, 16 Mar. 1697, and 6 Apr. 1697, ibid., 6: 41, 82–83.
43. CNM, pp. x–xi.

much less to prefer, the novel insights of the fertile brain of an upstart novelist.

Toland believed that the novel revelations of an author develop out of his feeling comfortable in numerous situations and surroundings. Toland's interests themselves were encyclopedic, his travels widespread, and his thinking broadly European; in short, his was an early example of the mentality of the true Enlightenment thinker. What individuals know, Toland remarked, depends upon the extent of their experience of the world. He believed that our ideas multiply and that our force of reasoning extends and augments itself as we learn more about the things around us and have frequent contact with men of different characters and of different countries.[44]

The fertility of the individual's mind (the self) depends upon his sense experiences. Toland explained that the infant has very few ideas because of its having experimented with only a few things. Inasmuch as the self has nothing else in its thoughts than what comes to it through the senses, the self is nothing else than the result of the impression of sensible things on the brain. A man finding himself originally in a void would not properly even be called a man, in that there would be nothing of the self. The self is defined in the correspondence between the brain and sensible things.[45] In this way, the fertile brain encompasses a great diversity of types of experience.[46]

If the education of the mind depends upon experience, Toland reasoned, then the best method of communicating the truth to others is to recount the experiences leading to one's having learned it himself.[47] As an example of this line of thinking, Toland referred to the educative value of writing freely about freedom: "Discoursing of Liberty, nay, assertaining and maintaining it, I cou'd not but act with the greatest freedom, and indeed it wou'd not only be improper, but, in my opinion, ineffectual to do otherwise: since the principal art of

44. Toland to Sophie Charlotte, undated, though probably sometime in 1702, commenting on Leibniz's discussion of reasoning without the senses, *Die Philosophischen Schriften von Gottfried Wilhelm Leibniz*, ed. C. I. Gerhardt, 7 vols. (1875–90; reprinted, Hildesheim: Georg Olms, 1960), 6: 511.

45. Ibid., p. 512.

46. In this context Toland noted that if after his death he became a soul, then he would no longer be himself, because as a man he was a body and soul (ibid., p. 514). This introduces a further meaning for his epitaph, in which he remarks that he will not be the same Toland after his death.

47. *CNM*, p. ix.

persuasion is to appear persuaded your self."[48] Persuading another to accept the truth is best accomplished by retracing the line of thought that led the author to it. This method is avowedly autobiographical in character and specifically intended to educate others. To describe the activity of coming to know the truth is to describe a historical series of events that are impressed on the brain in a particular order, upon which the truth is grounded. Much like a skill, truth is something an individual has in virtue of the development of his thinking in a certain way. It is not something the author can simply *tell* another: "To know the truth is one thing, to tell it to others is another thing."[49] The author must persuade the other by *showing* how he has been led through his experiences to this or that particular conclusion.

The responsibility of every reader—including the author as reader of his own previous works—is to reason for himself, testing the persuasiveness of the ordered experiences of others. But just as the experiences of men differ from individual to individual, so will their judgments differ about what is reasonable. In fact, Toland went so far as to say that it is *impossible* for reasonable men not to differ about intricate doctrines or the meaning of ancient books like the Scriptures.[50] As a proof for this claim, Toland observed that many of these doctrines and books were widely disputed among those who use their reason. In contrast,

implicite belivers, and such as make no use of their reason, swallow all books alike, without examining into their original or meaning; and consequently, not otherwise differing about them, than as they are taught to prate by rote. The same holds as true of Intricate Doctrines (as of the Trinity or Predestination) which occasions them to be so differently explain'd by reasonable men; whereas there is no disagreement about them among those, who never enquire into their meaning, nor reason a moment about them.[51]

The question Toland raised concerns how men can disagree with one another and still be considered reasonable. The outline of his answer indicated his belief that men are reasonable not because they agree on a particular interpretation or doctrine but because they do their own thinking. There is a further, perhaps even more surprising

48. Toland to unknown correspondent, 22 Jan. 1714, in *Collection*, 2: 431–32.
49. "Clidophorus," *Tetradymus*, p. 63.
50. *Second Part of State Anatomy*, p. 11.
51. Ibid.

implication in Toland's observation: when men agree with one another, it is almost a sure sign that they are no longer reasoning individually. This applies not only to the situation in which there is uncritical agreement or disagreement. It pertains as well to critical agreement, in that there is always a remaining zone of difficulty and obscurity in any human agreement, and hence a methodic need for disagreement to arise. Otherwise, critical-communal disagreement would degenerate into sheer uncritical disagreement (with the last state worse than the first).

Immediately after Toland revealed this rather paradoxical position, critics began to express amazement at the argument, which they saw as peculiar to Toland. Richard Fiddes, a chaplain to Harley (then, Lord Oxford) following the 1714 split between Toland and Harley, noted that Toland seemed to have overlooked ignorance or the passions of men as the causes of disputes:

I thought Reason had been rather a Means of composing the Differences of Men, and uniting them in the same Judgment whether of Books or Doctrines, than of dividing them in their Judgment of either. Had our Anatomist [Toland] said, what one would think should have occurr'd more naturally to his Thoughts, that 'tis impossible for very ignorant or passionate Men, not to differ about the Meaning of ancient Books or intricate Doctrines, there had been some Sense in this; but to found the Original of the different Opinions among Men, concerning these Things, exclusively of all other Causes, upon *Reason*, the only Principle which can and ought to unite them: This is such a Way of Reasoning, as no Man but our State Anatomist could have been guilty of.[52]

As in the case of many of Toland's critics, Fiddes touched upon something essential to Toland's method without recognizing it as such. Toland's way of reasoning was unique; and it was this uniqueness, he believed, that distinguishes the author as an individual reasoner. To imply, as Fiddes did, that disagreements among men are due to ignorance or passion instead of reason yields the embarrassing conclusion that learned, intelligent individuals are unreasonable insofar as they differ with one another. Furthermore, Fiddes missed Toland's point that reason cannot be considered exclusive of, or immune to, all other causes of disagreements, like ignorance and

52. *Remarks on the State Anatomy of Great Britain* (London: J. Morphew, 1717), p. 10; also, pp. 25–26.

human passions. Indeed, reason is constituted through experience, which itself can be impassioned or lacking in reflective perspicuity. In fact, Toland noted, men who inquire into a question very often do disagree with one another. On the other hand, there is often agreement among those who elect not to inquire. Using observations like these, Toland concluded that reasonable agreement was impossible; and he offered the above observations as a *proof* of his conclusion.

Fiddes had argued that disputes among the learned are accidental to the truths they seek to discover. It may just happen, furthermore, that truths are usually (perhaps even always) discovered as a result of such disputes. But, Fiddes continued, to say that truth is dependent upon the dispute would seem to indicate that disputes among passionate and ignorant men would reveal the truth just as much as would disputes among the learned.

This was exactly what Toland wanted to allow for in admitting the vulgar into the enterprise of human reasoning. At issue here was the very definition of what constitutes the reasonable; for it had yet to be shown that reason was not passionate and that it excluded ignorance necessarily. Toland thus identified a *necessary* characteristic of reason by means of his identification of a *universal* characteristic of reason. That is, the proof that reasonable men must necessarily differ to the extent that they are reasonable lies in the fact that when men give considerable thought to a question, they inevitably arrive at different insights and conclusions. Because thoughtful men have never universally agreed on important human questions, to say that universal agreement has been reached on such a question would indicate that communal reasoning on the question had ceased. In short, Toland argued, communal reason is essentially and necessarily disputative.

To some, this line of argument would appear to confuse a thing (reasoning) with a sign of its presence (disputation). The problem, of course, lies in defining something without necessarily resorting to a description of its signs. Or, more precisely, the problem lies in stipulating what serves as the sign of what. For example, we often speak of smoke as a sign of fire but feel uncomfortable saying that fire is a sign of smoke. However, without identifying fire as the source of the smoke we cannot be sure that a particular whitish cloud is smoke rather than water vapor or steam. Here, the fire serves as a sign of a type of smoke.

Toland used this kind of argument in a number of places. In *An Apology for Mr. Toland* (1697), he pointed out that bad tempers are "reasonably" associated with bad causes: "A *good Temper* and *sound*

Judgment usually go together, and if the absence of the former be no Demonstration that the latter is also wanting, yet questionless it creates a very reasonable suspicion of it; for a bad Cause is generally supported by Violence and ill Arts, while Truth establishes it self only by Lenity and Persuasion."[53] And in *Tetradymus* Toland provided a rule by which sincerity could be determined through this kind of backwards argument: "When a man maintains what's commonly believ'd, or professes what's publicly injoin'd, it is not always a sure rule that he speaks what he thinks: but when he seriously maintains the contrary of what's by law establish'd, then there's a strong presumption that he utters his mind."[54] With this argument Toland questioned the sincerity of those who adopted popular positions.

Applying this form of argument to the question of how the author determines not only the novelty of his ideas but also their importance for (a) making men sensitive to the obscurity of their beliefs and (b) highlighting the ambiguities of consensus, Toland found encouragement for his own project in the fact that it had given rise to disputes. "I know that to enterprize any thing out of the common road is to undergo undoubted envy or peril; and that he, who is not beforehand resolv'd to bear opposition, will never do any great or beneficial exploit: yet 'tis no small incouragement to me, that from the beginning of the world to this time not a single instance can be produc'd of one who either was or would be eminent, but met with enemys to his person and fame."[55] Toland seems to have thought that if he generated opposition, he would have some verification of his own eminence, novelty, and most especially, rationality.

Since the only way to discover the truth is to engage in reasoning, it was important for Toland that the individual recognize the disputational character of reason. Further, he should not try to limit the reasonable to any one position, because to follow one's reason—that is, to fulfill one's duty to God as a rational being—is neither characterized by nor knowable in terms of the products of reasoning:

He therefore that employs his Reason to the best of his Ability to find out Religious Truth, in order to practice it, does all that God desires: for God, who

53. P. 38.
54. "Clidophorus," p. 96.
55. "Life of Harrington," p. xxxvi. Toland uses the same passage verbatim in his *Vindicius Liberius*, pp. 161–62.

will not command Impossibilities, can require no more of him, than that he impartially searches after, and endeavors to discover Religious Truth, by the use of that Reason which was given him for that end. He that does this, may have the satisfaction of doing his Duty as a rational Creature, and may be sure, tho he misses Truth, he shall not miss the Reward that is due to him who obeys his Maker, in following as well as he could, and no more could be his Duty, the only Guide that God has given him to judg of Truth and Falshood. On the contrary, he that neglects to do this, is disobedient to his Maker, in misusing his rational Faculties; and tho he should light on Truth, the luckiness of the Accident will no way excuse his Disobedience: for God will judg us as we are accountable (that is, rational) Creatures; and consequently our Reward from him, whether we hit or miss of Truth, will be in exact proportion to the use we make of our Reason: And if God has oblig'd us to use it as the only means to distinguish Truth from Falshood, that alone must be the way to find the one, and avoid the other. . . . If two persons profess different Religions, one the true, the other a false one, yet if they have been equally sincere in their examination, they are equally in the way to Heaven; because in following their Reason, they both have done what God requires. . . . So that 'tis not *what* a Man professeth, but *how*, that justifies or condemns him before God.[56]

At least in regard to truths of religion, sincere reasoning is demanded by God. Although Chillingworth had earlier argued in much the same way, it is Toland who redefines the reasonable in terms of the sincerity of one's examination. The individual himself can recognize the sincerity of his own thinking—and thus whether he is really reasoning— only when he tests his ideas upon others. The attempt to use reason to do away with all dispute is the result of a misunderstanding and indeed undermines the very possibility of sincere individual reasoning.

The tendency to discourage novelty and the universal pressure to make reasoning uniform create a perilous condition for every "particular man" (as opposed to the "common man," the "vulgar"). It appears almost impossible for the individual to escape this "Infection, to obtain or to preserve his Liberty; since all the other men of the World are agreed in the same Conspiracy to deceive him."[57] Other men, as other sources of authority, threaten the individual's assertions of novelty in their attempt to deceive him into thinking that rationality is only communal and not individual. In this way, the conspiracy joined in by all other men of the world aspires "to deprave the Reason of every

56. *Letter to a Member of Parliament*, pp. 3–4, 17.
57. *Serena*, pp. 15–16.

individual Person."[58] This conspiracy, in effect, is the challenge presented by all other reasoners to the reasoning self. It exists simply by virtue of there being more than one way of thinking as part of the process by which reason is constituted.

Toland had not slipped into some type of philosophic paranoia. As he noted, this remark about a universal conspiracy to deprave individual reasoning should not be understood to imply that he was against learning, religion, government, breeding and nursing of children, professions and trades, ordinary conversation, or living in society. His opposition was only to the variety of abuses that threaten independent thought.

The conspiracy to deprave reason is that universal tendency, on the part of other men, to cast doubt upon the "pure and original Reason" of the individual. As Toland's language indicates, this conspiracy to deprave reason is a secularized and reason-centered version of original sin. Other men cast this doubt through their emphasis on how the individual's limited and imperfect exercise is determined by his particular "capacities and apprehensions, no less than different views of things, and different opportunities to examine them."[59] This type of claim—that individuals imperfectly exercise their reason—could not be justified with the testimony of other individuals, for they themselves would fall under the same criticism. Only a *conspiracy* of reasoners, who identify themselves and others like them as imperfect reasoners, can challenge the perfection of the reasoning ability of the individual and the authority of the author.

3. THE DEFINITION OF REASON AND ITS ACTS

The central role of the individual in Toland's discussion of reason can be seen in the following nine-point epistemic context for an outline of the movement of individual thought.

A. The individual's way of reasoning is a product of a unique personal history. Just as the self is the result of sensible impressions on the brain, so the individual's way of reasoning is the result of his personal experiences.

---

58. Ibid., preface, para. 10.
59. *Second Part of State Anatomy*, p. 12.

B. Because it is only through one's experiences (e.g., education and conversation) that he comes to know what particular terms mean, the terms refer to the *notions* with which reasoning deals. Propositions that are definitional or axiomatic and that involve no need for discourse or allow for no doubt once the terms are understood are self-evident. Because a self-evident proposition simply indicates the meanings commonly given to the words contained within the proposition, no reasoning occurs in regard to self-evident propositions:

When the Mind, without the Assistance of any other Idea, immediately perceives the Agreement or Disagreement of two or more Ideas, as that Two and Two is Four, that Red is not Blew; it cannot be call'd Reason, though it be the highest Degree of Evidence: For here's no need of Discourse or Probation, Self-evidence excluding all manner of Doubt and Darkness. These Propositions so clear of themselves, their Terms being once understood, are commonly known by the Names of *Axioms* and *Maxims.*[60]

Notions (or meanings) learned by the individual, and thus ordinarily ("commonly") used in the individual's reasoning, might differ from the notions communally ("commonly") used in the discourses of a particular group of language users.

C. Notions peculiar to the self ("self-evident notions") and notions common to a group of reasoners that perhaps includes the individual ("common notions") are the standards by which arguments are tested for truth. The only way for a man to discover the truth of arguments or proofs proposed by himself or by others is to compare the arguments or proofs "with his common and self-evident Notions, by means of which he finds out the agreement or disagreement of any Proposition with those Standards and Tests of Truth."[61] When something dubious or obscure is discovered to be certain by comparing it with something evidently known, the "method of knowledge" involved is properly called *reason*: "When the Mind cannot immediately perceive the Agreement or Disagreement of any Ideas, because they cannot be brought near enough together, and so compar'd, it applies one or more intermediate Ideas to discover it.... This Method of Knowledg is properly call'd *Reason* or *Demonstration* ... and it may be defin'd, that Faculty of the Soul which discovers the Certainty of any thing dubious

60. *CNM*, pp. 11–12.
61. *Letter to a Member of Parliament*, p. 4.

or obscure, by comparing it with something evidently known."[62] The certainty achieved through individual or group reasoning is *truth*.

D. "We cannot in this World know any thing but by our common Notions."[63] We cannot know what we do not understand or what does not mean anything to us. All knowledge, then, is nothing else but the perception of the agreement or disagreement of the ideas for which we understand some meaning.[64]

E. We are informed about meanings by experience and authority. Our own experience and the testimony of others provide knowledge without necessarily commanding assent: "The means of information I call *those Ways whereby any thing comes barely to our Knowledg, without necessarily commanding our Assent. By the Ground of Perswasion*, I understand *that Rule by which we judg of all Truth, and which irresistibly convinces the Mind. The Means of Information are Experience and Authority.*"[65] To assent to a proposition, the individual must be persuaded of its truth, which is based on its agreement with common notions. Any revelation, even a revelation from God, must be understood as intelligible and possible: "Now since by *Revelation* Men are not endu'd with any new Faculties, it follows that God should lose his end in speaking to them, if what he said did not agree with their common Notions. Could that Person justly value himself upon being wiser than his Neighbours, who having infallible Assurance that something call'd *Blictri* had a Being in Nature, in the mean time knew not what this *Blictri* was?"[66] A revelation must agree with the common notions of men; otherwise, individuals would not have any means to distinguish divine revelations from the imposture and traditions of men.[67]

F. "All *Faith* or Perswasion must necessarily consist of two Parts, *Knowledg* and *Assent*. 'Tis the last indeed, that constitutes the formal Act of *Faith*, but not without the Evidence of the first."[68] Originally, the individual must acquire words and notions from others. Subsequently, he cannot properly believe any testimony about something he thinks is impossible or is beyond what he understands. To believe in anything

62. *CNM*, pp. 12–13.
63. Ibid., p. 30.
64. Ibid., p. 11.
65. Ibid., p. 14.
66. Ibid., p. 133.
67. Ibid., pp. 41–42.
68. Ibid., p. 133.

(e.g., the divine source of the Scriptures) without a test of its claims and an examination of how those claims are evidently consistent with common notions, is to have faith in something without understanding it. Toland is unreserved in his criticism of this:

To believe the Divinity of *Scripture*, or the Sense of any Passage thereof, without rational Proofs, and an evident Consistency, is a blameable Credulity, and a temerarious Opinion, ordinarily grounded upon an ignorant and wilful Disposition; but more generally maintain'd out of a gainful Prospect. For we frequently embrace certain Doctrines not from any convincing Evidence in them, but because they serve our Designs better than the Truth; and because other Contradictions we are not willing to quit, are better defended by their means.... To be confident of any thing without conceiving it, is not real *Faith* or Perswasion, but a rash Presumption and an obstinate Prejudice, rather becoming Enthusiasts or Impostors than the taught of God, who has no Interest to delude his Creatures, nor wants Ability to inform them rightly.... what is once reveal'd we must as well understand as any other Matter in the World, *Revelation* being only of use to enform us, whilst the Evidence of its Subject perswades us.... *Reason* is not less from God than Revelation; 'tis the Candle, the Judg he has lodg'd within every Man that cometh into this World.[69]

Someone can legitimately assent to a proposition only when he understands it and only when he has some further reason to believe that this meaningful proposition describes a state of affairs. The testimony of others is always hypothetical for the individual. When it is no longer hypothetical, it is no longer the statement of another, but is the individual's own.

G. To believe or come to know something on the testimony of another is different from, though dependent upon, having learned from others the meaning of that which is known. However, the revelation of information by another man or by God need not be only a "means of information." It can also be the ground of persuasion if the individual judges (again, using his past experiences or common notions) that the source is dependable. "We should not confound the Way whereby we come to the Knowledg of a thing, with the Grounds we have to believe it. A Man may inform me concerning a thousand Matters I never heard of before, and of which I should not as much as think if I were not told; yet I believe nothing purely upon his word

69. Ibid., pp. 36–37, 132, 146.

without Evidence in the things themselves. Not the bare Authority of
him that speaks, but the clear Conception I form of what he says, is the
Ground of my Perswasion."[70] Under some pointed criticism by Peter
Browne and Richard Willis,[71] Toland clarified his position on this
matter in *Vindicius Liberius* (1702):

Instead of saying that "Revelation was not a necessitating Motive of Assent, but
a Means of Information," I ought to have said, "Revelation was not only a
necessitating Motive of Assent, but likewise a Means of Information." The most
distinct Ideas in the World are not a sufficient Ground of Persuasion, for they
prove no more than that such a Thing may be; but to be convinc'd that it does
actually exist, we must have our own Experience, or the Authority either of
divine or human Testimony.[72]

Toland realized that communication has more than simply informative
functions. In like manner, reason can inform us which testimonies are
consistent with common notions and can persuade us to accept such
testimonies.

   H. When reason is taken for the "Principle of Discourse" within us,
it is "whole and entire in every one whose Organs are not accidentally
indisposed."[73] There is nothing imperfect or limited about the human
ability to reason. The individual's ability to reason, however, is
challenged by "depravers of reason," who attempt to use the fact that
the individual depends upon others for his notions originally to argue
that the individual should likewise depend upon others to reason for
him.

   I. Apparently, the conspiracy to deprave the individual's reason is
quite successful, for men often misuse their reason, frame wrong
conceptions, and make erroneous judgments.[74] The right use of
reason, or "right Reason," is from Toland's point of view more obvious
in the context of practical (moral, political) matters than in that of
purely speculative matters. Or, to put the contrast another way, right
reason ("Common Sense, or *Reason* in general") is to be distinguished

   70. Ibid., p. 38.
   71. Browne, *A Letter in Answer to . . . Christianity Not Mysterious* (London: Robert Clavel,
1697), pp. 18–20; Willis, *Reflexions*, p. 3.
   72. Pp. 103–4.
   73. *CNM*, p. 57.
   74. Ibid., pp. 57–58.

from reason in particular, the principle of discourse within the individual. "Every one experiences in himself a Power or Faculty of forming various Ideas or Perceptions of Things: Of affirming or denying, according as he sees them to agree or disagree: And so of loving and desiring what seems good unto him; and of hating and avoiding what he thinks evil. The right Use of all these faculties is what we call Common Sense, or *Reason* in general."[75] The rightness of reason is determined in a communal context ("common sense"), because right reason refers specifically to matters affecting shared reasoning, reasoning "in general"—in short, matters in which the reasoning activity of the individual affects others through his actions. The emphasis of practical reasoning is communal; that of speculative reasoning is individual. The two become united in the communal process whereby the individual is educated in the notions by means of which he reasons.

These nine facets of Toland's discussion of reason indicate how reason and the reasoner can be autonomous and yet educated and how Toland's uses of "common" take into account both beneficial and harmful characteristics of public reason.

The communal process whereby the individual is educated in his notions is not to be confused with the attempt to deprave the individual's reason by limiting all reasoning to communal reasoning. Notional education is necessarily communal. Recognition of this prompted Toland to remark that his objections to the depraving of reason should not be interpreted as objections against human interaction and communication. He wanted to emphasize the point that reasoning is made communal by means of the communal activity of men educating one another in their meanings or notions. In essence, reasoning is individual, but the elements with which it deals (notions) develop out of communal intereducation. In this way, reasoning becomes communal indirectly. Any attempt to portray reasoning as directly communal results in the depraving of reason. The individual is the author and source for the development of meanings in community (common notions), as well as the judge of the rationality of notions

75. Ibid., p. 9. See also "A Letter Concerning the Roman Education," in *Collection*, 2: 2–3; *Pantheisticon*, p. 85 (pp. 67–68); and "Barnabas-Original," *Nazarenus*, pp. 65–66, where Toland acknowledges his dependence on Cicero.

related to one another. He is not, however, the final judge of the *meanings* or notions affecting the community.

Individual reason is a source of light (*lux*) that can illuminate the communal process of reasoning. Since it does illuminate communal reason, individual reason becomes resplendent (*lumen*) and life-clarifying. Toland's remark in the *Pantheisticon*—"Reason is the true and first law, the light [*lux*] and splendor [*lumen*] of life"[76]—indicates that he placed the revelatory character of reason in the context of its lawlike character. Although he used the phrases of Cudworth and the Cambridge Platonists (e.g., "the light of reason" and "the candle of the Lord"), Toland did not employ them to support the traditional Christian theology.[77] Instead, he preferred that such phrases be used in the practical contexts specified by Cicero. Sound reason (common sense) was, for Toland, an "eternal rule," a practical law according to which men labor to attain peace and happiness. The truth of such an eternal law is realized only when the individual intends it as a meaningful revelation and others recognize it as a meaningful revelation.

4. THE REASONABLE AUTHOR AS PROPHET AND PHYSICIAN

The author, Toland proposed, should not pretend (and indeed does not have to pretend) to any special intelligence from extrahuman sources. Reason illuminates nothing more than the results of conclusions necessarily inferred from correctly presented premises. No supernatural reasons are necessary; no larger share of "Spiritual Irradiation or Ecstatick Vision, of Impulse or Inspiration," is claimed —only the ability to compare natural observations of the world. Toland referred to this ability as "Comparative Prophesy."[78] To the extent that the author pulls together (compares) the signs of his times or the meanings of his age, his revelations point to (or prophesy) future, communally accepted notions. The author prophesies the conclusions to be inferred from his revelations (the premises) without being able, by himself, to follow through to assert the conclusions. In

76. P. 73 (p. 57).
77. See *Letter to a Member of Parliament*, p. 3; "Primitive Constitution," in *Collection*, 2: 196; and *CNM*, p. 146.
78. *Destiny of Rome*, pp. 6–7.

terms of its author-itative source, the light of reason as *lux* is *prophetic* and as *lumen* is *veridical*.

In his *Defence*, Toland referred to a rumor alleging that at age fourteen he said that he would be the head of a religious sect by the time he was thirty. Scoffing at such a report, he remarked that prophecies of this type were meaningful as prophecies only after they had been fulfilled and not a moment sooner. "I know you [again, speaking to himself] are not superstitious, and therefore I need not advise you to give little credit to any *Prophecy* of this kind; and for my part, except it had been foretold, and the Prediction confirm'd to me by unquestionable signs, I cannot believe such a thing will ever come to pass."[79] That is, knowing what Toland knew about the author, he saw little point in placing any credence in prophecies not supported by the appropriate signs, just as he believed that there is little justification for accepting a revelation that is inconsistent with or not encompassed by common notions.

The author's role as the prophet who interprets his own age and anticipates the future through his own revelations becomes unified, for Toland, in the theme of the author as physician. Discerning the causes and cures of the "distemper of modern times," Toland claimed that he wrote "without expecting thanks or reward for the Physician."[80] Like the physician of reason, the prophet of reason diagnoses the diseases attacking human reason and contributes his own suggestions for cures. The suggestions neither effect the cures nor are found to be inadequate unless adopted and tested by the community of reasoners.

Both Toland and Leibniz found the image of the physician of reason a provocative one. In a letter to Toland in which he cautioned against confusing true religion and superstition, Leibniz commented that "it would always be better not to put off the Antidote until after the

---

79. P. 15. See MS note in Toland's copy of Martin Martin's *Description of the Western Islands of Scotland*, 2nd ed., BM copy, shelfmark C. 45. c. 1, p. 318. Also see Toland to Molesworth, Jan. 1721, BM Add. MS 4465, fol. 23. The marginal notes in the BM copy of Martin's *Western Islands* are in Toland's handwriting, with additional handwritten marginal notes by Lord Molesworth. The Bodleian contains a copy of Martin's book (Add. MS 18313; Gough Scotland 185) with the notes of Toland and Molesworth transcribed from the BM copy by Joseph Ames (1689–1759). Ames was an antiquary and "deist by conversation." See Stuart Piggott, *William Stukeley: An Eighteenth-Century Antiquary* (Oxford: Clarendon Press, 1950), p. 100.

80. *Tetradymus*, preface, p. vii. Also see *The Declaration Lately Publish'd, In Favour of his Protestant Subjects, By the Elector Palatine* (London: A. Baldwin, 1707), p. 11.

poison." Almost a year later, apparently responding for the first time to Leibniz's letter, Toland toyed with medical imagery. Noting that he had sent Leibniz a copy of his book directed against the English divine Dr. Henry Sacheverell, Toland said that he published the book as an "antidote" against a sermon by Sacheverell.[81]

Proposing antidotes to correct the ongoing depravation of reason was necessarily a process of guesswork for the prophetic physician. "For the saying of Euripides will ever hold true, that *the best guesser is the best Prophet*. He that is nearly acquainted with the state of affairs, that understands the springs of human actions, and, that judiciously allowing for circumstances, compares the present time with the past: he, I say, will make a shrewd guess at the future."[82] The shrewd guesser depends upon his experience of and acquaintance with the social, political, and historical circumstances surrounding the actions of individuals. He cannot limit his experience to general social movements, excluding important individuals who make major decisions.

To become a shrewd guesser Toland immersed himself in scholarship, popular debates of the day, political intrigues, and (when he could afford it) financial enterprises like the South Sea Bubble. He never lost sight, however, of the importance of being close to the authors and authorities who had an impact on his contemporaries; for in knowing them personally, Toland learned the "springs of human action" that prompted individuals to act as they did.

Toland's concentration on the author united the tendency to be comprehensive with the tendency to experience personally as much as possible. The best prophet, he seemed to say, would be the individual who understands a thing as much as is necessary or useful and who can justify his claim to comprehend by evidential, firsthand experience.

The prophet is the author in potentia; he is actualized only in communal history. "He that comprehends a thing," Toland remarked, "is as sure of it as if he were himself the Author."[83] *The author* serves as the ideal that comprehension approaches. Just when an individual thinks he knows all that is useful and necessary about a particular thing,

---

81. Leibniz to Toland, 30 Apr. 1709, and Toland to Leibniz, 15 Feb. 1710, *State Papers and Correspondence Illustrative of the Social and Political State of Europe from the Revolution to the Accession of the House of Hanover*, ed. John M. Kemble (London: John W. Parker and Son, 1857), pp. 467–68.
82. "Druids," p. 30.
83. *CNM*, p. 36.

the conditions shift, and comprehension eludes his grasp once more. We can be sure, Toland observed, that comprehension does not mean knowing the essence of a thing, if by essence is meant some mysterious and unknowable characteristic of the thing. "Rightly speaking then, we are accounted to *comprehend* any thing when its chief Properties and their several Uses are known to us: for *to comprehend* in all correct Authors is nothing else but *to know*; and as of what is not knowable we can have no Idea, so it is nothing to us. It is improper therefore to say a thing is above our Reason, because we know no more of it than concerns us, and ridiculous to supersede our Disquisitions about it upon that score."[84]

Comprehension, then, is the grasp of what Locke had referred to as nominal essences. "When we knew as many of the Properties of any Thing as made us understand the Name of it, and as were useful and necessary for us, this was enough for our present Condition, and we might reasonably be said to comprehend it."[85] In comprehending a thing, we attain the certainty that the author has of it. But because authors themselves progress in their thinking, so must the quest for comprehension. Even the author-as-prophet does not fully comprehend the meaning of all that he writes or says; for once public, his pronouncements mingle with all other pronouncements ("facts") in the determination of meaning. Whereas the author-as-prophet is his own *projection* of himself, the author-as-physician is his own *correction* of himself. Based on as comprehensive a diagnosis as possible, the correction is ongoing, due primarily to the author's self-education through his experiences of others and of the world.

Toland continually emphasized the need for personal experience to justify one's claims. He missed no opportunity to note his wide travels and studies of men and nature in many different contexts. He was impatient with those who accepted the testimony of others when they could have tested a questionable proposition themselves.[86]

Toland's interests in geology, for example, prompted him to try to obtain samples of amber stones from Edward Lhuyd, the curator of the Ashmolean Museum in Oxford.[87] Even though Toland was not

84. Ibid., pp. 77–78.
85. *Vindicius Liberius*, p. 86.
86. MS notes in Martin's *Western Islands*, pp. 7, 92, 132, 254.
87. Edward Lhuyd to M. Lister, 13 Mar. 1694, Lister MS 36, fol. 90, Bodleian Library. Toland refers to his conversations with Lhuyd in "Druids," p. 32.

"conversant in these studies," as Lhuyd put it, he exemplified those of his age—like Lhuyd and Hans Sloane, secretary of the Royal Society— whose imaginations were fired by the interest in collecting specimens.[88] Whether he was gathering samples of ambergris or collecting superstitions about the Druids, Toland preferred to gather his information first hand.[89] In this regard, he felt a special affinity for Diodorus the historian, about whom he wrote, "He's very unlike them who go no farther than their closets for materials."[90] Whether the focal points of his interest were the superstitions of the Druids, geological formations that might have helped to debunk superstitions about biblical history, or the popular superstitions about political movements and leaders, Toland insisted on appealing to personal and (where possible) direct experience.

He scoured public and private libraries looking for unusual works (and often came into possession of rare books and manuscripts by employing apparently less-than-honorable means). He counted kings and queens, carpenters and tailors, as his acquaintances. Experience of the world, including experience of nature and man, fed Toland in his endeavor not to confine himself to anything. He did not wish to imitate

the servile drudgery of those mean spirits, who, for the sake of som one science, neglect the knowlege of all other matters, and in the end are many times neither masters of what they profess, nor vers'd enough in any thing else to speak of it agreably or pertinently: which renders 'em untractable in conversation, as in dispute they are opinionative and passionate, envious of their fame who eclipse their littleness and the sworn enemys of what they do not understand.[91]

In his quest for comprehension, Toland relished the diversity of the distinct sciences. Comprehension did not mean the union of all matters under one science, just as comprehension in religion did not mean for him (as it did for many of his contemporaries) the union of all sects in one church. A uniform comprehension in religion, he believed, would have been debilitating and depraving for reason; it would have

88. See Redwood, *Reason, Ridicule, and Religion*, pp. 117–18.

89. See MS notes in Martin's *Western Islands*, p. 39; and *CNM*, p. 18.

90. "The Fabulous Death of Atilius Regulus," written no later than 6 Aug. 1694, in *Collection*, 2: 31.

91. "Life of Harrington," p. ix.

undermined the growth of reason by excluding meanings (notions) outside of the discourse of "the professionals."

Toland's ideal of comprehension combined the notion of *an experience of a totality* (i.e., that which is useful and necessary enough for our present condition) with that of a *totality of experiences*. The task of the author is never to rest content in his own field, because men in other fields continuously modify the meanings of his pronouncements. One can never stand still in a world filled with fluid meanings. Comprehension is the response of the author to the world, and the starting point for the world's transcendence of him.

The mark of the true author is his expansiveness. He is never at a loss for a subject and always wonders what contribution he will make to the development of language. He anticipates what he and the world will become in the future without being apprehensive of his focal role in that process. "The whole World is the storehouse of the Materials I shall use; antient and modern, foreign and domestick Books; the Letters and Conversation of other persons; the face of Nature and my own particular Thoughts. So that 'tis impossible I should ever be at a loss for a subject, but rather in suspence which to prefer, and how with the exactest judgment to chuse properly among so many."[92] Because he is "the author," he comprehends his work without speaking or writing comprehensively. He impels himself beyond himself and beyond all he comprehends in his very act of speaking or writing. He is a new fact for himself and the world, revealed as the source of novelty and developing meanings (*rationes*) in Toland's methodological emphasis on biography. Biography thus highlights the authority of the individual by tracing the genesis of individual and communal reason.

Toland recognized that the prejudices resulting from fixation on the revelations of authors ("authorities") could only lead to the stagnation of reason and the generation of superstition. The conflicts resulting from misinterpreting the authority of authors involved in reasoning prompted many of Toland's most outspoken comments. We now turn to these conflicts, considering Toland's treatment of the educational bases of prejudices and superstitions.

---

92. "A Project for a Journal," in *Collection*, 2: 206.

III

The Tyranny of Custom in Prejudicial Education

ALTHOUGH MY DISCUSSION up to this point has not adhered strictly to the chronological order of Toland's works, a general thematic development occurs as we move through this early part of his publishing career. The early works focus on topics such as the stifling effect of priestcraft and the accessibility of Christianity to reason raised in *Christianity Not Mysterious*. Indeed, we might be tempted to refer to the years 1695–1704 as a period in which Toland's writings were devoted solely to religion; but we would do so at the risk of minimizing the importance to him of the biographical works. Toland appears to have been concerned with the two topics independently of one another, even though he did treat the concepts of reason and revelation as points of intersection between them.

If we understand the movement of Toland's thought according to the appearance of his major works, then *Christianity Not Mysterious* certainly serves as a focal point in the first stage; the biographies of Milton and Harrington, in the second. Some of Toland's responses to criticisms of *Christianity Not Mysterious* appeared even after the Harrington biography was published in 1700. Because Toland addressed religion and biography concurrently, to try to divide the years into smaller periods or to treat the works of these years under one dominant theme would make his thought at this time appear erratic or would dilute its rich and diversified character.

From the question of how a biography mirrors the experiences or impressions of a lifetime, Toland shifted to the role of experience or impression in general in the formation of opinions. The course from the "Life of Milton" to the *Letters to Serena* reveals a broadening subject matter, from particular opinions to their acquisition. Coming to hold opinions is an educational process, which occurs throughout the history of one's life, Toland believed. The prime motivation for his investigation of this process was his concern for the damaging effect of priestcraft—understood in this context as the reason-depraving effects of superstitions.

Thus a new topic is generated from my previous two chapters—the educational, historical bases of superstitions and prejudices. Toland's approach to this subject stemmed not only from the internal movement of the biography and priestcraft themes but also from his contacts with individuals outside England between 1701 and 1704. Like other Englishmen of his time who went abroad, Toland became acutely aware of his own superstitions and prejudices—particularly in regard to English customs and habits—in the course of his extended contacts in Hanover, Berlin, and Holland. The *Letters to Serena* was the central work in his theory of education, in that it addressed the question of how customs and regional *prejudices* could be distinguished from *superstitions*, even though both had the educational base.

This chapter consists of three sections. The first describes Toland's discussion of his attempt, as an author, to transcend the hopes and fears that dominate the superstitious writer. Superstitions, based on particular ways in which all men are educated, are distinguished in the second section from prejudices, which characterize specific regions, groups, or professions. Formal education, although susceptible to pedantry, can nevertheless refine the etymological and historical tools by which destructive and divisive prejudices can be overcome. Section three reveals how this formal training in etymology and history is important and yet fruitless, according to Toland, without travel and conversation.

Toland's concern for historical exegesis arose from his sensitivity to the need for correcting the superstitions found in formal and nonformal education. The third section of this chapter merely suggests the historical and exegetical aspects of Toland's philosophy. Because his treatment of historical exegesis should be understood in the context of travel and conversation ("commerce" in a wide sense), the thematic discussion of exegesis must be postponed until the following chapter.

1. WRITING "WITHOUT FAVOUR OR FEAR"

Toland's discussions of other authors (in the biographies) and of his own writings (in the responses or apologetic works after *Christianity Not*

Mysterious) increased his own sense of being an author. This awareness freed him from having to endorse or defend other authors or positions or to remain trapped by his earlier positions.

As his writings became more political (explicitly in *The Militia Reform'd*, implicitly in the works on Milton, Harrington, and Ludlow), Toland was faced with the problem of trying to reconcile his portrayal of himself as an autonomous author with his public reputation as a spokesman for the Whig faction of the Country Party. Often during these years, Toland said that he published his positions "wholly independent from the Fears or Engagements of any Party."[1] His adamant autonomy made it risky for any individual or party to employ him as a writer. He had disappointed the Presbyterians who had supported his studies in Holland; he also proved an embarrassment for his friends and patrons (as Harley later was to discover). Shaftesbury learned to be wary of Toland just as Locke had been. Independence, Toland found, was not without its costs—a bitter lesson for a man with great expectations. Electress Sophia tersely cautioned him to pay closer attention to his enemies, among which was poverty.[2]

Toland, however, valued his precarious authorial autonomy. It was a superstitious writer who feared poverty or had hopes for reward. Superstition in general he saw as grounded in fear and hope, but that of writers in particular arose from fear and favor. Toland gradually made explicit how he intended his discussion of his own writing "without fear or favour" to be seen as part of a larger discussion of superstitions in general. His growing awareness of his presence in his own writing brought recognition of the author's susceptibility to influences that undermine his autonomy.

In *The Art of Governing by Partys* (1701) Toland's awareness of himself as an author writing without fear or favor arose in the discussion of hope and fear. "I know my self to be neither aw'd by hopes or fears," he wrote, "nor gain'd by Favour or Bribes."[3] But the hope-or-fear idea, as it refers specifically to the author, did not become clear until Toland worked out its implication in the *Letters to Serena*. "The Impressions of Hope and Fear . . . are ever founded in Ignorance. . . . The fluctuating

1. *Amyntor*, p. 3; also see *Apology*, p. 18.
2. Sophia to von Bothmer, 18 July 1702, *Briefe*, 79: 220.
3. P. 1. Cf. *CNM*, p. 23; "Life of Milton," p. 5; *The State Anatomy of Great Britain*, 4th ed. (London: John Philips et al., 1717), p. ii. Also, recall Toland's epitaph remark, "Nor could frowns, or fortune bend him, to decline from the ways he had chosen."

of mens Minds between Hope and Fear, is one of the chief Causes of Superstition: for being no way able to foresee the Event of what greatly concerns them, they now hope the best, and the next minute fear the worst."[4] The author who writes out of hope or fear, ignorant of the reception his work will receive (as every author is), tries to win a favorable reaction rather than to express his true opinions. The superstitious author is concerned more with how he is received than with actually communicating his authentic positions.

Because Toland believed that hope is founded in ignorance and easily becomes the cause of superstitions, his remarks about what men hope for may well be interpreted as always having a surreptitiously negative implication. For example, in the preface to *Letters to Serena*, he noted his telling Serena (Sophie Charlotte) "that Divine Authority was the surest Anchor of our Hope [in], and the best if not the only Demonstration of[,] the Soul's Immortality."[5] In the context of the above quotation about hope and superstition, this implies that the foundation of our hope in the soul's immortality is ignorance and that divine authority is invoked for the doctrine when philosophers are ignorant of the causes of things.[6]

Throughout his life Toland remained ambiguous on this question of the immortality of the soul. He implied in a late work, however, that the question is probably irresolvable as a speculative issue, even though as a practical issue the denial of immortality, and consequently the denial of all future rewards, "is an opinion I think inconsistent with society."[7] This opinion repeated an idea first mentioned in a 1694 letter to an anonymous correspondent at Oxford. Without the belief in an afterlife he asked, "what incentives could move me to common honesty?"[8] Again and again Toland addressed the topic of immortality not as a speculative question but as a practical and even a political issue. He thus shared in an approach common to other Enlightenment thinkers: David Hume, for example, later developed this theme of human fluctuation between hope and fear in his *Natural History of Religion*.[9] In

4. Pp. 9, 78.
5. Para. 11.
6. *Serena*, pp. 157–58.
7. *Second Part of State Anatomy*, p. vi.
8. Toland to unknown correspondent, sometime during the second or third week of May 1694, in *Collection*, 2: 302.
9. See Sabetti, *John Toland*, pp. 189–90.

opening the introduction to the *Natural History*, Hume distinguished between considering the origins or foundation of religion in human nature (with which the *Natural History* was concerned) and considering the arguments or reasons for religion (with which the *Dialogues concerning Natural Religion* was concerned). Toland's emphasis, of course, was on the former.

In passing from the study of Milton to the letters to Serena, Toland softened his view that all people fluctuate between hope and fear and necessarily fall into superstitious beliefs. Although he gradually came to recognize the possibility of nonsuperstitious hope and fear as genuine human attitudes, he did not emphasize it in the *Letters to Serena*. There he pointed out that fluctuation between hope and fear is grounded in ignorance and can generate superstitions. As he worked through the hope-fear topic, originally from the standpoint of the attitude of the author, Toland was led to the position that any individual could be hopeful or fearful about his own ability to influence others. But insofar as the individual is ignorant of something (i.e., does not comprehend it), he is not the source of that which he hopes or fears and does not maintain a grasp over that which he does not comprehend.

Because the sources of the impressions of hope and fear are external to the individual, the key for understanding superstitions (and perhaps how they can be eradicated) lies in identifying that part of our education by means of which superstitions arise. Our education in superstition, Toland believed, is the product of a widespread and almost continuous effort by those around us:

I must observe on this occasion, that there's no part of our education so difficult to be eradicated as SUPERSTITION; which is industriously instill'd into men from their cradles by their nurses, by their parents, by the very servants, by all that converse with them, by their tutors and schoolmasters, by the poets, orators, and historians which they read: but more particularly by the Priests, who in most parts of the world are hir'd to keep the people in error, being commonly back'd by the example and authority of the Magistrate.[10]

The educational effort required to promote superstitions indicates the degree to which tutors of every sort attempt to keep individuals (and themselves) ignorant of what they could know. Though Toland did not

10. "Druids," p. 140.

argue that all education and contact with others result in superstitious beliefs, he did propose that the process by which men become superstitious is educational. Just as the best method to persuade someone of a position is to retrace the line of thought leading up to its acceptance, so the best way to eradicate superstitious beliefs is to retrace the historical (biographical) process through which the individual comes to accept something he does not understand.

2. THE FOCUS ON PREJUDICES IN THE LETTERS TO SERENA

Although superstitions and prejudices alike are grounded in education, they can be distinguished. *Superstitions* are beliefs about matters we are ignorant of and can gain no knowledge of by natural means. *Prejudices* are beliefs for which we have insufficient evidence, although it is in principle attainable. As far as Toland was concerned, superstitions persist only through our efforts to convince ourselves and others that some beliefs are meaningful and important, even though no human being could understand them. Prejudices, on the other hand, deal with matters that can become known through natural means. By inquiring into prejudices, we can distinguish between beliefs that cannot be humanly resolved (i.e., superstitions) and those that, when sufficient evidence is gathered, can be comprehended and thus known.

Notwithstanding his distinction between superstitions and beliefs-known-to-be-true, Toland regarded both as prejudices originally. He believed that until an individual understands something he is taught, incorporates it into other beliefs, and tests its consistency, plausibility, and meaningfulness, his belief must be understood as a prejudice. Such an individual prejudges the matter at hand in accepting it without a critical evaluation of whether he understands what it means for him to believe it.

Superstitions are beliefs that no amount of human investigation can make clearly understandable. There can be prejudices about superstitions, in that an individual might adopt a certain belief before *attempting* to gain evidence for it. If he tried to gain such evidence about a superstition, he would not find it. Discussion with others may dissolve the prejudice concerning a belief, but it would do so precisely by showing that evidence cannot be gained, thus leaving the superstitious belief intact. To understand human prejudices is to understand both what men can know and what they cannot know but superstitiously think they should know or believe.

Five years after publishing the *Letters to Serena*, Toland singled out the first letter as the point where one may begin to appreciate the overall thrust of his writings. "The reading of this letter could serve as key to all my works. *The origin and the force of Prejudices* is its subject, which I explain as much through their physical reasons as through their moral causes."[11] From the first letter we learn not only that the concept of prejudice brings together a number of Toland's themes but also that the consideration of origins is necessary to appreciate the force of prejudices as well as to correct the misleading characteristics of prejudices.

In quoting the above remark from Toland's manuscripts, F. H. Heinemann suggests that Toland intended the first letter to Serena to be concerned *more* with the "moral" than with the physical causes of prejudices.[12] Toland's text says that he explains the physical reasons for prejudices *just as much as* their moral causes ("j'explique tant par les raisons physiques, que par les causes morales"), but Heinemann attributes the discrepancy to Toland's incorrect French. After all, Heinemann argues, in the preface to the *Letters to Serena* Toland said that the subject of the first letter was the moral causes of prejudices, not the physical causes.[13] It is possible, however, that in the five years between the *Letters to Serena* and this manuscript letter, Toland came to believe that his description of practical, human interaction and intereducation exemplified physical laws of motion. In fact, the laws of social interaction might prove to be as suggestive for the scientist or physicist as physical laws might be for the student of human nature.

The key might lie in recognizing the mutual influence of the two frameworks, or models. The last two letters published in the *Letters to Serena*, but not addressed to Serena, proposed that motion is essential to matter. The 1709 manuscript letter might indicate how Toland became aware of the implications of these subsequent letters for the earlier ones. That is, the apparently purely speculative concern of the final letters must be united with the practical (moral) concern for the force and origin of prejudices. Prejudices could not be treated solely in

11. Toland to (perhaps) Hohendorf, 23 Dec. 1709, BM Add. MS 4465, fol. 7; quoted in Heinemann, "Toland and Age of Reason," p. 42. See Giuntini, *Panteismo*, p. 225.

12. "Toland and the Age of Reason," p. 44.

13. Para. 10.

a practical-moral framework, nor could questions about matter be consigned to purely speculative considerations. The structure of topics addressed in the *Letters to Serena* was intended to indicate this.[14]

The structure of Toland's *Letters to Serena* is similar in a number of ways to William Coward's *Second Thoughts concerning the Human Soul.*[15] Not only did Toland address much the same topic as Coward; he also seems to employ a similar order of treatment. Coward began his work with a discussion of prejudices ("Of the Power and Prevalence of Prejudice contracted by Education, especially in Matters of Religion") and then considered the bases for beliefs in general. He next dealt with belief in an immortal soul (concluding that the soul dies with the body). His work ended with a brief history of the concept of soul.

Unlike Coward, Toland was not satisfied with ending the discussion of the soul on an etymological note without relating etymology to the metaphysics of soul-talk. For that reason, the three letters to Serena were followed by two that dealt with Spinoza. The latter explained how an etymological correction of prejudices about the soul could be supported by a metaphysics that started from, and was limited by, practical concerns and methods based on experience. Moving from the consideration of prejudices, to that of one, often prejudicial belief (immortality), to that of the mystification of immortalized individuals (idolatry), and finally to that of Spinoza's failure to see how immortal matter could be individuated, Toland's *Letters to Serena* showed the effect of expanding speculation to include practical activity. In speaking about "moral causes," he pointed out that we cannot overlook the speculatively moral or the physical (motion-of-matter) character of practical activity.

As early as 1702 Toland refused to allow Leibniz to impose upon him a methodology that begins with a metaphysical-physical description of sensible things. In a letter to Sophie Charlotte, Leibniz expressed frustration with Toland's apparent refusal to answer metaphysical-physical questions about the nature of things.[16] Instead, Toland limited his discussion with Leibniz to "figures and movements," which provoked the remark from Leibniz that Toland did not appear to be well versed in the doctrines implicit in his claims. Toland's participation in

14. Cf. Redwood, *Reason, Ridicule, and Religion*, pp. 142–43.
15. London: Richard Bassett, 1702.
16. No date (but written in response to a 1702 letter by Toland to Sophie Charlotte), *Schriften*, 6: 519–20.

pure speculation waned when the immediate practical implications similarly faded from the discussion, or when the discussion seemed to wander from the actual state of affairs in this world of men and things. Leibniz thought that Toland's model was Hobbes: he appears to have recognized Toland's inclination toward the "politics of motion" high-lighted in Hobbes—that is, the description of figure and movement as directed toward practical social and political considerations.

Toland responded to objections like Leibniz's by portraying himself as concerned with "the Physical Reasons of what every person allows."

The Mathematicians compute the Quantities and Proportions of Motion, as they observe Bodys to act on one another, without troubling themselves about the Physical Reasons of what every person allows, being a thing which does not always concern them, and which they leave the Philosophers to explain: tho the latter wou'd succeed better in their Reasons, if they did more acquaint themselves before hand with the Observations and Facts of the former, as Mr NEWTON justly observes.[17]

Toland's position emphasized the speculative-physical explanations of the "philosophers" (like Leibniz) only insofar as they remained tied to *the interests of every person* and limited to the observations and facts with which the "mathematicians" (like Newton) dealt.

In characterizing physical reasons as the concern of every person, Toland expanded the speculative enterprise of professional philoso-phers, mathematicians, and theologians to include the practical concerns of nonprofessionals. Concern for the practicality of reasons helps one resist the temptation to yield to professional prejudgments. Such prejudgments refer not only to beliefs for which there is insufficient professional evidence (i.e., evidence accepted in one's profession), but also to beliefs accepted by professionals before their consistency with political or social concerns has been determined. A person without a profession, Toland noted, is "more likely to be freer from prejudices, as he has more leisure maturely to consider; neither being ty'd down by Articles upon Oath, too frequently productive of perjury, nor crampt by any other partial or politic restraint."[18] The leisure and flexibility of one who does not profess exclusively any particular creed or occupation allow him to avoid hasty or restricted

17. *Serena*, p. 177.
18. *Nazarenus*, preface, p. iv. See *CNM*, p. xxiv.

judgments. That flexibility is essential for freeing the "philosopher" or the "mathematician" from concern for speculative constructs unrelated to the de facto constructs of political and social life.

Toland prided himself in representing men, in regard to political or legal matters, not as they ought to be but as they are: "In all *Political* or *Legislative* Proceedings, we are not so much to mind what Men ought to be, as what they are."[19] This does not mean that he was content with men as they are. It does mean that social progress, particularly in correcting prejudices, would not occur—at least insofar as Toland was a participant—through abstract, general, and utopian proposals for human action. Rather, the true philosophic dreamer concentrates on *source-explanations* of human nature in regard to *social* development, and he focuses his *goal-oriented* attention on developing the uniqueness of the *individual*. In short, Toland's utopian thought (at least up to 1705) centered on the individual. But the characteristics that distinguish the individual from others can be discerned only through an examination of the historical and biographical method by which men are united in prejudices.

To confuse future concentration on the individual with past-and-present concentration on the uniformity of opinions or practices results in the hope for *uniformity* as a future ideal for mankind. However, future unity among men or even among Christians alone, Toland argued, is an impossible ideal generated out of a methodological mistake. The mistake lies in taking one of the characteristics discerned in a historical study of mankind (viz., that some men are or have been united in their opinions or practices) and proposing this characteristic as an ideal for all men. The attainment of such an end would contradict the situation of men as they are (i.e., nonunited individuals or individuals within nonunited groups). Furthermore, because people become united through prejudices, the ideal of a united mankind is not only destructive of the individual—because it would make a union of *individuals* impossible—but also it could promote the universalization of prejudices.

Toland's emphasis on the historical analysis of prejudices in the *Letters to Serena* was balanced in the following year (1705) by his recognition that considering the controversies of men as necessary could provide little hope for general, nonprejudicial human unity. In

---

19. *Memorial of the State of England*, p. 47.

Socinianism Truly Stated (1705) he wrote to a correspondent that this recognition could result in peace of mind, which would be preferable to the despair of those who believed that nonprejudicial unity was impossible:

I very well remember the Result of our last Discourse was this, that you hated and that I lov'd those Controversys, which so much divide the World in their Affections and Interests, as well as in their Opinions. And yet after frankly discovering our Thoughts to one another, and impartially examining our several Dispositions, it appear'd, that you who so carefully avoided all Disputes, cou'd never enjoy any Tranquillity, occasion'd by your Concern for the differences of others; and that I who industriously engag'd my self in the Consideration of all their Quarrels, was nevertheless extremely easy and unconcern'd. The reason of these contrary Dispositions in two, who agree in most other things, I take to be, that you, who no less expect than wish to see the different Partys reconcil'd, must needs have a Detestation for every thing that widens their Breaches or retards their Union; and that I, who despair of any Uniformity in Mens Opinions or Practices (which I hold to be impossible) must needs be pleas'd with examining the Grounds of those Notions, and the Springs of those Actions, which tho I cannot help or prevent, yet give me a further Knowledg of human Nature. With submission therefore to your Judgment, I think our whole Difference to be, that you represent Mankind to your self, such as they ought to be, and that I consider 'em but just such as they are; or that you are uneasy to see 'em continue their own Enemies, and that I am easy since they cannot become their own Friends.[20]

An examination of "our several Dispositions" shows that even when we consider the disputes among various groups and the possibility for their resolution, our own individual education, prejudices, and preferences determine our hope or despair about future human unity. The lover of controversies and disputes finds tranquillity and peace in this world of quarreling parties; he who hopes for the day when mankind is united can enjoy little serenity with men as they are now.

Two themes demand some recognition in the present context.[21] First, Toland endorsed the prospect of human unity without uniformity. That unity, though, is not of opinions but of temperament—that is,

---

20. *Socinianism truly Stated, Being An Example of fair Dealing in all Theological Controversys* (London, 1705), p. 5.

21. These themes will receive more detailed treatment in the chapters on toleration and metaphysics.

a unity of men who tolerate one another's often conflicting opinions. This toleration was not grudging or involuntary; rather, it was an attitude found where disagreement was eagerly expected. Toland even showed a certain nationalistic pride in the partisan differences of the English: "There is no Contry in *Europe* more divided than *England*; and . . . we cherish all the kinds of Differences which in any place or Time disturb'd the Peace of the World."[22] Toland's "despair" of uniformity in opinions or practices was not as disappointing to him as it might sound to a modern ear; for he saw the impossibility of uniform opinions or practices as grounded practically, in de facto sectarian disputes, and also speculatively, in the demands of metaphysical individuality. Nature itself prohibits such uniformity (e.g., in religious opinions and practices); and even if this uniformity were possible, it would not be desirable: "Tho I cannot say, that I wish there was but one communion of Christians, since this in nature is impossible, neither is it in itself desireable, nor the thing intended by the communion of Saints."[23] Just as the "communion" of saints includes a wide variety of religious viewpoints and personalities, so nature allows and promotes a diversity of opinions and practices.

The second theme—concerning the contrast between what men are and what they ought to be—ties back into the question about the type of union men can attain. Toland's analysis of the grounds of opinions and springs of actions indicate his recognition of individual diversity and distinction in the context of *actual* disagreement. By means of his emphasis on how men *are*—distinct individuals who test themselves and one another through polemic—he hoped to generate sympathy for disputation and acceptance of it. To hope for a uniformity of opinions is to disregard the need to gain knowledge of human nature in terms of the *origins* of opinions, prejudices, and ontologically distinct individuals themselves. Toland implied in almost all that he wrote that human nature in general is not to be explained teleologically.

Toland refused to discuss the possibility for future human unity without first raising the metalevel question of why not all reflective thinkers would hope for such a unity. The question is not particularly *epistemological* (nongenetic): it does not deal with an evaluation of why

---

22. *Propositions for Uniting the Two East India Companies; in a Letter to a Man of Quality, who desir'd the Opinion of a Gentleman not concern'd in either Company* (London: Bernard Lintott, 1701), p. 1.

23. "Barnabas-Original," *Nazarenus*, pp. 70–71.

men should or should not hope to attain a nonprejudicial unity. Rather, it is *psychological* (genetic), treating the attitudes, "dispositions," or prejudices of reflective thinkers themselves.

The question Toland asks his correspondent and his reader is, Why do you and I, reasonable men and considering the same basic information, adopt two fundamentally different attitudes toward the future of man? It is this type of metalevel question about Leibniz's *need* to define sensible things apart from figures and movements that frustrated Leibniz and prompted him to conclude that Toland did not really want to search after the truth. But, for Toland, the more pressing question was not whether we should engage in the search but rather why we should not do so freed from the prejudices that disturb our inner quiet and joy.[24] Differences of opinion among reflective thinkers should not, of themselves, generate disturbing conflicts. When men are mistreated because of their different opinions, however, conflicts do result.[25]

The *Letters to Serena* addressed the psychological history of prejudices while recognizing individual efforts to be free of them. The first letter, on the origin and force of prejudices, was followed in the second by a history of the pre-Christian doctrines of the immortality of the soul and (in the third) by a discussion of idolatry, particularly the adoration of ancestors as divine. In the next, a "confutation" of Spinoza, Toland argued that Spinoza's philosophy failed to account for the individuality of material things. The final letter, a response to questions raised by an anonymous correspondent about the fourth one, included Toland's constructive suggestion (concerning the problems left by Spinoza) that motion is essential to matter.

At this point, my concern is not so much to describe Toland's positions on the topics treated in the letters as it is to show the line of thought exemplified in their arrangement. The transition from the second and third letters (addressed to Serena) to the fourth and fifth (addressed to a Dutch gentleman) hinges on the central place of *mummies* in the history of the doctrine of the immortality of the soul. Mummies serve as immortal images of the material individual: at death, the material individual, taking on the immortal character of the gods, becomes a proper object of adoration. In his attempt to respect the importance of matter and immortality, Spinoza failed to give a

24. *Serena*, p. 16.
25. *Second Part of State Anatomy*, p. 70.

metaphysical explanation of how individual bodies actually become individual, Toland believed. In short, Spinoza emphasized the immortal character of the material individual, as the Egyptians had done in their treatment of mummies; but as a metaphysician, Spinoza should have explained how something immortal could be individual as well as how an individual could be immortal. Until psychological prejudices concerning immortality were revealed in a historical analysis, metaphysical and epistemological questions such as those raised by Spinoza could not be satisfactorily addressed.

Our indoctrination in prejudices, as the first letter makes clear, begins even before we are born. Receiving good and bad impressions in the womb, we can correct the foundations of our prejudices and dispositions toward particular habits and biases only through the utmost efforts and with the exercise of reason.[26] The "grand Cheat" and depravation of reason begins almost as soon as we are born. Those around us endeavor to instill in us the fruits of their own erroneous credulity, and they hope (often with success) that as we grow older we will readily accept the mysterious and incomprehensible as part of some natural revelation:

We no sooner see the Light, but the grand Cheat begins to delude us from every Quarter. The very Midwife hands us into the World with superstitious Ceremonys, and the good women assisting at the Labor have a thousand Spells to avert the Misfortune, or to produce the Happiness of the Infant; making several ridiculous Observations, to discover the Omen of his future State of Life. Nor is the Priest in some places behindhand with these Gossips, to initiate him betimes into his Service, by pronouncing certain Forms of Words as so many powerful Charms, and using the gentle Symbols of Salt or Oil, or the severer Applications of Iron or Fire, or by marking him after some other manner, as his own Right and Property for the future. The Child, it's true, is not yet affected by any of these or the like Foolerys, whatever Virtue he may be afterwards persuaded to allow them: but this shows how early those about him begin to infect him (if they cou'd) with their own mistakes, and how industriously every one with whom he has afterwards to do, endeavours to deprave his Reason from the very beginning; so that not remembering when, or where, or how he came by many of his Notions, he's tempted to believe that they proceed from Nature it self, and is astonish'd to find that any shou'd call the Truth of 'em in question. . . . what may be conceal'd from a Child in a prudent Family, he's sure to hear of it at School, where so many Children are brought together, not to improve one another (which cannot be suppos'd of

26. *Serena*, p. 2.

such Conversation) but to communicate their mutual Mistakes and vicious Habits, to grow the more idle, and to meet with bad Examples. We greedily devour the Poets, Orators, and Mythologists, committing great Extracts of their Fictions to our memory, being surpriz'd and gain'd by the Charms of their Stile, Numbers, and Composition; whereby it comes to pass that we swallow the Poison of their Errors with inexpressible Pleasure, and lay a large Foundation for future Credulity, insensibly acquiring a Disposition for hearing things rare and wonderful, to imagin we believe what we only dread or desire, to think what we are but puzzl'd that we are convinc'd, and to swallow what we cannot comprehend.[27]

In order to appreciate the similarity between this passage and remarks by Locke, we need only consult Locke's *Essay concerning Human Understanding*.[28] Both Toland and Locke appear to have expanded on Cicero's *Tusculan Disputations* (3.1.2–3) in their descriptions of the origins of prejudices and superstitions. Toland, of course, gives the topic the most extensive treatment.

Toland believed that one's early training and education establish the dispositions upon which he acts later in life. He thought that it was particularly important to apply this observation to the training of future governmental leaders. In a work published two years before the *Letters to Serena*, he expressed concern that the electoral prince of Hanover (later, George I) should have the most early impressions of love and kindness for Britain, arguing that George should have been invited to England while still young, "to make the Customs of this Country habitual to him like those of his native Place; and, in a Word, to have him Educated in the Language, Laws, and the establisht Religion of the Nation he's to govern, not by his own Will and Discretion, but according to certain Rules and Limitations, whereof he shou'd not remain ignorant till the Time they are to be put in practice."[29] Judging from the subsequent animosity many Englishmen held for George after his accession to the throne (1714)—an animosity encouraged by his German mannerisms and refusal to learn English—

27. Ibid., pp. 2–6.

28. P. 712 (4.20.9). Also see Locke's *Reasonableness of Christianity*, ed. George W. Ewing (Chicago: Henry Regnery Co., 1965), p. 178.

29. *Reasons for Addressing His Majesty to invite into England their Highnesses, the Electress Dowager and the Electoral Prince of Hanover. And likewise, Reasons for Attainting and abjuring the pretended Prince of Wales* (London: John Nutt, 1702), p. 1. For the Hanoverian reaction to this work, see Leibniz to Burnet of Kemnay, 27 Feb. 1702, *Werke*, 8: 341–42; *Schriften*, 3: 288; and Baron von Schutz to Leibniz, 30 June/11 July 1702, *Werke*, 8: 356–57.

Toland's early suggestions may have been occasioned by premonitions about the young prince that he formed during his trip to Hanover.

Toland did not want to limit the discussion of prejudicial education solely to the question of the Protestant Succession, however. The principle could be more broadly applied in the political domain. For example, he noted that free peoples had always forbidden children of tyrants from succeeding their parents to positions of authority.[30] The prejudices of our parents; of the region or society in which we are raised; of rural, urban, political, or military settings—all are firmly ingrained in us.[31] "No sort of Prejudices stick closer to us, or are harder to be eradicated, than those of the Society wherein we live and had our Education. This holds equally true of their civil Customs and religious Rites, of their Notions and Practices."[32] Because the self is the result of sensible impressions, the social context in which the self is defined exercises a formative and unmistakably prejudicial influence.

Although Toland adhered strongly to the belief that prejudices characterize every society and that their educational origins often go unnoticed, he did recognize certain values in promoting them. Even superstitious prejudices might have a role in maintaining civil order:

In civil society, there are certain superstitions which might be called tolerable, because, even though they cannot be rooted out entirely, still the prudent political leader should strive to temper them to the general status of the commonwealth, in order that it may not be thoroughly destroyed. Atheists, however, ought not to hope at all to be tolerated under any conditions, since they are bound to the profession of an opinion by no chain of conscience (either by the dread of punishment or the love of reward). However silly he may continually be, the Superstitious man nevertheless can sometimes be harmless; but the Atheist, intent upon his own interest, never dissents from established Religion, and he evades suspicion by whatever subterfuge is necessary and wishes that all others conform to established Religion. Atheism, in short, involves the consideration of few individuals, whereas Superstition involves the consideration of almost all.[33]

Public and universal (or almost universal) compliance to the laws and

30. *Reasons for Addressing His Majesty*, p. 15.
31. See Toland's French version of *Serena*, sent in manuscript to Hohendorf in Vienna, ONB MS 10325, fols. 92–93.
32. *Serena*, p. 12.
33. *Adeisidaemon, sive Titus Livius a superstitione vindicatus. To which is added, Origines Judaicae* (The Hague: Thomas Johnson, 1709), pp. 77–78.

accepted practices of a commonwealth is essential for the maintenance of civil order. Insofar as communal—particularly religious—superstitions can be employed to maintain the general stability of the commonwealth, they will be tolerated by the prudent *political* leader. At least they will be tolerated much more than the individualistic beliefs of the atheist.

To the extent that the political leader is concerned *only* with men's public, political behavior, he prefers the uniformity and universal effectiveness of superstitions. Following the example of Hobbes, Toland observed that dread of punishment and love of reward are the only effective means of insuring *universal* compliance with the law or with accepted practices. And in this regard—that is, politically and publicly speaking—Toland saw papists and atheists as supporting politically subversive positions. He did not imply, however, that atheists should not be *tolerated* within a commonwealth; indeed, religious toleration must be extended to include Catholics and atheists. He endorsed only the position that the individuality of atheistic positions cannot serve political leaders as the basis upon which to build the uniformity essential for political stability. Toland agreed with Shaftesbury and Bayle that the atheist's personal morality does not have to contradict that of the theist; in fact, he viewed the *personal* morality of the theist as much more troublesome to political stability.[34]

A distinction between the superstitious man and the atheist also serves to explain further why Toland's opinion about the common man's wisdom seemed to change after *Christianity Not Mysterious*. Politically speaking, the common man, as Toland came to perceive him, lacked discretion. When scholars and respectable ministers objected to Toland's positions, the dispute occasioned a flurry of pamphlets and heated philosophic exchange. Even though in some of these exchanges the bounds of philosophic decorum were exceeded, responsible authors mutually agreed to limit their disputes to a battle of words rather than of fists. Such restraint, however, did not characterize the behavior of demogogic clerics like Sacheverell, who provoked artisans and apprentices to physical violence against authors like Toland through appeal to their superstitions and prejudices.[35]

---

34. Cf. Shaftesbury's *Characteristicks of Men, Manners, Opinions, Times*, 3 vols. (London: [probably John Darby], 1711), 2:46 (treatise 4, bk. 2, pt. 3, sec. 2). Also see Giuntini, *Panteismo*, pp. 445–47.

35. Cf. Redwood, *Reason, Ridicule, and Religion*, p. 218.

In the years after the publication of *Christianity Not Mysterious*, Toland recognized the need to distinguish the form of toleration necessary for free thought from that concerned with social stability. This is paralleled by the distinction between atheism in speculative matters and atheism in practical activities. To charge someone with this second type of atheism, Toland noted, is much more grievous than to label him a traitor, murderer, or parricide; "for such a Person is not only justly lookt upon as one that has no Reason or Reflection, but likewise as under no Tyes of Conscience, of Obligations or Oaths, when he has the Opportunity of doing Mischief; and so not to be trusted in any privat or public Capacity."[36] Besides, when told that someone is an atheist, Toland continued, many people conclude that he is guilty of all those immoralities they take to be the natural consequences of his opinion; and without further examination, they charge him with everything imaginable.

Leibniz warned Toland that he seemed to equate religion and superstition in his *Adeisidaemon*, particularly in arguing that religion involved dread of punishment and hope of reward. Toland responded that because religion played a politically stabilizing role, it encouraged tolerable superstitions.[37]

3. THE PRACTICAL CONTEXTS OF HISTORY IN FORMAL EDUCATION

Toland was careful to point out that the prejudices in which men are educated from the cradle to the grave, far from being corrected, are

36. *Vindicius Liberius*, p. 38. See also *Apology*, pp. 18–19. Cf. Locke, *Epistola de Tolerantia; A Letter on Toleration*, ed. and trans. Raymond Klibansky and J. W. Gough (Oxford: Clarendon Press, 1968), p. 135.

37. Many of Toland's remarks in *Adeisidaemon* ("The Unsuperstitious Man") about atheism and superstition had not been included in the original MS, entitled "Livius Vindicatus" and dated 1 Jan. 1707 (Rawlinson MS D. 377, fols. 132–39, Bodleian Library. See Giancarlo Carabelli, "Un inedito di John Toland: Il *Livius Vindicatus*, orvero la prima edizione [mancata] dell'*Adeisidaemon* [1709]," *Rivista critica di storia della filosofia* 31 [1976]: 309–18). Less polemical than the published version, the early draft did not include any remarks concerning superstitions about celestial phenomena (which are contained in *Adeisidaemon*). Additions to the early draft seem to have resulted from Toland's reading of Bayle's *Pensées diverses sur la comète* [1683], translated into English in 1708. In *Adeisidaemon* Toland quoted Bayle and spoke favorably of his ideas; but Bayle was not referred to in "Livius Vindicatus." Toland recognized a kindred spirit in Bayle

often augmented by the "prejudice of education" itself. Because of his concern for the general procedures by which notions and practices become habitual or customary, he took special interest in the practical functions and effects of formal education. Education, he maintained, should be understood in the context of the public needs of the nation. In line with this thinking, he pointed out that a classical education, especially for large numbers of poor children, delays the movement of children into the labor market, contributes to idleness, and "spoils their handwriting, figuring, and true English, the only accomplishments requisite for the Populace."[38] Overly educated manufacturers and laborers fail to devote themselves earnestly to their trades and prove to be financial burdens on the public, through added education subsidies and higher production costs.

On the other hand, Toland favored a classical education for children whose families could afford the tutorial costs, because he believed that it could engender the development of virtuous attitudes.[39] However, because from those to whom much is given, much is also expected, he did not hesitate to accuse the nobility and the gentry of failing to maintain the tradition of the ancients, in which those who were distinguished by birth or fortune were also educated to fill the offices of religion, law, the military, and politics. "Among the Moderns, on the contrary, the noble and the rich quit the use of Letters as well as of arms to the meaner sort, thinking their knowledg shou'd be carry'd about by their servants like their cloaths, tho' with this difference, that they will not use the one as they wear the other."[40] Unlike the ancients, the modern nobleman or man of means is led blindly by his inferiors in matters related to the common welfare. He acquiesces because he assumes that the specialist's observations are grounded upon information available only to those learned in particular professions.

The clergy, in particular, hold a special dominance over the nobility

---

and sought to disseminate his ideas to correspondents such as Prince Eugene of Savoy, to whom he sent a personally dedicated copy of *Adeisidaemon* (ONB Autographen 45. 83. Cf. Bayle, *Miscellaneous Reflections Occasion'd by the Comet*, anon. trans., 2 vols. [London: J. Morphew, 1708], 1: 269–80). These correspondents depended on Toland for the latest information on the writings of clandestine or suspect authors.

38. "A Memorial to a Present Minister of State," in *Collection*, 2: 251.
39. French MS version of *Serena*, ONB MS 13025, fol. 93.
40. "A Letter Concerning the Roman Education," in *Collection*, 2: 4.

and the gentry, because they often serve as schoolmasters and tutors.[41] Always recommending a subservient and unquestioning attitude toward the unknown (at least unknown to others), the clergy maintain positions of political importance, teaching their students at an early age to defer to the opinions of "professionals." At the same time, they fail to make it clear that the professions have their own prejudices.

Toland considered education too important to be left to the clergy or to scholars. A plan of education must, first, respond to the needs of a society through the development of educational policies for the general population and, second, recognize the dangers of clerical domination or pedantry in advanced education:

Nothing can be of nearer concern to any country than Schools and Universities, Education being of that importance, that Princes and States ought to take this matter (as the wisest have ever done and do) into their own immediate Inspection: for such as is the Education of their Youth, such will be the genius of their Elders, such will be their Posterity, such will be their Government; knowing or ignorant, polite or rude, virtuous or vitious, and so on. . . . Schools therefore being instituted for the publick Good, must be kept to their Institution by publick Authority.[42]

Formal education should have an essentially practical and social orientation. As educational institutions lose sight of this orientation they degenerate into cloisters of "speculative men," the domains of those who are "strangers to the world" of business, experience, and conversation. In contrast to the moderns, the learned of the ancients were not

cloister'd up from society; nor under the whips and fines, the scanty dyet and barren lectures of speculative men, accustomed to a retir'd and sedentary way of living: for such persons are commonly strangers to the world, which (with the want of practising mankind by the advantage of travelling) makes 'em imperious and austere, vehemently addicted to dispute, impatient of contradiction, noisy and passionate in conversation, and, what's worst of all, more concern'd to preposses the understandings of their Schollars with thos particular doctrines which make for the profit and credit of their own

---

41. "A Memorial to a Present Minister of State," in *Collection*, 2: 241. Also see *The Jacobitism, Perjury, and Popery of High-Church Priests* (London: J. Baker, 1710) p 15.

42. *State Anatomy*, pp 70–71.

profession, than to fit them for business, to give 'em gentile accomplishments, and to advance 'em in the liberal Arts and Sciences.[43]

The educator who would not be a stranger to the world or an "insufferable Pedant" engages in the art of "practising mankind by the advantage of travelling." The truly intelligent man augments his reading of books about the customs and ways of thinking in other countries with conversation and travel in order to recognize his own academic and cultural prejudices. Travel and conversation are the means by which men *practice* the humanity upon which *speculative* men dwell.

Toland took his clue on this point from Milton. In his "Life of Milton," he noted that Milton was persuaded "that he could not better discern the Preeminence or Defects of his own Country, than by observing the Customs and Institutions of others; and that the study of never so many Books, without the advantages of Conversation, serves only to render a Man either a stupid Fool, or an insufferable Pedant."[44] Travel and conversation outside strictly academic circles frees the man who would be educated from the prejudices of pedantry. "Pedantry," Toland noted, "is perhaps a thing, more or less, inseparable from all Universities, I say, from a mixture of old recluses and unexperienced striplings; as the getting rid of it is one advantage a man has by coming abroad into the world."[45] Coming abroad into the world, the learned man can recognize how a university education itself contributes to the bewitchment of reason by means of its own prejudices.

Although universities have the potential to foster recognition of previously unnoticed prejudices, they often simply substitute new prejudices for old ones. The university, Toland claimed, is

the most fertile Nursery of Prejudices, whereof the greatest is, that we think there to learn every thing, when in reality we are taught nothing. . . . our comfort is, that we know as much as our Masters, who affect to speak a barbarous Jargon which commonly has no Signification; and the main Art that fits their Disciples to take their degrees, is to treat of very ordinary Matters in

---

43. "A Letter Concerning the Roman Education," in *Collection*, 2: 5.

44. P. 7. Also see Toland's introductory letter (probably addressed to Molesworth's son) in his edition of *Letters from the Right Honourable The Late Earl of Shaftesbury to Robert Molesworth* (London: J. Peele, 1721), p. xv.

45. *State Anatomy*, p. 74. Also see p. 44.

very extraordinary Terms. Yet this dos not render them half so insupportable to People of Sense, as their formal Stiffness and Pedantry, their perpetual Itch of Dispute and Contradiction.... for, in one word, there is scarce any thing learnt at the University, but what a man must forget, if he would be understood, or not appear ridiculous and troublesome, when he comes into other Company.[46]

Toland might have had Spanheim or some of the Oxford dons in mind when he wrote so critically about university teachers. For according to a questionable story about his days as a student of Spanheim, he had argued with his master and had been hooted out of the classroom by his fellow students (for whom Toland also had little respect).[47]

To break free of the prejudices of pedantry, Toland prescribed a regimen of experience and conversation in the business of the world. In his own case, this meant not only personal travel throughout Europe but also expansion of his interests to include matters beyond the areas of his academic training. In order to move freely into areas for which he had no explicit academic credentials, Toland felt that he must travel in nonacademic circles. His guides in such an enterprise were Locke and, to a lesser extent, Newton; and the question of *coinage* provided a theme for movement beyond the closed domain of university discourse. Locke's concern for coinage and monetary matters and Newton's activities as warden of the mint (1696) and master of the mint (1699) had their philosophical parallels, Toland thought, in the attempt to coin new forms of discourse capable of bringing together the experience and conversation of the business world with the speculations of philosophy.[48]

In his translation, in 1696, of *A Discourse upon Coins*, by Bernardo Davanzati Bostichi (1529–1606), Toland spoke of his desire to know more about matters dealing with coinage:

for neither my Years, nor Employment at the Schools (which I left but t'other day) will allow me to be Master enough of a thing, whereof the Knowledg depends so much upon Business, and more acquaintance with the World than I

---

46. *Serena*, pp. 7–8.
47. See *Nazarenus*, preface, p. iv.
48. See Locke's *Several Papers relating to Money, Interest, and Trade* (New York: Augustus M. Kelly, 1968); and *The Correspondence of John Locke and Edward Clarke*, ed. Benjamin Rand (Cambridge, Mass.: Harvard University Press, 1927).

can boast of. And indeed I benefited little (tho most willing to learn) by all the Pieces written upon this Subject, till Mr. *Lock* was pleas'd to favour the Publick with his Thoughts upon it. It seems as impossible for that great Man to write obscurely, as to publish any thing he does not thorowly understand. He has by this, and his other Treatise concerning *Lowering the Interest of Money*, given a convincing Demonstration that Business and Observation are not incompatible with the speculative part of *Philosophy*: but if you compare his Book too, with what others have said of *Coin*, you have there a Demonstration how ridiculous it is to write from abstracted or Closet-Notions of what must be only learn'd by *Experience* and *Conversation*.[49]

The notions of closeted university scholars lacked the kind of novelty and authority that characterize the development and growth of reason. New and vital notions or meanings could be coined only in the context of practical experience and in interdisciplinary and international conversation.

Toland did not want to give the impression, however, that he objected to formal education. Though he referred to universities as nurseries of prejudices, he also recognized them as nurseries of good literature:

No man is a greater admirer of such Nurseries of good Literature, and had I not past a considerable part of my time at the University, even this *Memorial* had not been in every respect such as it is. . . . He must be savage and unpolish'd indeed, an enemy to all Religion and Politicks, who's an enemy to Schools and Universities: tho such as from their love to solid Learning and just Government, wou'd reform or improve those Seminaries of both, are often made to pass for their enemies.[50]

Far from being an enemy of formal education, Toland supported the reform of universities, so that students might learn to be "polite Gentlemen as well as profound Scholars."[51] Tutors, he argued, should be required to lecture regularly. Such a regulation might even curtail their pompous attitudes. Furthermore, if fellows and masters were not required to become clerics, not only would the growing ecclesiastic influence be checked, but the academic garb and contrived modes of

---

49. (London: Awnsham and John Churchill, 1696), translator's preface, pp. iii–iv.
50. *State Anatomy*, p. 69.
51. *Ordinances, Statutes, and Privileges*, p. 40.

behavior could be replaced in ways that would reflect more closely the extra-academic (public, business) aspects of a university education.[52]

The great benefit of a university education lies in its potential to give individuals the tools for discerning their own prejudices and those of others. This process of educating oneself out of prejudicial notions paradoxically involves the immersion of oneself in the study of how these notions become customary. The etymologist traces the history of words that rule equally over princes, priests, and common people through the authority of "our most mighty Master, the irresistible Tyrant Custom."[53] Toland believed that custom exercises a stranglehold on our words and meanings only to the extent that we are not the original sources of meaningfulness. When an etymologist traces the history of words, he reminds us of the human origins of our language and the human ability to effect changes in word meanings. Too long, Toland argued, have men considered custom as unassailable as nature itself; for too many custom is indeed a second nature. "Custom (which is not unfitly call'd a second Nature) has imprest such a Stamp on the very Language of the Society, that what is deliver'd in these or those Words, tho never so contradictory or abstruse, passes ordinarily for current Truth."[54] We are so used to thinking that terms like "mystery," for example, make perfect sense in regard to religious doctrines that we do not detect the inappropriateness of their usage in certain contexts until they are analyzed etymologically. In the first few pages of *Christianity Not Mysterious*, Toland carried out precisely such an analysis of the word "mystery" in order to show that later arguments depended on an initial recognition of the customary and prejudicial uses of the word. Etymology can prevent our becoming slaves to habit and unwitting pawns of custom.

Toland's tendency was always to describe the weakness of a position or idea by tracing its history.[55] Even his critics recognized his use of this fundamental technique when he discussed the rise of "vulgar errors."[56]

Indeed, according to Toland, tyranny of custom in linguistic usage is parallel to tyranny of the priestcraft in religion. Bound to language and naming, thinking is never free from words. But the free thinker is not

---

52. "A Memorial to a Present Minister of State," in *Collection*, 2: 241–48.
53. *Serena*, p. 15.
54. Ibid., p. 13.
55. See, for example, *Serena*, p. 213.
56. See William Wotton, *A Letter to Eusebia* (London: Tim. Goodwin, 1704), p. 69.

as easily dominated by his language as other men are. The more the laity can control their meanings and limit their language to words that are not mysterious, the more they can think for themselves.

This examination of how word meanings (notions) are controllable was important for Toland because of its implications for the discussion of superstitions. Superstitions persist only because men convince themselves that certain beliefs or words are meaningful even though they cannot be understood. Such meaningfulness independent of language users can be undermined only through a careful etymological analysis of the beliefs or words. Without that analysis, the beliefs or words maintain the power and status of superstitions and thus control thought and action.

Less than a year before his death, Toland expressed amazement at how old superstitions are—"almost as old as [names and] writing."[57] This marginal manuscript remark is interesting because it has a line through the words "names and." On the following page, he decried the fact that superstitious taboos in many cultures limit the speaking of "unlawful" names: names themselves can thus be treated as superstitions. By combining the remarks on these two pages, one might interpret Toland as saying that superstitions are not *almost* as old as names but, in fact, are *as* old as names. That is, the very activity of naming begins the process of objectifying the meaningfulness of that which is named; and the more one loses sight of the fact that the thing named was originally recognized as meaningful through the act of naming, the more names themselves (supported by custom) contribute to superstition.

The key to dealing with the tyranny of linguistic custom lies in evaluating the prejudices of language and of notions, using the same historical techniques employed in the evaluation of practices. Again and again, Toland's use of the phrase "notions and practices" focused attention on the need to apply the criteria used in historical studies to the study of the development of customary notions and habitual practices. By concentrating on history, he implied that the resolution of many theological and political problems may depend upon understanding the historical sources of disagreements.

Toland reiterated and reinforced Spinoza's "theologico-political" concentration with his own *historical* concentration on etymology and

---

57. Marginal MS note in Toland's copy of Martin's *Western Islands*, p. 16.

on the study of our adherence to particular opinions and practices. Insofar as he emphasized the need to return to consideration of the historical sources of beliefs—whether of the Judaic roots of Christianity or of the appropriate role of the clergy in civil government—Toland looked to the worldly-wise scholar to direct his energies toward developing a social sensitivity for history.[58]

A historical sensibility permeated Toland's writing. It appeared on the personal level in his showing how biography reveals the origins of an individual's prejudicial notions and practices. It appeared on a universal level in his etymological and historical procedures for discerning the prejudices of entire cultures. Toland's attempt to develop these techniques through his exegetical work, in order to inspire in men the confidence to assert a *new authority* in dealing with history, is the next topic.

58. For an explicit treatment of Toland's concern for Jewish law as the core problem of the Christian-Jewish relation, see Max Weiner, "John Toland and Judaism," *Hebrew Union College Annual* 16 (1941): 215–42.

IV

Historical and Literary Exegesis

MUCH OF TOLAND'S WORK on biblical criticism and the treatment of classical sources occurred during his sojourn in Holland from 1708 to 1711. Works such as *Adeisidaemon* and *Nazarenus* resulted from the research conducted at this time when his friends and correspondents were asked not to write to him about matters of political intrigue in England.

Toland's research in the writings of the ancients and in the interpretation of scriptural and ecclesiastical sources extended back at least as far as his studies with Spanheim in 1692–93. Soon after his arrival in Oxford, in 1694, Toland completed a treatise challenging certain classical authors on their description of the death of the Roman consul Marcus Atilius Regulus. Combining critical techniques with a tenacious drive to obtain manuscripts or personal testimony, Toland also exposed a work attributed to Charles I, the *Eikon Basilike*, as a forgery. In his "Life of Milton," Toland suggested applying critical techniques to what are usually regarded as scriptural sources. Divines on both sides of the Channel worried that if there were the same critical techniques used in the study of pagan classical sources, Scripture would lose its place of literary preeminence. Coming from the author of *Christianity Not Mysterious*, such suggestions were seen as the exegetical equivalent of the attempt to rid religion of the mystery by which it maintained prominence over other aspects of life. When Toland pointed out, in the *Letters to Serena*, that prejudices and superstitions become customary through the uncritical adoption of notions and practices, he again focused attention on the need for etymological and historical research.

Many of Toland's ideas for biblical and historical exegesis appear to have come from Spinoza, Bayle, and Richard Simon. However, his was distinguished by an emphasis on drawing connections between pagan sources and biblical texts to unite the business and conversation of the world with scholarship. With Toland, biblical and historical exegesis became a means for incorporating the elegance and insight of antiquity into the "practicing of the world," that is, into ongoing conversation throughout history. The exegete contributes to the authority of the texts he studies since he makes the text *eloquent* to, or expressive in, the world of commerce and conversation. His task is not only to study that which is eloquent but also to be eloquent himself.

Divided into three sections, this chapter begins with Toland's attitudes toward testing Scripture; for superstitious prejudices in religion can be undermined only by pinpointing the origins and tracing the traditions of inelegant commentators ("authorities"). The elegant writing of ancient pagan authors provides a point of reference and a model for the historian concerned with the practical implications of the past for the present: this serves as the theme of the second section. The third section treats of Toland's insistence that the historian-exegete be a man in the world, who expresses well the elegance of history's learned authors.

1. BIBLICAL EXEGESIS AND THE DEBASING IMPACT OF THE CHURCH FATHERS

Like Locke before him, Toland portrayed himself as clearing away the rubbish that inhibits the attainment of clarity in knowledge. The business of such an under-laborer is "to take away and pull down, to mend and contract; and not to lay any new Foundations, where there has been too much building already."[1] This caution against the development of further prejudicial foundations of knowledge has specific application, especially in the *Letters to Serena*, to the *customary* interpretation of biblical texts. The very words of biblical sources should be understood in the context of the *practical* orientation of religion, not as supports for the *speculations* of philosophy. A "world of words" is invented, Toland pointed out, "to help our Imagination, like Scaffolds for the convenience of the Workmen; but which must be laid aside when the Building is finish'd, and not be mistaken for the Pillars

---

1. *Defence*, p. 15.

and Foundation."[2] The interpreter of the Scriptures coins terms to clarify how the religious message can be acted upon. Religion becomes superstition laden with prejudices when the false coinage becomes confused with the true—that is, when the interpretive scaffolding (like the writings of the Fathers) is mistaken for the original sources.

Toland's endeavor to "take away and pull down" the respect given to apocryphal works and to the opinions of the church fathers embroiled him in debates about the canon of the New Testament. At issue was the question of which critical techniques to employ in determining the genuine books of divine revelation. Toland's discovery of the forged *Eikon Basilike* was an example of the use of both internal references and external testimony in determining authenticity. The discovery provided him an opportunity to extend the question of forgery to ancient Christian sources themselves:

When I seriously consider how all this happen'd among our selves [concerning the counterfeit *Eikon Basilike*] within the compass of forty years, in a time of great Learning and Politeness, when both Parties so narrowly watch'd over one another's Actions, and what a great Revolution in Civil and Religious Affairs was partly occasion'd by the Credit of that Book, I cease to wonder any longer how so many supposititious pieces under the names of Christ, his Apostles, and other great Persons, should be publish'd and approv'd in those primitive times, when it was of so much importance to have 'em believ'd; when the Cheats were too many on all sides for them to reproach one another, which yet they often did; when Commerce was not near so general, and the whole Earth intirely overspread with the Spuriousness of several more such Books is yet undiscover'd, thro the remoteness of those Ages, the death of the Persons concern'd and the decay of other Monuments which might give us true Information.[3]

Determining the authenticity of the canon not only entails justifying the inclusion of a work but also involves explaining why certain works, at one time treated as authentic by some authors, are excluded from the canon.

Toland's emphasis on the questionable means by which canonical works are designated as authentic implied that modern scholars should be able to determine authenticity on grounds stronger than appeal to tradition. The return to the study of the texts themselves, rather than

---

2. *Serena*, p. 174. On p. 137, Toland refers to a system of philosophy as a "new World."
3. "Life of Milton," p. 29.

blind dependence upon traditional interpretations, demonstrates the right of each age to use the techniques at *its* disposal to determine the sources and meanings of its beliefs. The exegete should not depend upon the word of early Christian writers that a work is authentic; their era was no less superstitious and prejudicial than his own. Toland challenged biblical scholars to justify the inclusion or exclusion of works from the canon on grounds other than the often contradictory testimony of the church fathers.

Although many biblical scholars remained silent in the face of Toland's challenge, realizing the difficulties in authenticating canonical works, some divines objected that he had raised doubts about the reliability of accepted canonical books as sources for the Christian faith. In a sermon preached before the English House of Commons on 30 January 1699, Ofspring Blackhall attacked Toland's allusions to the canon in the "Life of Milton." In response to such accusations, Toland produced, in *Amyntor*, a twenty-page list of works attributed to Christ, Mary, and the Apostles and endorsed as authentic by early Christian writers and church fathers. In preparing a work to be entitled "The History of the Canon of the New Testament," he expanded the list; and he continued to revise it as late as 1718.[4]

Quite apart from showing his familiarity with the Fathers, Toland's inquiries into the status of the canon revealed that their authentication of scriptural texts had been haphazard. Their attempts to justify inclusion of certain works in the canon had often resulted in disagreement. To make matters worse, later scholars usually glossed over those disputes. Toland thus called for a reevaluation of the works of the canon, and of those excluded from it, using critical techniques not available to the church fathers. He realized that this would involve *testing the metal* of the Canon, in an effort to distill the sources of true religion from the dross of superstitious and prejudicial writings. His investigation of the coinage of terms as a way to identify how religious and philosophic prejudices were established was directly related to the money metaphor. In the introduction to his translation of Davanzati's *Discourse upon Coins*, he noted his pleasure at finding in that work an

---

4. *Amyntor*, pp. 20–41; "A Catalogue of Books mention'd by the Fathers," in *Collection*, 1: 360–403. On the history of the canon, see Werner Georg Kümmel, *The New Testament: The History of the Investigation of Its Problems*, trans. S. McLean Gilmour and Howard C. Kee (Nashville, Tenn.: Abingdon Press, 1972).

account of the origin and names of money, of the persons who first invented it, of the evil consequences of debasing or inflating its value, and of the origins of monetary commerce in general.[5]

Those remarks are striking when compared with the *Letters to Serena*, for his method there parallels Davanzati's. After describing the origins of prejudices in general and then focusing on prejudices and superstitions about immortality in particular, Toland named the Egyptians as the source of the belief in immortality, traced the belief's gain in importance, and revealed the evil consequences of misunderstandings about its origin and appropriate role in society. This methodic pattern—an exegesis of origins to explain later degenerations—abounded in Toland's writings, giving them a unity discernable only when they are viewed comprehensively.

As in the economic sphere, many problems in religion and philosophy can be traced back to the "coinage" of belief. The coinage of particular words or commerce in particular actions is best understood by adopting the stance of the exegete or the historian. Toland recommended the same approach to evaluating the process by which works become customary in lists of canonical books.

Following the suggestions of Spanheim and LeClerc, Toland applied to the Scriptures the same rules of interpretation used for classical pagan sources. He argued, for example, that just as classical writers sometimes resort to hyperbole to emphasize a natural event otherwise explicable in terms of ordinary experience, so too did scriptural writers. Of course, New Testament authors wrote with good sense and an easy, natural style that undermines attempts to explain the simplicity of the Gospels in terms of the Apostles' enthusiasm or lack of education.[6] But

the stile of the *Old Testament* is extremely hyperbolical, even in the books that are written in prose; but [especially] in the poetical books wonderfully magnificent, and this somtimes in the description of the most ordinary events. Thus a storm (for example) is often represented in such pompous terms, as if the whole frame of nature had been convuls'd, and the Universe on the point of dissolution. Every thing great, or beautiful, or excellent in its kind, is attributed to GOD, or denominated from him. . . . Every thing therefore that's hyperbolical is not strait to be counted supernatural, nor what's only magnificent to be

5. P. iv.
6. *CNM*, pp. 49–50.

admir'd as miraculous: besides that whatever can be explain'd by ordinary means, any thing whose phenomena are easily solv'd, and wherof the like has often happen'd elsewhere, will by no man, who's not strongly prepossess'd with the errors of his education, be counted a miracle.[7]

Modern interpreters are quick to recognize such literary devices as hyperbole in pagan authors, Toland noted, and they should not hesitate to do so with biblical authors as well. With this in mind, he declared that not one-third of the miracles reported in the Pentateuch, for example, are really miracles and that the same applies proportionately for the other books of the Old Testament.[8] But, following Bayle, he accepted the *possibility* of miracles, which he described as actions "exceeding all humane Power, and which the Laws of Nature cannot perform by their ordinary Operations.... The *miraculous* Action therefore must be something in it self intelligible and possible, tho the manner of doing it be extraordinary."[9] Because God is the author of nature, when he "assists" it (as in a miracle) he is acting as its author.

Toland suggested that his questions about the authenticity and divine origin of Scripture were intended to defend it from attacks by nonbelievers. He conceded, however, that his technique could be interpreted as implying doubt. But without such a critical and methodic attitude, nothing could be verified as genuinely scriptural, and nothing could restrain the claims of whimsical interpretations of the Scriptures.[10]

The method Toland used in ecclesiastical history is much the same as that of Spinoza, Bayle, LeClerc, and the younger Spanheim. Subverting medieval theology and political theory, whether based on Scripture, canon law, dogma, or the judgments of the Fathers, Toland drove all who sought the final answer in Christian religion back to the Gospels. "The Religion taught by JESUS CHRIST and his APOSTLES (but not as since corrupted by the subtractions, additions, or other alterations of any particular man or company of men) is that which I infinitely preferr before all others."[11] The investigator must carefully

---

7. *Tetradymus*, preface, pp. iii–iv. See also "Hodegus," *Tetradymus*, p. 27.

8. "Hodegus," *Tetradymus*, p. 5.

9. *CNM*, p. 150. See Ogonowski, "Le 'Christianisme sans mystères'," p. 210. Cf. Bayle, *Miscellaneous Reflections*, 1: 186 (sec. 91).

10. "Mangoneutes," *Tetradymus*, p. 181. Also see *Apology*, p. 30.

11. "Mangoneutes," *Tetradymus*, p. 223. See also *Apology*, p. 17; and Evans, "Toland's Pantheism," p. 26.

distinguish between gospel sources and *traditional* nongospel writings, just as he should differentiate between written tradition and oral tradition ("the most uncertain rule in Nature").[12] Tradition in general is to be considered suspect; it is "the pretence for supporting all the superstition, tyranny, and other abuses, which have so much disfigur'd and perverted Christianity in most parts of the world."[13] As that which has debased the true religious coinage of the Gospels, tradition serves as a major prejudice in dealing with Christian religion.

The "New Divinity" that Toland proposed depended upon the development of confidence in the *new authority* of modern readers.[14] Not only do they surpass the old authorities (church fathers) in knowledge of languages, philology, and history; they also have the advantage of having written and read after the Fathers:

> I have always declar'd (I go not about to deny it) a soverain contemt for most of the *Fathers*; as well as for other material causes, regarding their Integrity, their knowledge, and certain other disqualifying qualifications. Not above three of the Greec *Fathers* of the four first centuries (if I may strictly allow so many) knew any thing of the original Hebrew; and the Latin *Fathers*, no greater excepted, understood as little either of that or the original Greec. Yet, in spite of common sense, these must be the best interpreters of *Scripture*. . . . Tis mere illusion, errant sophistry to say . . . that the *Fathers* having liv'd nearer than we to the times of the Apostles, they are therefore better interpreters of *Scripture*.[15]

It is the modern scholars who should be considered the authorities, because they are *older* (and supposedly wiser) than those who wrote in the very youth of the Christian era.

At the roots of the Christian theological and religious disputes and prejudices are the Fathers, who appear again and again in Toland's writings. If a new authority is to be established in modern interpretations, it cannot be based upon patristic and medieval interpretations. To the contrary, freedom from the mystifying prejudices and superstitions of early Christianity entails the utter repudiation and disparagement of the church fathers. The focus of Toland's attack was the

---

12. *Amyntor*, p. 58; also *Nazarenus*, appendix, p. 16.
13. "Mangoneutes," *Tetradymus*, p. 209.
14. *Defence*, p. 6.
15. *Tetradymus*, preface, p. xv. Cf. Jean LeClerc, *A Treatise of the Causes of Incredulity* trans. Toland (London: Awnsham and John Churchill, 1697), translator's preface, p. iv.

appeal to, use of, and respect accorded to the Fathers without realization that exegesis of *their* remarks would reveal their failure to transcend the prejudices and superstitions of their own times.

Even as historians, Toland observed, the Fathers were very sorry writers.[16] A "damning crew," depraving and corrupting the Scriptures, forcing interpretations through writings unpleasant to read, their only claim to predominance over modern writers is their priority of birth. "In short, there's nothing on which the Fathers laid their hands that they did not deprave and corrupt, but above all things the sacred *Scriptures*, which no men in the world were less fit to explain; as appears by their forc'd allegories, delirious etymologies, fanciful allusions, their impertinent and farr-fetch'd interpretations."[17] That they lived near the times of the Apostles does not in itself make the Fathers good interpreters of Scripture. To grant them authority because of their antiquity is to treat religion as a historical rarity. Those persons who think that no doctrine is confirmed or any doubt dissolved "unless they run to that indigested heap and fry of Authors which they call Antiquity"[18] consider ecclesiastical resources valuable because of their age rather than because of their insight and applicability. But the Scriptures must have practical, daily impact, Toland argued. Their value lies in their accessible and nonmysterious message. As historical oddities the doctrines of the Fathers might appeal to some; but they should never be preferred, as interpretations of the Scriptures, over the easily understandable teaching of the Bible.

No other group or topic received such critical treatment from Toland. Although his animosity toward the Fathers was perhaps more extreme than that of Milton or of Archbishop John Tillotson, it was nevertheless in keeping with their assessment, he argued.[19]

2. "TO WRITE APTLY, DISTINCTLY, ORNATELY"

The desire to use the gospel sources of Christianity is only one example of a recurring aspect of Toland's methodology—recognition of the

16. Sophie Charlotte, *A Letter against Popery*, trans. Toland (London: A. Baldwin, 1712), dedicatory letter, pp. 17–19.

17. "Mangoneutes," *Tetradymus*, pp. 208–9. Also see "Barnabas-Original," *Nazarenus*, p. 60; and *CNM*, pp. 3–4.

18. "Life of Milton," p. 12.

19. Ibid. See *A Letter Against Popery*, dedicatory letter, pp. 23–24.

need to return to the primary texts. When commenting on a particular
work or author, he often went out of his way to say that he had the
speech, letter, or manuscript in front of him.[20] The exegetical historian
refuses to depend upon summarizations by others or personal recollec-
tions. Apparently adopting a technique he learned from Spanheim,
Toland always went straight to available Greek or Hebrew sources of
biblical texts when a dispute arose.

Constantly relying on the text as the starting point for his discussion,
Toland concentrated on historical accuracy as the central feature of
exegesis. Whether concerned with a biblical text or a biography, the
historian "must observe the rules of any faithful historian, remaining
indifferent to his subject in all things but accuracy."[21]

This does not mean that the historian, the grammarian, or the
textual critic is justified in using a dry, unentertaining style.[22] Often
disappointed by the writings of grammarians and critics, Toland
nonetheless recognized the usefulness of grammatical and critical
approaches to the writing of history and the process of historical
exegesis:

That I despise Grammarians and Critics, I deny with justified reason; nor will I
allow that any man at all ever gives more credit than I to the art itself or to those
who apply it intelligently. For who but one thoroughly grounded in grammatical discipline can express himself appropriately, plainly and gracefully—not to
speak of teaching the derivations and etymologies of languages? Who, except
for the individual who is strong in the art of criticism, picks out things correctly
and appropriately, distinguishing the false from the true, the sublime from the
shallow, the genuine from the spurious? Who exposes ambiguities, and
explains perplexities? Who, finally, deprived of these aids, is able to write
APTLY, DISTINCTLY, ORNATELY? This precept of Cicero, first master of the art,
have I chosen as a motto for myself—and may it be a good omen.[23]

The grammarian and critic perform services necessary to uncover the
history of prejudiced or superstition-laden terms or beliefs. That

---

20. *The Art of Restoring*, 3rd ed. (London: J. Roberts, 1714), p. 15. Also see *Dunkirk or Dover*, 2nd ed. (London: A. Baldwin, 1713), p. 20; and "Life of Harrington," p. xxvii.

21. "Life of Milton," p. 47; "Druids," p. 15; "Irish Manuscript," *Nazarenus*, pp. 2, 48, 50.

22. "Druids," pp. 19–20.

23. "Cicero Illustratus," in *Collection*, 1: 285–86. Cf. *Philippick Oration*, pp. xli–xlii.

Toland considered their tasks central in his own work is evidenced by his claim that their skills or techniques are to be found in all that he did.

In order to combine his concerns for elegant writing and historical insight, Toland portrayed the historian (ecclesiastical or secular) as a writer aware of obligations to his readers to write aptly, distinctly, and ornately when appropriate:

> For as every thing in the Universe is the Subject of writing, so an Author ought to treat of every subject smoothly and correctly, as well as pertinently and perspicuously; nor ought he to be void of ornament and Elegance, where his matter peculiarly requires it. Some things want a copious style, some a concise; others to be more floridly, others to be more plainly handl'd: but all to be properly, methodically, and handsomly exprest. Neglecting these particulars, is neglecting, and consequently affronting, the reader.... In my opinion, therefore, the *Muses* themselves are never agreeable company without the *Graces*.[24]

The writer who yields to the historical Muse is a simple antiquarian or chronicler *unless* his writing incorporates the charm of the ancient sources themselves. He does not have to write in the style of the ancients, but his style must respect the presence of the historical reader.

The union of the techniques of the grammarian and the critic mirrored Toland's concern that the scholar and the man of business —the speculative and the practical—be conjoined. Contact between commerce and learning provides for *elegance* in historical writing and also, because such writing adapts to improvements in communication, for *fidelity* and *perspicuity*. Historical writing restrains the tendency to allow elegant sources to generate superstitions or prejudices. Even the use of Roman instead of Irish characters in printing and writing is due, Toland claimed, to developments in commerce and learning that occurred in most of Western Europe but not in Ireland.[25]

To bring the elegance of ancient writers before the general reader, Toland proposed that works of writers like Cicero be published in editions that would be not only accessible but also intelligible to statesmen, magistrates, and businessmen.[26] These editions, including

---

24. "Druids," pp. 18–19. Also see *The Description of Epsom* (London: A. Baldwin, 1711), pp. 2–3.

25. MS notes in Martin's *Western Islands*, p. ii.

26. See "Cicero Illustratus," in *Collection*, 1: 249–55.

the always important biographies of the authors, would make explicit the critical-historical principles of their editors and would indicate how the study of Greek and Roman authors could improve practical human learning.

Of all the ancient authors, Cicero was Toland's favorite. He complained that Cicero was read very little, even though he was often quoted.[27] He deplored the sorry state of editions of Cicero's works and was genuinely disappointed when he could not find financial backing for his own projected new edition.[28]

In contrast to his attitude toward the church fathers, Toland often repeated his admiration for ancient pagan authors. Closer to modern thought than to the medieval Schoolmen regarding the connection between commerce and learning, the Greeks and Romans appealed to Toland because of their aversion to the superstitions of religion devoid of elegance. "I will always hold all the Roman and Greek authors (many of whom survive the advances of superstition and barbarism) as dear to me; not only that I might disclose, with a great deal of pleasure, the writers of more polished speech and refined culture: but also in order to extract from them the true notions of things; as well as to learn better the principles of this (so to speak) book-of-the-world."[29] Greek and Roman authors shared with Toland a world of elegance, of learned conversation, and of disdain for superstition.[30] He turned to them, as Harrington had done, to "imitat whatever was excellent or practicable in them" and to support his speculations with the authorizations of the "wisest men in all nations."[31] The ancients were sources of fact —authorities to whom the historian must appeal—and models of elegance—teachers to whom any communicator concerned with relating commerce to learning should turn.

Toland's references to paradoxical scriptural passages, to remarks by church fathers, and to flourishes by pagan authors appeared to

27. See Günter Gawlick, "Cicero and the Enlightenment," *Studies on Voltaire and the Eighteenth Century* 25 (1963): 669. Also see Gail Allen Burnett, "The Reputation of Cicero Among the English Deists (1696–1776)" (Ph.D. diss., University of Southern California, 1947).

28. Quintus Tullius Cicero, *The Art of Canvassing at Elections*, trans. Toland (London: J. Roberts, 1714), translator's preface, p. v.

29. *Adeisidaemon*, pp. i–ii.

30. "A Letter Concerning the Roman Education," in *Collection*, 2: 2.

31. "Life of Harrington," pp. xix–xx.

some critics simply as a show of learning or, as one put it, as an opportunity to empty his commonplace book.[32] Indeed, Toland often said that in his transcription of passages he did not refer to all the commonplaces at his disposal. Although no commonplace book survives among his manuscripts, his works reveal a wealth of references dealing with topics he addressed. As he noted, his practice was to refer to enough passages that "a Man running may read with Conviction what I defend."[33] The commonplace format not only facilitated Toland's writing but also enabled his readers to assimilate and remember pertinent passages.

The importance to Toland of the commonplace heritage becomes apparent when we consider (*a*) the relation of his writing to the process of thinking and speaking, (*b*) his attempt to unify his ideas in terms of theorems or propositions, and (*c*) his development of mnemonic techniques under the influence of writers like Giordano Bruno. It should be remembered, especially in regard to the third point, that in the seventeenth century controversialists made a point of developing collections of quotations in ways that would facilitate quick recall.[34] Whereas the mnemonic compilation of texts did allow Toland to *write* for the "man running," he gradually came to realize that it failed to capture the stylistic elegance of the ancients and the learned insights contained in their writings. In other words, writing for the "man running" demanded a different *method* than that of the commonplace book, even though its techniques could still be employed in other contexts.

As early as his days at Oxford, Toland had been recognized by his contemporaries as a methodizer. In 1694 Edmund Gibson was busy working in London on his edition of William Camden's *Britannia*. In April he wrote to a friend in Oxford, Thomas Tanner, requesting that he ask Toland to help with the edition.[35] Even though Gibson broke off relations with Toland in May because of Toland's "insolent and conceited way of talking," he still recognized Toland's ability "to

---

32. See, for example, Mangey, *Remarks Upon Nazarenus*, p. 3.

33. *CNM*, p. 97. Also see "Clidophorus," *Tetradymus*, pp. 63–66; and *Serena*, preface, para. 12.

34. See John G. Rechtien, "Thought Patterns: The Commonplace Book as Literary Form in Theological Controversy during the English Renaissance" (Ph.D. diss., St. Louis University, 1975), pp. 4–14.

35. See Piggott, *William Stukeley*, pp. 98–99.

methodize" a catalog of manuscripts by English historians.[36] And six years later, when Toland's edition of the works of Harrington was published, the subtitle noted that the project was "Collected, Methodiz'd, and Review'd" by Toland.[37]

Not only did Toland's boisterous mannerisms cloud his methodological abilities, according to observers, but his introduction of commonplace quotations also had a numbing effect, often causing readers to miss a passage's individuality and elegance of style. The techniques of the commonplace book had a tendency to develop a momentum of their own, sweeping the author and reader along without allowing the time or leisure for either to appreciate the content and style of particular texts.

Such techniques also had the effect of confusing Toland's readers. On the one hand, he appeared to focus attention on the *content* of the passages he arranged for consideration; on the other, he chided writers who failed to appreciate and incorporate into their own writings the *stylistic characteristics* of ancient authors. But he realized that his readers demanded clear statements from him, particularly about his religious beliefs. Thus after outlining his positions in a number of works, he decided to present his ideas in "naked theorems," stripped of the elegant characteristics of literature. "Seeing learned disquisitions are not for every body's taste or capacity, however grateful to the curious, and necessary for the proof of things; I shall hereafter (God willing) give a more distinct account of my Religion, stript of all literature, and laid down in naked theorems, without notes of any kind."[38] However, Toland never did get around to writing such a religious manifesto. This might indicate how difficult he found it (or how unwilling he was) to present his own ideas according to a geometrical or propositional method. After all, he had always emphasized that the method of the historically sensitive writer respects the life of the texts themselves, without fixing them according to a structure of theorems or propositions.

In two relatively early works, though, Toland did experiment with the propositional method of writing. In spite of his recognition (in

36. Gibson to Arthur Charlett, 23 July 1694, MS Ballard 5, fol. 50, Bodleian Library, Oxford.

37. Also see "Barnabas-Original," *Nazarenus,* p. 69; "A Project for a Journal," in *Collection,* 2: 208.

38. *Nazarenus,* preface, p. xiv. Also see *Second Part of State Anatomy,* p. 23.

Propositions for Uniting the Two East India Companies, 1701) that the method was intended to help the memory rather than the understanding, he proposed it as useful in indicating how his plan could be implemented. And in *The Militia Reform'd* he said that his purpose was

to deliver an intelligible and practicable MODEL of disciplining and maintaining [a military force] with very little Charge, and no Trouble at all. My Method shall be to lay down a few *Propositions*, and those very short, to each of which I subjoin a Discourse confirming or explaining it, and containing what other Remarks might be naturally made in that Place. But I am so far from writing all I have read or observ'd upon this Subject, that I shall omit several useful things wherein the World seems to be already well satisfy'd, or that are not absolutely essential to my purpose.[39]

In this work, as in the work on the East India Companies, Toland appears to have been dissatisfied with the limitations of the method that forced him to omit useful information. Even the geometrical method of Spinoza, although absolutely certain in itself, was very much open to misuse, according to Toland.[40] For within a geometrical framework, the use of beliefs accepted as self-evident or as true based on the authority of others or one's own prepossessions can be highly deceptive.

Toland hesitated to adopt a propositional-summary format for historical writings, but not simply because the format was unentertaining. He was more concerned that such a format would rob the ancients of their vitality. Because human nature is ever the same, he reasoned, the purpose of reading ancient history is to converse with the dead to learn how to deal with the living.[41] And however much we might pride ourselves on knowing various languages, "no language is really valuable, but as far as it serves to converse with the living, or to learn from the dead."[42] Knowledge of languages opens the doors of historical scholarship as well as of conversation and commerce. Experienced in the business of the world, the linguist learns firsthand, from ancient and modern alike, the truths of human nature (revealed

39. (London: John Darby, 1698), pp. 17–18.
40. *Serena*, p. 153.
41. *Philippick Oration*, pp. vii–viii; *Art of Restoring*, p. 12.
42. "Druids," p. 6. Also see Elisha Smith's letter to Thomas Hearnes, 23 Jan. 1706, Rawlinson MS C. 146, fol. 49, Bodleian Library, Oxford.

through the efforts of the critic) and the expressiveness of elegant and effective style (through the researches of the grammarian). For this reason, Toland took pride not only in his knowledge of ten languages but also in his wide travels and in his residence in London—the commerce and business capital of the world. These conditions linked him in spirit to the ancients and moderns.

3. FROM ELEGANCE TO ELOQUENCE

In spite of attempts of historian-exegetes to justify their activity by pointing out that mankind repeatedly makes the same mistakes or commits the same atrocities, the argument that history and exegesis are useful for practical reasons sounded weak to Toland, as it did to many. Most would agree that awareness of some historical detail might provide occasional moments of entertainment and might even contribute, in some measure, to the education that makes a man *learned*. But as elegant as the writings of the ancients appear to those sufficiently schooled in the appropriate languages, the existence of such works in history does not seem to make any real difference for the magistrate, the businessman, the politician. The major challenge for the historian-exegete is not justifying his techniques or even discerning important events or authentic meanings. Rather, it is answering the question, Why bother? Why should merchants or magistrates be concerned with the elegance of the ancients, when that can be left to scholars in their universities without a noticeable loss to daily living?

In response to questions like those, Toland proposed that the historian-exegete is in fact the channel through which the ancients *converse* with us. When the scholar speaks in and to the world, he does so to *facilitate* the ordinary conversation of men more immediately concerned in the "practice of the world":

I could give but an ill account of my time, if, having sometimes the Happiness of keeping good Men company, I should not entertain more exalted and generous Notions. Truly I'm so far from desiring to live meerly to my self, and from preferring a solitary Life, that I set no value upon all the Books and Leisure in the World, further than they contribute to render me fit for *Business* and *Society*, especially the Service of God and my Country. Those Creatures, who perhaps are not to be blam'd for shutting themselves up all their days, I judg as useless and contemptible as the Worms that help 'em to consume their Papers.[43]

Truly learned men understand very well "the Art of making Study a help to Conversation, of reading to good purpose by practising the World, of distinguishing Pedantry from Learning, and Ceremony from Civility."[44] Through study, the man of practical concerns *understands* the rationale and meaning of what he practices: he is the artist, aware of why he does what he does, rather than the artisan, the practitioner who lacks such understanding.

The historian-exegete himself acquires knowledge of his subjects very often through *good* conversation.[45] Often, conversation is nothing more than banter without sensitivity for the history of practices and notions referred to. In fact, because the historian's conversation is not only *about* the ancients but also *with* them, he develops an understanding of conversation not limited to a particular time or its interests or to oral communication alone.

Toland extended the notion of good conversation to include even marginal notations in books he owned. In at least one instance, he and Molesworth engaged in a written exchange in the margin of Toland's copy of Martin's *Western Islands*. Martin had made a comment about a small fish called an "eel" found on one of the western islands of Scotland. Toland wrote in the margin, "They are indeed call'd *sand-eels*, but are real Smelts, & are so dug out of the sands in the north of Ireland. In Irish they're call'd *maghr*." Molesworth replied, "You are much mistaken Mr. T——d: they are a different fish from Smelts, whereof I never saw any in Ireland." Toland then responded, still in the margin, "I am not at all mistaken, My Lord: and if you have not been in every part of Ireland, that's none of my fault."[46] This exchange is an example of Toland's great respect for the conversation format. Not only did he feel it necessary to keep the exchange as a *recorded* conversation; he also wanted to show that the conversation format allows the exchange to remain alive, still open to further development,

---

43. *Discourse upon Coins*, translator's preface, p. v.
44. *Serena*, preface, para. 2. Cf. "Life of Milton," p. 5.
45. "The Fabulous Death of Atilius Regulus," in *Collection*, 2: 29.
46. P. 58.

even after the ink has dried on the page. Elsewhere in Martin's book, Toland explained the marginal comments:

After the first cursory reading of Dr. Martin's book, I perus'd it a second time with pen in hand (as is often my custom) and in the same manner a third time. My remarks serve partly to explain, and partly to correct him; some to supply his defects and others to expose his negligence. These strictures are all extemporaneous, many of 'em abrupt, and not a few particulars omitted well worthy [of] notice; which was necessarily occasion'd thro want of room in so narrow a margin, and in some instances for want of competent information: tho I have taken much pains about those Islands, as well by reading books as consulting men, not without a view of seeing them myself. . . . Having lent this book, thus mark'd, to the Lord Viscount Molesworth, and he adding several other notes, I thought fit to distinguish him by L. M. and my own by J. T.[47]

These comments themselves appear to be addressed to still other readers than Toland and Molesworth.

That open-ended exchange indicates how intrigued Toland was by the scholarly use of conversation. But *good* conversation presses the true scholar to keep in touch with the practical matters. "Mere Scholars, when they meddle with anything that requires Reasoning or Thought, are but mere Asses: For Being wholly occupy'd about frivolous Etymologies, or the bare sound of words, and living most of their time excluded from Conversation, bury'd in dust among Worms and mouldy Records, they have no exact Knowlege of things, and are perfect strangers to all the useful business of the World."[48] An exacting knowledge of the world depends upon the life-infusing character of conversation—not only because conversation provides information (which could easily be obtained through *reading* newspapers and letters), but also because it emphasizes the place of eloquence in the communication of information.

The historian-critic seeks to transmit information and also to *transform* it in terms of eloquence or art. Without "Eloquence or Art," the commonplace method of writing appears as "nothing else but a huge heap of Rubbish, consisting of injudicious Quotations, very disorderly piec'd together."[49] The *order* of topics treated by an author,

47. P. ii.
48. "Life of Milton," p. 31.
49. Ibid.

then, reveals whether eloquence has been considered in the writing.[50] When the elegance of ancient works is not *properly* presented by the historian—that is, when the historian is not attuned to the interests and business of the world through conversation—their *elegance* is lost through the historian's lack of *eloquence*.

By "eloquence" Toland did not mean oratorical ornaments provided to make simple observations appear more learned or straightforward expressions of truth more palatable to superstitious or prejudiced minds.[51] Eloquence is intended to demonstrate that the historian is explicitly engaged in an ongoing conversation with (*a*) the ancients, (*b*) the practical world of commerce, and (*c*) his reader. His role in this conversation is to develop his abilities as an orator by respecting the elegance of ancient authors (especially the poets) while maintaining the complete historian's search for truth.[52]

Eloquence became a topic to which Toland often returned. In *Clito*—subtitled "A Poem on the Force of Eloquence"—his concern for the poetic force of eloquence was related directly to the project of motivating himself and his reader to action. The quotation he took for the motto of this "scheme of his studies" was from Cicero. "There is no subject inappropriate for the orator, provided that it be treated ornately and impressively. It is the task of the orator, when advising on matters of great importance, to present his opinion as a man of prominence: it is also his duty to arouse a listless populace, and to moderate its unbridled impetuosity."[53] Even the Druids recognized the power of the orator in their portrayal of Hercules as an old man who led a multitude of people connected by means of almost imperceptible chains linking their ears to his tongue. Embodying the "force of eloquence," Hercules gradually developed into the symbol of the protector of learning for the Druids.[54]

Toland believed that when a historian remains faithful to ancient sources and understands that their elegance can become eloquence for his own age and society, he attains the Herculean posture of one in control of the force of eloquence.

---

50. *Mr. Toland's Reflections on Dr. Sacheverelle's Sermon* (London: J. Baker, 1710), p. 7.

51. "A word to Honest Priests," in *Appeal to Honest People*, p. 2; *Clito*, p. 19.

52. *Phillippick Oration*, p. vi. Also see *Declaration Lately Publish'd*, p. 11; and *Description of Epsom*, pp. 2–3.

53. *Clito*, title page; taken from Cicero's *De Oratore*, 2, chap. 9.

54. "Druids," pp. 33–35.

Toland's own literary style employs the straightforward though often exaggerated eloquence of coffeehouse exhortation. Full of catchy, easily remembered witticisms and maxims about weighty religious and political issues, his style underscores his presence as an author in control of his medium. He was sensitive to the effect of both written and spoken language on his readers and concerned that they realize that the authorial self is not dominated by false eloquence and scholarly mannerisms.[55]

As far as Toland was concerned, the key for *testing* his own eloquence was to be found in the "promiscuous communication" of polemical exchanges. A characteristic of his writings and activities, polemic united (*a*) the historian-exegete's desire for conversation in the context of a developing history of meanings with (*b*) the philosopher's desire for techniques to overcome prejudices and to establish an autonomous identity. The role of polemic in Toland's thought and life is the subject of the next chapter.

55. For more on Toland's style, see Robert E. Sullivan, *John Toland and the Deist Controversy* (Cambridge, Mass.: Harvard University Press, 1982), pp. 43–50.

V

The Method of Polemic

THAT MANY THINKERS become embroiled in vociferous disputes about their ideas is often considered accidental to their work itself. Attributable to personality clashes or competition for notoriety, such disputes do not appear to be important for future generations of readers —except perhaps for the historian who tries to understand the personalities or politics behind certain remarks. Particularly in philosophy—often regarded as a science of eternal verities—are the results of personal conflicts, although occasionally considered interesting, overshadowed by the force of the ideas dealt with.

With John Toland, however, dispute, confrontation—polemic in general—was not accidental. His writing became but one means by which he *lived* a life of polemical confrontations. For him, philosophizing meant reflecting on the human condition. And because the human condition contains elements of conflict and dispute, philosophic reflection needed to incorporate them in some methodic or thematic way. But he went one step further: philosophy is not only a *description* of how men live; it is also a reflective *way of living* itself. To consider Toland as a polemical philosopher we turn (*a*) to his writings to see how he commented upon the function of conversation, polemic, and retirement in philosophizing and (*b*) to descriptions by others to see how his activities and manners were perceived as being polemical.

Although most of this chapter deals directly with Toland's written comments, it emphasizes descriptions of how he *practiced* a philosophy of polemic. In surveying his acquaintances and correspondents we can begin to share in what he heard from those who responded to his methods of conversation and polemic. Testifying to the importance his contemporaries placed on the *oral* character of his philosophizing, there are even accounts of debates and discussions in which he participated. The existence of such material underscores the need to move beyond Toland's written word in this chapter.

Since polemic ran throughout Toland's writings and life, the interjection of the topic at this point—between a chapter on his treatment of exegesis and one discussing toleration and the need for esoteric forms of response to intolerance—may seem to imply that roughly after 1709 a major work appeared or special event occurred, related to polemic. But that was not the case. As I mentioned in the previous chapter, Toland's concern that the historian-exegete be able to overcome contemporary prejudices through eloquent applications of the wisdom of the ancients prompted him to value conversation with individuals outside academic circles. The same concern had arisen in his treatment of formal education: only when the scholar becomes *practiced in the world*, through conversation and travel, does he overcome the special prejudices of university pedantry. In addition, the toleration theme resulted from his realization that inhibiting the free exploration and communication of ideas frustrates the progress of reason. His response to such intolerance, in the form of esoteric communication, involved recognizing and respecting the polemical character of reason. Thus, discussion of the particular types of toleration with which Toland was concerned requires some familiarity with the type of polemical communication he saw as necessary for the development of reason.

In addition to these thematic reasons for the chapter's location, there are chronological grounds. In addressing Toland's use of polemic, one should not move too far away from the volatile years surrounding the 1696 publication of *Christianity Not Mysterious*. During that period Toland spent much of his time in coffeehouses and taverns (railing, as one critic put it, against religion and politics). In so doing he embodied the public and active character of his philosophizing among men of business and commerce. This activity engaged the attention of patrons like Shaftesbury and Harley but also brought words of caution about his methods of polemic.

In response to these cautions and to the prospect of prosecution, which he had undergone in Ireland, Toland began to temper his polemical reasoning. After returning to England from Germany in 1702, he lived a quiet country life in Epsom, supported by Harley. This period of relative retirement and study extended into his three-year stay in Holland (1708–11). Even after his return to Epsom in 1711, Toland continued to write like a man at peace in retirement but not in *solitude*. That kind of retirement, he often hinted, was not a repudiation of the philosophy of polemic but was rather a refinement of an essential part of it.

The three sections of this chapter deal with the place of *conversation*, *polemic*, and *retirement* in Toland's thought. The maturing of his philosophy is described, from "promiscuous communication" to the rules of reasonable polemic to the guidance of retirement-based publication. His continual emphasis on his individuality and on his ability to lead others to attainment of their own sense of individuality lies beneath this movement. Toland believed, though, that to attain a particular distinction one must *contrast* himself with others, using information obtained in conversation. This process of gathering information, questioning argumentation, and guiding others through reflective publication serves as a theme to unite much of Toland's life.

1. CONVERSATIONS IN COFFEEHOUSES

Toland believed that there are fundamentally two types of problems: those whose resolution requires critical scholarship and those that can be resolved through rigorous public debate. Furthermore, scholarly problems are, in a sense, resolved only through appeal to debate outside the academic community. Legitimate scholarly questions (those not the product of pedantry) must be intelligible and important to any well-read individual. And the *well-read* individual (including the scholar) must test his understanding of what he reads by appealing to the public forum, where the individual prejudices of a solitary reader or the mutually supportive prejudices of an academic community are not allowed to go unchallenged by men of *practical* concerns.

Toland saw himself not as an academic representative acting in the domain of business and commerce but rather as a reflective thinker who dealt with ideas foremost in the minds of men of wit and fashion. When "the daily Talk of the Exchange, in Coffee-houses, and all manner of Conversation" turned to the East India Companies, for example, Toland made the topic an object of his study. "I have ... conferr'd with Men of all Stations whether in or out of the Trade: not with any privat View, being intirely disinterested; but to inform my Judgment, and to improve my Knowledge in the Affairs of the World."[1] Wishing to discover where the various dissenting religious

1. *Propositions for Uniting the Two East India Companies*, pp. 2–3.

sects stood on the question of toleration, he wrote to their leaders, mentioning that he had come to his judgment about them "after a carefull perusal of [their] best books, after hearing many of [their] celebrated Preachers, and Conversing with some of the most intelligent in every Communion."[2] Unwilling to limit his contacts to any one group, which would bind him up in particular prejudices, Toland sought out men of all stations in life in order to make informed judgments about affairs of the world.

In some instances, Toland's wide range of contacts led to a situation that insulted an acquaintance. For example, Lord Raby, the English ambassador to Berlin, wrote to Harley from Berlin (in November 1707) reporting that Toland had the audacity to bring a friend of his—a German tailor—to sit and chat with Raby. To Raby's subsequent objection Toland responded that in England, at that time, a rich tailor was thought a fit companion to any nobleman and that "little or no difference was made between them."[3]

Some of Toland's enemies charged that his frequent contacts with members of some religious sects showed sympathy for their views and that he could thus be identified by means of his associations. If that were the case, he responded, "they may as well conclude me a Quaker, or a Jew, or any thing else; since I am acquainted with men of all persuasions, and very well pleas'd to be so with many, that differ the widest from me in Religion."[4] Toland recognized that encountering different ideas entailed communicating with those who held them. The attainment of truth, he declared, is an eminently interpersonal and human process. The philosopher does not confront *ideas in abstracto*; rather, he deals with *individuals*, whose lives as well as ideas are the focus of the reflective thinker:

I frankly declar'd in NAZARENUS, that I convers'd with men of all nations and religions; provided they were masters of any art, science, or other good quality, by which I might reap benefit or entertainment. They, who teach their followers to avoid any, except men of flagitious lives, are afraid their ignorance or their deceit may be discover'd. But let it be owing to what motive you will, it

2. See Toland's letter to the Dissenters, Jan. 1706, Gibson MS 933, 8, fol. 1, Lambeth Palace Library, London. Toland quotes the letter in *Second Part of State Anatomy*, p. 53.

3. See *Manuscripts of the Duke of Portland*, 8: 289.

4. *Second Part of State Anatomy*, p. 22. Also see *Some Plain Observations Recommended to the Consideration of every Honest English-Man* (n.p. 1705), p. 1.

cannot procede from the knowledge of truth, which must be proof against all the attacks of error; nor yet from the love of truth, which leads to inquiry, and consequently to promiscuous communication. How little this social virtue is practis'd needs not to be told, since men of different opinions in religion are taught to shun each other, as if it were a fundamental article of their faith.... men who differ about the true Religion, may very well agree and receive mutual improvement in all things besides: otherwise the true Religion must be the foundation of agreement in critical learning, poetry, painting, mechanics, and what not. If the philosophers and travellers of antiquity had made the tenets of their peculiar sects, or of the religions of their country, the tests of intercourse and endearment wherever they dwelt or travell'd; we had been ignorant at this time of a thousand things, no less useful than ornamental to life, which they learnt by a free and friendly communication with all men.[5]

To further the investigation of truth and to defend it from attack, the lover of truth engages in *promiscuous* communication. Apparently intending to draw attention to both the diverse and the unorthodox connotations of promiscuous communication, Toland refused to limit truth-seeking conversation to anything less than "a free and friendly communication with all men." As we shall see in the following chapter, Toland was aware that this ideal of a universal, promiscuous communication was not practically attainable, because of intolerance toward free thought. Thus he gradually incorporated the theme of promiscuous communication into that of esoteric communication.

Among those who doubted the benefits of communication was Leibniz. He believed that it was precisely the atmosphere of toleration in England that explained why so many individuals had come to have a bad opinion of Toland.[6] Toland should have been firmly advised to restrict his communication so that others might be more receptive to his ideas. In general, Leibniz argued, England had too much writing and conversation, especially about religion; and this disputational characteristic seemed to have infected Toland. Toland's response to this type of objection came in 1705:

We have as many Controversys agitated among us as any Nation whatsoever; which I am so far from thinking a Disgrace or Unhappiness, that on the contrary I count it our Felicity and Glory, being the surest Sign of an inquisitive

---

5. "Mangoneutes," *Tetradymus*, pp. 183–85. Also see *Destiny of Rome*, pp. 3–4.
6. Leibniz to Thomas Burnet of Kemnay, July 1701, *Schriften*, 3: 273; *Werke*, 8: 276.

and active Genius, of the love of Truth and increase of Knowledg, and of the envy'd Liberty we enjoy of professing our Judgments about every thing. The Concord of those Places where this Freedom is not allow'd, nor any such Controversys discust, is like Men agreeing about Colours in the dark, or like the Peace restor'd to his Country by a Tyrant after he has made it a Desart; such a Silence being an infallible Symptom of Ignorance, Sloth, and Servitude, of abject and broken Spirits, but not of Union or Science.[7]

From Toland's point of view, the philosophic decorum Leibniz advocated commanded too high a price—loss of freedom of thought.

English acquaintances were also among those who cautioned Toland against adopting an attitude in which conversation with men of all stations was not only justified but actively sought after. Remarking that Toland should respect his position as a member of the English delegation to Hanover, Shaftesbury advised him to act in a way befitting all those he represented.[8] But Toland questioned the propriety of such admonishments: "The man, of what color or profession soever, wou'd be counted no less unmannerly than strangely assuming, that shou'd prescribe to another what company he ought to keep."[9] One who tries to limit another's choice of acquaintances is, in Toland's view, practicing a personalized form of priestcraft—trying to think for another and to restrict access to new, possibly more vibrant, notions and perspectives.

Similar cautions had been relayed to Toland from Locke through William Molyneux. Both Molyneux and Locke expressed an initially favorable impression of Toland, but their feelings toward him gradually cooled as he got into deeper trouble in Ireland, where he visited Molyneux. Locke wrote to Molyneux (3 May 1697) that he hoped that Toland would put his talent to good use and that he was sorry that Toland had not visited him while in London. Locke appears not to have corresponded directly with Toland, for he told Molyneux (15 June 1697) that he had never written to him and had no plans to do so.[10] In

7. *Socinianism Truly Stated*, p. 10.

8. Shaftesbury to Toland, 21 July 1701, *Original Letters of Locke; Algernon Sidney; and Anthony Lord Shaftesbury*, ed. T. Forster (London: J. B. Nichols and Son, 1830), p. 146; quoted in Heinemann, "Toland and Age of Reason," p. 48. Cf. Shaftesbury's letter to Benjamin Furly on the same day, *Original Letters*, p. 146. Also see Jacob, *Radical Enlightenment*, p. 60.

9. *Description of Epsom*, pp. 17–18.

10. For the correspondence between Molyneux and Locke about Toland, from 16 Mar. to 11 Sept. 1697, see *Correspondence of Locke*, 6: 41, 82–83, 132, 191–93.

the case of the Molyneux-Locke correspondence, however, the issue concerning Toland was not so much the breadth of his contacts as it was the *setting* in which he chose to engage in his promiscuous communication—namely, the English coffeehouse.

The environment of the coffeehouse was special for Toland. There he had the chance to converse with men of taste and policy. Just as public opinion, at that time in English history, was determined more by "men of wit and fashion" than by divines or theologians, so the coffeehouse replaced the pulpit as the platform from which came the impetus to engage in theological debate.[11] Unlike university lecture halls or church assembly buildings, the coffeehouse captured the atmosphere of irreverence and ridicule that permeated much of the thinking of seventeenth- and eighteenth-century gentlemen. The age, as John Redwood notes, was ready for polemical forms of writing and for dispute, and it was one in which gentlemen were willing "to doubt a God in order to savour a joke."[12]

The proliferation of coffeehouses, inns, taverns, beerhouses, and brandyshops indicates the popularity of establishments where such an atmosphere was nurtured. Although the first coffeehouse was not established in London until 1652, there were nearly 3,000 coffeehouses, inns, taverns, beerhouses, and brandyshops there by 1708. By 1739 specific numbers were available, and they reveal an amazing growth of such establishments: in London alone, there were 551 coffeehouses, 207 inns, 447 taverns, 5,975 beerhouses, and 8,659 brandyshops.[13]

For Toland, the coffeehouse was more than simply a place to test ideas or to refine argumentative skills. It fulfilled a demand of effective philosophizing: a place where men of divergent opinions could converse about matters of religious or political importance and, moreover, where personal invective and flights of speculative fancy were not allowed. Unrecognized by his contemporaries as an essential part of his methodology, Toland's presence in coffeehouses in London, Oxford, Dublin, and elsewhere became the focus of attacks by his enemies and bewildered his friends.

---

11. On this point, see Gerald R. Cragg, *From Puritanism to the Age of Reason* (Cambridge: Cambridge University Press, 1950), pp. 138–47.

12. Redwood, *Reason, Ridicule, and Religion*

13. Bryant Lillywhite, *London Coffee Houses* (London: George Allen and Unwin, 1950), p. 23; John Ashton, *Social Life in the Reign of Queen Anne* (London: Chatto and Windus, 1919), p. 163.

Molyneux, having only a month before told Locke that Toland had impressed him as a candid freethinker and a good scholar, wrote to him again, on 27 May 1697, concerning Toland's behavior in Dublin: "I do not think His management since he came into this Citty has been so prudent; He has raised against him the Clamours of all Partys; and this not so much by his Difference in Opinion, as by his Unseasonable Way of Discoursing, propagating, and Maintaining it. Coffee-houses and Publick Tables are not proper Places for serious Discourses relating to the Most Important Truths."[14] Molyneux's distinction between Toland's opinions and his "unseasonable" way of discoursing overlooks Toland's insistence that (*a*) serious discourse should not be bound by the cermonies of university disputations or scholarly pedantry and that (*b*) the "most important" truths are those recognized as such by the *generality* of men.

Toland's trip to Dublin followed the publication of *Christianity Not Mysterious* in 1696. Barely had he arrived in Ireland before he heard his name and book attacked from the pulpits—and still he did not shun the coffeehouses, even as the prospect developed that the Irish Parliament would take action against him. Even in his early days at Oxford, Toland had frequented coffeehouses. A 1694 letter from Edward Lhuyd to Martin Lister describes Toland as "railing in the coffeehouses against all communities in religion and monarchy."[15] From the early days of his public career, Toland thus seemed to draw strength and insights from his coffeehouse contacts—even in the face of criticism from more traditional, usually university-associated, scholars. He attracted attention because he was an academic heretic, trained in and familiar with the skills of university disputation but attuned to their application outside the university.

The coffeehouse served Toland as a place where issues of practical importance could be discussed without endangering the peace of society. Religious and political questions, to be avoided as much at the dinner table as in church itself, should be discussed *primarily* in coffeehouses.[16] It was there that a sensibility for toleration and social virtue in general could develop.[17] Without recourse to the coffeehouse,

---

14. *Correspondence of Locke*, 6: 132.
15. See Simms, "Donegal Heretic," p. 307.
16. *Descriptions of Epsom*, p. 17.
17. Ibid., pp. 15–16.

men often found that their words too quickly resulted in actions. Without the delay provided by coffeehouse discussions men began to expect action to follow immediately upon their words; and therein lay the grounds for intolerance.

Toland used coffeehouses as an office, a mailing address, and a means for publicizing his relations with well-known figures.[18] When charged with burning a common-prayer book, he was "arraign'd and convicted," as one contemporary puts it, in the coffeehouses—not in a civil or ecclesiastical court.[19] In fact, Toland continually took his case to the coffeehouses, testing himself not so much against ideas or ideals as against other men, in a setting that attracted widely different temperaments and frames of mind.

Among Toland's favorite coffeehouses in London were the Grecian and the Rainbow. Frequented by scholars, scientists, lawyers, and statesmen, the Grecian provided fertile soil for developing and testing his ideas on political theory and religion. At the Rainbow (the central meeting place of the London group of French Huguenots), he developed contacts with thinkers like Pierre Desmaizeaux and broadened his appreciation and understanding of a comprehensive and cosmopolitan approach to philosophy.[20] These contacts also taught Toland that the French refugees who lived in England deserved admiration and gratitude because of their contributions to England's financial, intellectual, and political development.[21]

In the years following his return from Hanover, Toland visited coffeehouses less frequently. He made note of this in a letter to Shaftesbury, in which he described his "not sauntering any longer in Coffee-houses, nor keeping so much tattling Company" as he formerly had.[22] Apparently his early interest in the promiscuous communication

18. Toland to Shaftesbury, 10 Mar. 1702, in Heinemann, "Toland and Age of Reason," p. 49; *Nazarenus*, appendix, p. 5, footnote; anonymous correspondent to Toland, 7 May 1694, in *Collection*, 2: 298; Will Stephen to Toland, 27 May 1717, BM Add. MS 4465, fol. 12.

19. Edmund Gibson to Arthur Charlett, 9 Apr. 1694, Ballard MS 5, fol. 27, Bodleian Library, Oxford.

20. On the Rainbow Coffeehouse, see James O'Higgins, S.J., *Anthony Collins: The Man and His Works* (The Hague: Martinus Nijhoff, 1970), p. 210; Ashton, *Social Life*, p. 168.

21. See *Art of Restoring*, p. 44.

22. Toland to Shaftesbury, 22 Oct. 1705, Shaftesbury Papers, 30/24/20, fol. 105, PRO, London; Heinemann, "Toland and Age of Reason," p. 50.

afforded by coffee-houses became tempered by the realization that neither he nor the men of wit and fashion who debated there could control how their debates were presented outside. This ultimately led him to concentrate on the methodological importance of esoteric communication. But he never seemed to lose confidence in the atmosphere of the coffeehouse, where debate was lively and tolerant.

2. CHARACTERISTICS OF POLEMIC

Expanding treatment of methodology beyond the written word to include comments about *oral* communication is, of course, nothing novel in the historical study of philosophers. Students of Plato and Aristotle, for example, often wonder about the relationship of the written and oral doctrines of their authors. Some philosophers guard the presentation of their ideas by insisting that we see them only through their written word; others are quickly forgotten by succeeding generations because of the paucity of their writings. Even in the case of many of Toland's contemporaries and successors we often have only vague ideas about the manner of conversing or debating or about the importance placed on oral communication as complementary to written.

Toland, on the contrary, allows us to watch him in action. Conversation was not simply a means by which he gathered and tested information; it was an art form, a methodic endeavor employing techniques that needed to be explicitly recognized, he felt. When he wrote about his conversational techniques, it was in the context of *an art* that was pursued in earnest while being playfully enjoyed:

I therefore hear and see every thing. I have the pleasure very often by cross questions, or a seeming compliance, to draw that out of some people, for which they wou'd be ready to hang themselves, if they thought I rightly understood them; tho', after starting their designs, to the best of my ability, their persons for me shall be always safe. Bantering and fooling, indifference and doubtfulness, are successful engines in this art of disburthening, which you know the French call *tirer les vers du nez*, and we English *pumping*. In short, I set up not pretendedly, but in downright earnest, for conversing with all men and about all things.[23]

23. Toland to anonymous addressee, 9 Feb. 1711, in *Collection*, 2: 204.

To get men to say what they think, Toland suggested that the successful interlocutor play the fool, feign indifference, or pretend now to agree, now to object. The key lay in the *interaction*, in not only hearing what is said but also in seeing how it is expressed on the face or in the movement of the hands.

Toland expressed impatience with wranglers, those who think that polemic should be employed on topics of personal or passing political interest. The false polemicist argues for the sake of argument; the fashionable topics he treats soon are replaced by more timely issues. It is precisely for these reasons that Toland objected to the indiscriminate inclusion of some of Harrington's political pamphlets among works intended for "universal benefit." "'Tis obvious by the bare perusal of the titles, that these are but pamphlets solely calculated for that time; and it certainly argues a mighty want of judgment in those editors who make no distinction between the elaborat works which an author intended for universal benefit, and his more slight or temporary compositions, which were written to serve a present turn, and becom afterwards not only useless, but many times not intelligible."[24] Whereas more cautious individuals think that significant religious and political issues ought not be raised in coffeehouse settings "to serve a present turn," the philosophical polemicist openly discusses them, to show that they are treated adequately in polemic.

Polemic provided a setting—much like that in the coffeehouse—in which, by attacking their arguments, Toland continually subjected himself and his ideas to the criticism of others. As Leibniz noted, Toland presented himself as a contradiction, a challenge to the staid wisdom of those who viewed polemic as foolishness at best.[25] Indeed, Toland suggested that the best arguments for any good cause come from those who experience the force and vivacity of a counterposition. "None can be so well furnish'd with Arguments for a good Cause, like such as were Sufferers under a bad one; the Writings of unconcern'd and retir'd Persons being either an exercise of their Parts, and the Amusements of idle time, or, what is worse, pitiful Declamations

24. "Life of Harrington," p. xxiv. On the question of whether there is anything lasting about the method of polemic as Toland himself treats it, see Albert Lantoine, *Un précurseur de la franc-maçonnerie, John Toland 1670–1722* (Paris: Librairie Critique Émile Nourry, 1927), pp. 171–72.

25. Leibniz to Spanheim, 24 June 1702, *Werke*, 8: 353. Cf. Sabetti, *John Toland*, pp. 111, 233.

without any Force, Experience, or Vivacity."[26] Polemic embroiled Toland in issues he had to struggle with to overcome conflicting proposals. In challenging others, he challenged himself. Calling him forward to be the "heroic adventurer," his pen led the first attack against error and prejudice.[27]

As a heroic adventurer, Toland hoped to give others the courage to follow his guidance and example. Even though he saw himself as "wandering guideless through a wilderness of dangerous paradoxes," he hoped that the path he lit up as *Hodegus* ("the guide") would aid those who followed after him.[28] But to identify the arguments used in justifying errors and prejudices, someone must indict them, exposing himself to the charge that he is simply trying to make a name for himself.

To some extent, Toland accepted with gratitude Leibniz's observation that he distinguished himself by "his novelty and singularity."[29] What begin as his singular and novel opinions, Toland remarked, often tend to become the adopted sentiments of those who were the first to criticize them.[30] In this regard, the opinions themselves were not what really concerned Toland and Leibniz. It was the singularity of Toland's polemical *attitude*—spirited, lacking moderation, bold, sometimes abrasive—that appeared all the more vividly to those who conversed with him after having read some of his writings.[31] For them, the polemical character of his writing took on the added significance of being consciously formulated to provoke a response directed to the issue rather than against Toland himself.

This attempt to adopt a highly personal method of engaging individuals in conversation (about topics having highly personal

---

26. "Life of Milton," p. 21.

27. See *Defense*, p. 2; *Second Part of State Anatomy*, p. 8.

28. *Serena*, preface, para. 12.

29. Leibniz to Electress Sophia, sometime between 13 and 16 Sept. 1702, *Werke*, 8: 364; and *Schriften*, 6: 502.

30. See *Nazarenus*, preface, p. ix.

31. For a sampling of impressions about Toland as a man of spirit, lacking moderation, see: Leibniz to Thomas Burnet of Kemnay, July 1701, *Schriften*, 3: 273; and *Werke*, 8: 171; Sophia to Leibniz, 15 and 22 Oct. 1701, *Werke*, 8: 289, 293; Leibniz to Burnet, 27 Feb. 1702, *Schriften*, 3: 281; and *Werke*, 8: 333; Sophie Charlotte to von Bothmer, 14 July 1702, *Briefe*, 79: 14; Leibniz to Lord Raby, 29 Dec. 1707, *State Papers*, pp. 462–63; Pierre Coste to Locke, 23 June 1699, in Heinemann, "Toland and Age of Reason," p. 42.

implications for the interlocutors) yielded mixed results for Toland. On the one hand, because his method was so closely bound up with his treatment of topics, some readers took his emphasis on the need for methodological singularity to be an attempted singularity of opinion. Put more briefly, his method of singularity was often interpreted simply as a cover for his supposed vanity and ambition. On the other hand, Toland's writing usually did occasion a great deal of discussion and response. But more often than not, his critics spent as much time attacking its unorthodox character as they did in presenting their replies.

Even Toland's friends agreed that some of his behavior (in Dublin in 1697, for example) was inappropriate for his condition of life. As one wrote to him:

Mr. Methwen[32] as well as your other friends agree in censuring your Conduct since you came to Dublin, they say you have acted a part very different from what was given you here [London], and that it was no ways fitt for a Private man, who had no publicke Employm^t: and whose interest it was not to pretend to any (at present) nor to own any hopes or expectation of any, to make visits in form as you have don to all the ministers and persons in any considerable Post. You have laid claime to more respect than was due to your Quality, and drawn much envy and censure upon your self, and given occasion to the party, who are afraid of you in that Country, to believe that you have (whatever you say to the contrary) some great expectations, such as may justify the advances which you have made towards an acquaintance with all the great men in the Kingdom.[33]

Those who got to know Toland were surprised that his vanity and lack of moderation were not sufficient to justify his wicked reputation. The Electress Sophia wrote to von Bothmer that she could not understand what all the objection to Toland was about. He is not really that bad personally, she remarks; in fact, she agrees with Pilate, "ich

32. Lord Chancellor of Ireland in 1697, to whom Toland was sent by Whigs in London to seek employment as his secretary.

33. Will Simpson to Toland, 20 Apr. 1697, Gibson MS 935, 74, Lambeth Palace Library, London. Also see the letter to Toland, 1 June 1697, probably from Will Simpson, Gibson MS 933, 55 and 74, Lambeth Palace Library; M. C. Jacob, *The Newtonians*, p. 207, footnote. Cf. Charlett to Thomas Tennison, 25 Oct. 1695, Gibson MS 942, 110, fol. 1, Lambeth, quoted by S. R. Maitland, "Toland," *Notes and Queries*, ser. 3, 1 (1862): 6–7. Also see *Serena*, preface, para. 16.

sehe nichts an dem Menschen."[34] And Lord Raby makes much the same comment about Toland in a letter to Leibniz: "I found the devil not so black as he was painted."[35]

Toland himself noted that his writing expressed a creative urge, a "noble fury," that no opposition could control and that was furthered by all communicative contacts.[36]

> A noble Fury dos posses my Soul,
> Which all may forward, nothing can controul;
> The fate of Beings, and the hopes of Men,
> Shall be what please my creating Pen.[37]

Possessed by such a *noble* fury, Toland did not underrate the importance of the type of thinking he proposed. He did not err on the side of humility when referring to his "systems"; his was "not a System of Accomodation, such as those which some invent to reconcile other different Systems, tho they are not certain that their own is more true than the rest."[38] Because he considered his general interation with other men as complementary to his writing, and because his writing allowed for little *accomodation*, he did not tend toward flattery in other forms of communication.[39] In this way, autobiographical topics, such as his personal attitude toward vanity or flattery, became focal points for philosophical discussion.

Toland believed that polemic should not involve attacking, defending, flattering, or accommodating personalities. The adversary's is a noble role, which is degraded when attacked:

---

34. 24 June 1702, *Briefe*, 79: 219; see also Sophia to Leibniz, 29 Oct. 1701, *Werke*, 8: 294; and her letter to von Bothmer, 18 July 1702, *Briefe*, 79: 220.

35. 17 Jan. 1708, *State Papers*, p. 465.

36. Toland's reference to this noble fury of the writer recalls the "heroic frenzy" of Bruno, whose writings he had first encountered three years before. See Giovanni Aquilecchia, "Nota su John Toland traduttore di Giordano Bruno," *English Miscellany* 9 (1958): 83–86. More detailed comments on Toland's connection with Bruno appear below in Chapter 7.

37. *Clito*, p. 8.

38. *Serena*, p. 160. Cf. Paolo Casini, "Toland e l'attività della materia," *Rivista critica di storia della filosofia* 22 (1967): 24; and Toland, *Short Essay upon Lying*, p. 17.

39. "A Memorial for the Earl of Oxford," 17 Dec. 1711, in *Collection*, 2: 232; also see "Primitive Constitution," in *Collection*, 2: 126; and *Vindicius Liberius*, p. 31.

To reflect on Men's Persons when we oppose their Errors is not only expressly contrary to the sacred Precepts of the *Christian* Religion, but also to the common Dictats of Reason, and below the Dignity of human Nature. We are rather oblig'd to make the most candid Construction of their Designs, and if their words admit of a double Sense, (which is hard to be always avoided in any Language) we ought to allow the fairest Interpretation of their Meaning. This is the practice of those who really love and esteem the Truth, who labor for the Reformation and not the Destruction of their Adversaries: for their Intentions can never be good who seem apprehensive lest those they attack shou'd be able to justify themselves, who wiredraw their Expressions to Things that were never in their Thoughts, who charge 'em with Consequences they reject or did not foresee, who accuse 'em of impious or seditious Designs, who suspect the plainest Apologies they can make, and discover a hidden Poison in their words even when they are of their own prescribing.[40]

Writers who attempt to *destroy* their adversaries seem to be unaware of the *rules of polemical disputation*, which respect the importance of personality without making it a focal concern of debate. Instead of following "the old fashion'd Way of *soft Words and hard Arguments*," many of Toland's contemporaries engaged in a politically motivated form of polemic characterized by the "new fashion'd Method of much *Railing and no Reasoning*."[41] "I am pretty well convinc'd, that it is not always so much an Earnestness and a Zeal for the Truth of their own Opinions, nor a Dislike and Aversion to the Falsity of others, that make the Disputants so eager against their Adversarys, but rather a certain political Conduct, which they hold themselves oblig'd to observe in order to render their Vigor no less serviceable than their Sincerity unsuspected."[42] Especially in the case of personal attacks this "new" method undermined Toland's attempt to show that spirited proposals should not be rejected simply because they lack moderation. Indeed, the very lack of moderation—the heroic adventure or fury of the author—legitimates debate as a truly human enterprise in which *reasoning* is always recognized as an essentially human endeavor. Toland refused to allow his concentration on techniques of dispute that respect and enhance the individuality of the disputant to be

40. *Vindicius Liberius*, pp. 6–7. Also see *Second Part of State Anatomy*, p. 8.
41. *Vindicius Liberius*, p. 149.
42. *Socinianism Truly Stated*, p. 6.

interpreted as implying that the focus of reasoning is individuality. Rather, he tried to blend disputational individuality with a *regulation* of disputational techniques.

Toland insisted that adversaries acknowledge each other as personalities and understand that the process of reasoning is essentially an interpersonal enterprise. The presence of individual thinkers is needed to legitimate claims that *reasoning* is in fact occurring. The major difficulty with this emphasis on the individual is that it easily becomes grounds for justifying the use of personal attacks. To prevent this, Toland proposed that just as reasoning has to be *legitimated* by appeal to the presence of individuals, so appeal to the presence of the individual in polemic must be *regulated* according to certain standards if any claim of genuine reasoning is to be justified. Otherwise, personal attacks might be claimed as part of the reasoning process.

Because disputes inevitably arise from human interaction (in fact, Toland considered them necessary for discovery and the development of reason), Toland's description of the *dispositions* required of the disputant and of the *rules* under which he should act was directed toward two ends. First, it showed that disputational reasoning was not destroyed by the adoption of rules. He did not want to imply that dispute is sufficient for discovery or that all polemic is necessarily productive. Second, his description portrayed dispute not as a human fault to be overcome but rather as the healthy condition in which, with the control of rules, discovery is possible.

Toland's rules of dispute were products of his observations and of his experience with attacks on his own writing, which he interpreted not only as confusing the issues but also as prostituting the ends of polemic. For example, in his "Life of Harrington" he noted that some persons had resolved to be angry at whatever he wrote.[43] He seems to have been justified in such claims, for a number of years later, a writer named Thomas Mangey wrote that "whenever [Toland] is so good as his Word to print his promis'd History of the Sacred Canon, he shall have me once more for his Adversary."[44] And Richard Fiddes admitted that he wrote his response to Toland's *State Anatomy of Great Britain* after having read only two or three pages of it.[45] Faced with such

---

43. P. xxxvi.
44. *Remarks Upon Nazarenus*, p. iii.
45. *Remarks on the State Anatomy of Great Britain*, p. 7.

adversaries, Toland formulated many of his rules in a way that emphasized how these and similar practices could be avoided.

Among the destructive devices unregulated polemicists typically employ against an opponent, Toland included the following "artifices and wiles."[46] (*a*) They often misrepresent the issue in question, over- or understating its importance. (*b*) They summarize his view rather than quote him directly; when they do quote him, it is in a disjointed or confused way. (*c*) They conceal his strongest arguments, nibbling at unguarded expressions or inaccuracies of style "into which, thro more attention to the matter than to the words, the correctest writers are somtimes apt to fall, especially in a work of any length." (*d*) They attribute aims to him other than those he expressly intends. (*e*) They call him stupid here, cunning there. (*f*) They draw out unintended consequences of his ideas. (*g*) They accuse him either of being innovative or of reviving old teachings. (*h*) They charge him with insincerity or singularity, accusing him of trying to make a name for himself. (*i*) If he writes intelligibly, without the "enthusiastic cant of the *Fathers*, the barbarous jargon of the *Schools*, and the motly dialect of later *Systems*," they consider it dangerous. (*j*) They attack his learning as ostentatious. (*k*) They charge him either with heresy or, if he should agree with *one* sectarian belief, with belonging to a sect. (*l*) They attack his background, upbringing, or appearance. (*m*) Finally, they charge him with atheism, if for no other reason than that the term alone will cause many to avoid reading his writings or associating with him.[47]

The rules countering these violations of polemical techniques are intended to produce disputes that allow the possibility for genuine discovery. Every just disputant should act without passion or prejudice; he should distinguish the opinions of individuals from the positions of groups they belong to; he should not confuse fundamental with incidental positions, nor use the summaries of a person's adversaries as the basis for making judgments about him; and he should avoid personal attacks and malicious insinuations.[48] "Since . . . for want of equal Help, Application, or Capacitys, Men must necessarily differ; what a happy Use might they make of their Controversys, and what numerous Discoverys in Nature might their

---

46. The following points (including the two quoted passages) are from the *Nazarenus*, preface, pp. xviii–xx.

47. *Apology*, pp. 18–19.

48. *Socinianism Truly Stated*, pp. 8–9.

Contests produce, wou'd they but manage their Disputes with these or the like Rules, and with such a peaceful Disposition of Mind!"[49] The task of the philosopher of polemic is not to undermine controversy but rather to channel it, allowing disputants peace of mind even while engaged in dispute.

Descartes and Spinoza had indicated that rules might facilitate discoveries in nature, but their rules did not emphasize public communal exchange as much as Toland preferred. Rules for the direction of the mind (in Descartes) or for the correction of the understanding (in Spinoza), while allowing for some input from other sources, had been expressed primarily in personal terms: the individual was their focus. Toland shifted the emphasis to the explicitly communal, necessarily disputational arena of public polemic.

Although he might have been a "lover of controversies," Toland found that dispute was satisfying only when learning resulted.[50] And he believed that the only way to achieve learning in polemical encounters is to treat the process of polemic as a rule-governed activity.

3. "BOOKS, BREAD, AND COMPANY ENOUGH"

Surrounded as a matter of course by enemies and detractors, Toland used his posture of polemicist as the basis for justifying and defending his ideas. Of course, when attacked in print, he claimed the right to defend himself publicly. While recognizing "the defender" ("Amyntor") as an essential stance in the polemicist's enterprise, he did not wish to give his readers the impression that the polemicist is always on the defensive.[51] His defensive stance was only part of an overall technique: (a) aggressively attacking a position uncritically held by an adversary, (b) getting the adversary to adopt his method of addressing the issue, and (c) defending himself from counterattacks. Counterattacks implied the legitimacy of Toland's own position insofar as they adopted his method. If an adversary failed to adopt these polemical techniques—as occurred when the rules of polemic were violated—then the move to the role of self-defender was undermined.

49. Ibid., p. 9.
50. Cf. *Nazarenus*, appendix, p. 2.
51. On the possible multiple meanings of "Amyntor" in Toland's work, see Franz H. Mautner, "Noch ein Wort zu 'Amintor'," *Deutsche Vierteljahrsschrift für Literaturwissenschaft und Geistesgeschichte* 32 (1958): 111–12.

Toland's polemical techniques become most noticeable in nonpublic, personal confrontations, which included not only face-to-face debates but also correspondence.

The most famous and perhaps the only surviving complete record of Toland in a debate, appeared in the *Bibliothèque germanique* in 1723.[52] Isaac de Beausobre, theologian and minister of the French Protestant church in Berlin, described a discussion he had with Toland in 1702 at the invitation of Sophie Charlotte. A close look at the debate reveals how in the brief span of two hours Toland encapsulated the general methodology of polemic. In written form, the entire methodology could take years to emerge, through an author's writings, objections by others, and his replies.

Beausobre described the debate in the following way. One evening, he had been called upon by Princess Sophie Charlotte to help her defend the foundations of her faith against doubts raised by Toland. No sooner had Sophie Charlotte introduced the two men and explained why she had called Beausobre than Toland boldly expressed doubts about the authenticity of the books of the New Testament. Beausobre, stunned at first by Toland's lack of reserve in his comments to a stranger, asked why he was trying to place him on the defensive. Because Toland appeared to be such a staunch spirit, Beausobre suggested that Toland take the part of the defender of the faith. But first, Beausobre argued, Toland should state his own beliefs, for only then could it be determined whether they survived the same critical analysis Toland applied to the study of the New Testament.

Toland continued by explaining to Beausobre that he felt justified in doubting the authenticity of some of the books of the New Testament because of doctrinal inconsistencies in them. When Beausobre appealed to the authority of the church fathers, Toland's replies turned to banter, mockery, and nit-picking. What Beausobre failed to notice was that by his answers Toland intended to show that appeal to the contradictory testimony of the Fathers inevitably led to just that response.

The conversation ended, without resolution, in a general dispute over the authenticity and veracity of the sources quoted by both speakers. The question at hand—about the canon of the New

52. 6: 39–50; reprinted in J.-P. Erman, *Mémoires pour servir à l'histoire de Sophie Charlotte, Reine de Prusse* (Berlin: G. F. Starke, 1801), pp. 203–11.

Testament—had receded into the background, and the debate had gradually come to focus on the techniques one should employ in addressing the question. This was characteristic of Toland's *writing* also: to raise doubts about an issue that normally goes unquestioned so that he could expand on the *method* whereby such doubts become plausible. By the end of the debate, Toland had involved Beausobre himself in the use of suspect texts and had invited him to be critical when he suspected the authenticity of Toland's own sources. In short, by involving his counterpart in his own techniques of polemic, Toland succeeded in communicating a method rather than a particular position; and he did so by *practicing* the method.

Toland seldom wrote anything without directing it toward some individual. Whether addressing an adversary or composing a biography or a history, he repeatedly used the format of the letter writer.[53] Presenting even his "Account of the Druids" (1718) in the form of three letters to Molesworth, Toland used the focus of an addressee and specified date and place to emphasize its personal character. Unified by the polemical enterprise, his writing demands that the reader be "present" to the writer, and this was quite effectively accomplished in the letter form.

Toland took his correspondence seriously. Less than two weeks before he died, he wrote that he "was never a careless correspondent."[54] He always let his reader feel that he anticipated a personal response (even from readers of published letters). Nor did he write without referring often to himself. Without the lively involvement of others, his solitary work was barren and unentertaining: "Instead of the public News or the private Intrigues of this part of the World, I'll send you some account of my own Studys. 'Tis, I readily confess, one of the barrenest and least entertaining Themes I cou'd take."[55] Removed from the context of polemic, his studies lost their appeal. This writer-in-polemic, whom adversaries charged with vanity, saw little value in his own work when others were not involved in criticizing, modifying, or adopting it.

Even though Toland thought it very important to be actively involved in business and commerce, he was aware that even the

---

53. See Toland to a Mr. Phillips, 17 Aug. 1703, BM Add. MS 4465, fol. 3.
54. Toland to Molesworth, 2 Mar. 1722, in *Collection*, 2: 494.
55. *Serena*, preface (addressed to a gentleman in London), para. 1.

polemicist must attain a certain reflective distance from the "public news and private intrigues" of the world.[56] But that distance could have a chilling effect on intellectual endeavors if allowed to isolate the individual:

Solitude . . . I take to be quite another thing from Retirement. I am ready to own that without Retirement one is in a perpetual hurry: it reiterates all our enjoyments by recollection; and furnishes us with materials as well as desires for new pleasures, when we produce our selves again upon the theatre. Solitude, on the contrary, not only deprives us of both the past and the future, but always inclines the present hour to joyless melancholy, which sooner or later ends in something intractable, Timonean, (pardon the word) or perhaps more fatal.[57]

As the means by which the polemical present is linked to the past and future, retirement prepares the thinker for his public encounters. The excitement and business of London yielded at times to the pastoral serenity of Epsom so that Toland might be able to balance "the splendid hurry of the city" with "the innocent amusements of the country."[58]

The appeal of the pastoral setting represented the general tendency of nature toward economy. The reflective thinker, attuned to such economy, asks only for "books and bread enough" and for the opportunity to converse with agreeable company:

NATURE IS CONTENT WITH A LITTLE, and he wants least who has fewest desires, or keeps the strongest control over his passions. Books and bread enough, with select company in an agreeable Retirement, give the solid satisfaction, which is fruitlesly expected from the scraping or hording of treasure, from sollicitously counting or profusely spending it. Wherfore I preferr the innocent amusements of the country (where alone real pleasures are best injoy'd) its frugal but salubrious diet, the purity of the air, the charms of the earth and water, and the traquility of my walks unconfin'd as my thought, to all the pomp and delicate entertainments of the Court, to all the wealth and splendid hurry of the City. . . . There I shall contribute my best endeavors for the good of mankind,

---

56. Ibid., p. 162.
57. Toland to anonymous woman correspondent, no date listed, in *Collection*, 2: 412. Also see *Serena*, p. 132.
58. Cf. "Life of Milton," p. 47; *Adeisidaemon*, pp. iii–iv.

and never do any thing to disturb the public peace, which is the nurse of the common welfare.[59]

The difference between the *solitary* thinker and the man in *retirement* lies in this consciousness of the need to relate one's thoughts in retirement back to their promotion of the common welfare:

I prefer Retirement to Solitude, and so wou'd have it in my power to be alone or in company at pleasure.... let me have Books and Bread enough without Dependence, a bottle of Hermitage and a plate of Olives for a select Friend, with an early Rose to present a young Lady, as emblem of discretion no less than of beauty; and I ingloriously resign (from that moment) my share of all titles and preferments to such as are in love with hurry, pay court to envy, or divert themselves with care, to such as are content to square their lives by the smiles or frowns of others, and who are resolv'd to live poor that they may die rich.... grant me, ye powers, luxurious Tranquillity!... O refreshing Zephirs, ... O ye wild fruits and berries, ... O cooling shades and grots, ... I call you all to witness, that, tir'd with sport or study, and sleeping on the grass under a spreading beech, I enjoy not a more solid and secure Repose, than the proudest monarch in his gilded Palace? In such places ... you'll imagine to see me wandring as void of care as of ambition, and always a book in my hand or in my head: yet still with a design of returning more entertaining to private conversation, or more serviceable to publick Society.[60]

Even in retirement, the "theatre"-conscious thinker looks forward to the pleasant conversation of others. If privacy entails restricting the extent to which one allows himself to return to the public eye, then that privacy becomes solitude instead of retirement. The distinction between solitude and retirement depends not so much upon what one does as upon whether the period is seen as anticipating a return to active polemical enterprise.

Toland suspected that Shaftesbury's notion of privacy bordered too closely on solitude. Shaftesbury wrote to him, "My greatest Desire is Privacy and Retirement. I am not so well fitted to bear the World; and whatever good I may do Mankind it must still be in the same Private Character."[61] Although Toland could not adopt such a retirement, he

59. *Tetradymus*, preface, pp. xx–xxi.
60. *Description of Epsom*, pp. 30–32, 34–35. Also see *Serena*, preface, para. 3.
61. 21 July 1701, Shaftesbury Papers, 30/24/21, fol. 231, PRO; quoted in Heinemann, "Toland and Age of Reason," p. 48. Also see Toland to Shaftesbury, 22 Oct. 1705, Shaftesbury Papers, 30/24/20, fol. 105; also in Heinemann, p. 50.

did not lose his respect for Shaftesbury. He once remarked that Shaftesbury went into retirement from public affairs after being disappointed by his friends who had compromised the goals of the Glorious Revolution. Toland very much admired Shaftesbury and had decided to follow his studies of Milton and Harrington with only one more full-scale biography—that of Shaftesbury. After Shaftesbury's death, Toland wrote, "Perhaps no modern ever turn'd the Ancients more into sap and blood, as they say, than he. Their Doctrines he understood as well as themselves, and their Virtues he practis'd better."[62] Shaftesbury could have been more active in conversing with his contemporaries, Toland believed, but he was unsurpassed in his personal appreciation and application of the ancient teachings.

When in London, writing about and discussing volatile political or theological issues, Toland often tested his ideas on friends and acquaintances before publishing them. The nine-year delay in the publication of *Nazarenus* is a case in point. In criticizing Toland's *State Anatomy of Great Britain*, Daniel Defoe complained that the work was merely edited by Toland, because segments had been publicly discussed and then reworked by Toland before publication.[63] Toland, however, considered the prepublication period as much a part of the communal project of polemical investigation as is the time after publication. In fact, he expressed disappointment that this practice of communicating ideas before publication, so much in use with the ancients, had been neglected in modern times.[64]

Publishing his own ideas as well as those of others was an obligation for Toland. "It's Mens mutual Duty to inform each other in those Propositions they apprehend to be true, and the Arguments by which they endeavour to prove them; which cannot be done so well as by *Printing* them ... By *the advantage of which, Men, tho at never so great distance, may, with a great deal of Ease and little Charge, be exactly acquainted with each others Sentiments.*"[65] Toland felt a responsibility to his contem-

62. Introduction to *Letters from Shaftesbury to Molesworth*, p. vii. Also see John A. Dussinger, "'The Lovely System of Lord Shaftesbury': An Answer to Locke in the Aftermath of 1688?" *Journal of the History of Ideas* 42 (1981): 156.

63. *An Argument Proving that the Design of Employing and Enobling Foreigners, Is a Treasonable Conspiracy...With an Appendix; wherein an insolent Pamphlet, Entitled, The Anatomy of Great Britain, is Anatomiz'd; and its Design and Authors detected and Exposed* (London: Booksellers of London and Westminster, 1717), pp. 7–8.

64. Toland to unknown correspondent, no date listed, in *Collection*, 2: 145.

65. *Letter to a Member of Parliament*, p. 4. Also see *Nazarenus*, preface, p. i; *Serena*, p. 161.

poraries first, and only then to succeeding generations. For it was his own generation from whom his conversational and polemical spirit benefited most directly and immediately. One who refrains from publishing cuts himself off from a world of minds who could challenge him to move beyond anything he could otherwise have imagined.

Toland's concern to provide his generation with food for thought prompted him to publish manuscripts by Shaftesbury and Molesworth without their approval. In 1699 he published Shaftesbury's *Inquiry concerning Virtue*.[66] Annoyed by this unauthorized act, Shaftesbury bought all the copies he could find and published a revised edition of the work as part of his *Characteristics of Men, Manners, Opinions, Times* (1711). In 1721, over the objections of Molesworth, Toland published some letters by Shaftesbury to Molesworth, arguing again that their generation deserved to hear the insights of great minds:

What reason can be given, why the Moral and Instruction, the Incentives and Examples, contain'd in the Letters I send you, shou'd not be communicated to those who live now, as well as to such who shall live hereafter? especially, since the present Generation stands as much in need of them, as the future can possibly do. Why shou'd I promise myself to out-live all concern'd in these Letters, since some of them are considerably Younger? or who can secure me, that others will publish them after I am dead?[67]

Concerned with the development of reason and with its benefit to future generations, Toland refused to allow others to shirk their responsibility to the polemical enterprise of communal reasoning —even if that meant pirating their manuscripts for publication. The fact that a particular author's work was intended as a private communication to a specific individual did not distinguish it from any other contribution in the development of reason.

Anything meaningful, Toland always maintained, can be communicated to another, and that which cannot be communicated is not meaningful. He thus eliminated mysteries from Christianity: they could not be understood. Communicability is the key for determining whether a pronouncement is meaningful and useful; and the more widespread the communication, the more meaningful and useful the pronouncement becomes. It is for this reason that Toland published

66. London: A. Bell.
67. *Letters from Shaftesbury to Molesworth*, introduction, p. vi; also see *Serena*, p. 161.

his own letters and those of Shaftesbury. And again, it explains why Toland preferred the letter format: anything that is meaningful implies an audience. More than the treatise, the essay, or the written dialogue, the letter was directed to an explicit reader, through whose understanding the communication became meaningful.

Just as Toland's letter format always included a specific (although sometimes anonymous) addressee, so his published writings often indicate the specific audience to whom his appeal was directed.[68] By including certain readers in his personalized form of polemic he also narrowed the audiences of potential coreasoners and revealed his growing doubts about the viability of the polemics-project on a large scale. That is, the society in which Toland found himself failed to appreciate or understand unrestricted and public reasoning. To the extent that it did tolerate such reasoning, it did so only at great expense to such reasoners (as Toland had experienced in regard to *Christianity Not Mysterious*). Toland doubted that with the passage of time, large-scale polemic would become more acceptable. He did not adopt the utopian outlook of Harrington or the millenarian attitudes of Ludlow and some of his own contemporaries.

Faced with intolerant individuals supported by doctrines of intolerance, Toland proposed a response that those who saw the purpose of rule-governed polemic could adopt. Not only must a *theory of toleration* be formulated to allow for polemic; but *esoteric* ways in which people might circumvent intolerance to engage in polemic must be developed. Toland's turn to these two tasks is taken up in the next chapter.

---

68. See *Appeal to Honest People*, pp. 2–3.

VI

Toleration and the Appeal to Esoteric Communication

BECAUSE TOLAND WAS INVOLVED in sectarian debates and political activity and intrigue, he devoted much of his writing to questions of religious toleration and civil liberty. He started his public career with issues of interest to the religious sects, but his experience with their wranglings and with the uproar occasioned by *Christianity Not Mysterious* dissuaded him from engaging in further disputes with the divines.

In *Christianity Not Mysterious* Toland had intended to convince people that everything in their religion must be intelligible. Considering this task accomplished, he decided to take up studies that could be addressed without embroiling himself in the rancor of Christian apologetics.[1] In his *Apology for Mr. Toland*, he gave further reasons for his turn away from religious disputes. He realized that disputes between the divines of the Church of England and those of dissenting sects were based on civil and not religious differences.[2] Quoting Tillotson, he expressed doubts about pursuing sectarian debates that so often involved violations of polemical decorum and that led to a detachment from the practical interests of men of business and commerce: "Being (I hope) releas'd from that irksom and unpleasant work of *Controversy and Wrangling about Religion*, I shall now turn my Thoughts to somthing more agreable to my Temper."[3] Toland found

1. *CNM*, p. 184.
2. *Apology*, pp. 16–17.
3. This sentence from Archbishop Tillotson's preface to his "Sermon concerning Resolution and Stedfastness in Religion," delivered 3 June 1684, is used as an epigraph by Toland on the title page of *Vindicius Liberius*. For the location of the Tillotson quote, see *The Works of the Most Reverend Dr. John Tillotson*, 3 vols. (London: J. and R. Tonson et al., 1752), 1: 471.

that what was more agreeable to him concerned the political means by which religious toleration was insured and public debate protected.

For Toland, the topic of toleration was related not only to the question of the dissenters; it also was involved in the general methodology of the growth of knowledge through polemic. This chapter describes how toleration became the foundation for productive dispute and industry—and even population growth. Toland's treatment of toleration united his concern for the individual's freedom to hold and communicate *opinions and ideas* with the need for civil regulation of *actions* in society.

When he shifted his primary area of concern from religious and theological questions to the practical aspects of political activity, Toland recognized that political settings were not much more conducive to philosophic polemic than were religious ones. On the one hand, men of wit and fashion, whose practical experiences and inclination to conversation attracted him, were involved closely with politics. If there was to be any hope for enlightenment and toleration, he believed that its major support had to come from men in positions of political authority. On the other hand, Toland's actual experiences with Harley, Shaftesbury, and other members of the Whig and Tory factions indicated that open, philosophic dispute was not (and perhaps, could not be) supported by government. Whereas civil government may have been able to provide the conditions for tolerating small-group polemic, it did not appear to be capable of the toleration necessary for polemic on a large scale. Small groups often had to conceal their philosophical activity from public view to avoid repression and so that candid polemical activity (which does not have a detrimental effect on society) could continue.

My intention here is to show that Toland restrained his enthusiasm for the polemical activity described in the previous chapter. Insisting that men be considered as they are rather than as they ought to be, Toland liked to be regarded as much a political realist as philosophic champion of free speech. Although some of his early critics found him indiscreet, as the years passed he discerned a need not only to be more discreet himself but also to incorporate group discretion into his thinking as an important part of his methodology.

This chapter focuses on two overlapping movements in Toland's thought. The first, concerned with developing a theory of toleration, began in the years immediately following the publication of *Christianity Not Mysterious* and continued at least to the 1717 publication of the two

parts of *The State Anatomy of Great Britain*. The high point of Toland's
interest in developing such a theory appears to have come when he
submitted a series of comments and questions to dissenting ministers in
1706. Until that time, he seems to have been seeking social realization
of his theory of toleration. After that time he began treating the theory
more and more as an ideal, in reference to which the actualities of the
social and polemical enterprise could be evaluated, and his break with
Harley in 1714 accelerated this process.

As the theory of toleration became more of an ideal for Toland,
his concentration on the distinction between esoteric and exoteric
communication increased. Very rarely mentioned in his writings
before 1704, the esoteric-exoteric distinction became his ultimate
philosophic expression of political and social discretion. Works like the
Letters to Serena and *Socinianism Truly Stated* briefly alluded to the
distinction, and correspondence in the following years hinted at it.
Only with the 1720 publication of *Tetradymus* and *Pantheisticon*,
however, did the distinction become an explicit part of Toland's
philosophical enterprise.

This chapter's two sections deal, respectively, with Toland's themati-
zation of the toleration topic and with why an esoteric-exoteric response
was needed to deal with intolerance.

1. THE FUNCTION OF TOLERATION

Toland's opinions on toleration began and ended with concern for the
freedom of speech, the freedom to communicate one's thoughts to
others. Life, he believed, resolves around such commerce in ideas.
Polemic, debate, discussion, conversation—all demand that people
and their ideas not only grow and change but also that they be tested
against others.

The dignity of human nature itself depended upon this freedom to
feel one's own life and power in testing one's thoughts in conversation.
The greatest advantage of living in a free government is that one can
"employ one's Thoughts on what he pleases, and . . . speak as freely as
he thinks. . . . [Without] it to live, is, in my Opinion, worse than Death."[4]
A life without the ability to share one's thoughts with others is a
self-refuting life, for the very principle of reflective, reasoning life—in

---

4. *Militia Reform'd*, pp. 4–5. Cf. *Letter to a Member of Parliament*, pp. 24–27.

general, fully *human* life—is founded, Toland maintained, upon intellectual exchange regulated by practical concerns.

Toland believed that freedom of speech—particularly liberty of the press—is at the base of all liberties; however, he did not hesitate to suggest regulation of the press, especially where sedition, licentiousness, or personal attack were involved.[5] This suggestion recalls his proposals for regulation of polemical debate in general. Just as polemic must respect the integrity of individuals, so must the publication of ideas avoid harming society. Freedom of speech is a social, or communal, requirement for rationality. The greater the variety of opinions in a society, the greater the possibility that men can live and think freely. "A great variety of Opinions is a certain sign of a *Free Government*; and no wonder, since Men are there permitted to live as Men, making use of their Reasoning Faculties, and speaking what they think, as they think what they please."[6] This position was the social application of Toland's belief that individuals should expose themselves to as many divergent personalities and ways of thinking as possible.

Twenty years after Toland proposed this freedom as essential for human life itself, he still insisted that the freedom of men to converse and to share their ideas openly was requisite for discovering truth. Even though he recognized the seeming unattainability of total freedom of speech, he did not let his readers forget that the discovery and dissemination of truth depends upon free communication. "Now if it be a desirable thing to have the Truth told without disguize, there's but one method to procure such a blessing. *Let all men freely speak what they think, without being ever branded or punish'd but for wicked practises, and leaving their speculative opinions to be confuted or approv'd by whoever pleases: then you are sure to hear the whole truth, and till then but very scantily, or obscurely, if at all.*"[7] After twenty years of struggling against intolerance toward the free communication of ideas and resigned to the practical difficulties of universal polemic and its lack of acceptance, Toland acknowledged that some may not *desire* his kind of universal truth seeking. The dignity of human nature was still to be found ideally in

5. See "Proposal for Regulating yᵉ News-papers," BM Add. MS 4295, fols. 49–50; published in Laurence Hanson, *Government and the Press 1695–1763* (London: Oxford University Press, 1936), pp. 135–38.

6. *Memorial of the State of England*, p. 44.

7. "Clidophorus," *Tetradymus*, pp. 95–96.

the freedom to share ideas. But he gradually realized that a fundamental question must be answered first, namely, whether all men really want to know the "whole truth." To tolerate free and universal discussion is to risk attaining something—the truth—traditionally reserved for political, religious, or academic insiders—or even God Himself. Only late in his life did Toland appear to become expressly aware of the powerful forces that simply could not afford universal toleration of free speech, because it entailed loss of their authority.

Nonetheless, Toland never repudiated his earlier accounts of the meaning and implications of toleration and of its importance for him. Less than two years before his death, he recalled that his widely disparate writings were united by the themes of civil liberty and toleration of religious opinions and beliefs. "CIVIL LIBERTY AND RELIGIOUS TOLERATION as the most desirable things in this World, the most conducing to peace, knowledge, and every kind of happiness, have been the two main objects of all my writings."[8] Although he never produced a formal treatise on political philosophy or the philosophic study of comparative religions, Toland identified the character of his writings as an attempt to show that his methods of dealing with political liberty and religious toleration promoted peace, knowledge, and happiness. He noted that the *general* principles upon which he acted—principles he called "unalterable and indispensable," his "conditions *sine qua non*"—were "civil Liberty, religious Toleration, and the Protestant Succession." The *special* principles upon which he acted were serving Harley and "securing a competent maintenance" for himself.[9]

As Toland despaired of the possibility of government support for free and open debate (exemplified in Harley's lack of enthusiasm for his work), he began to consider his concern with the Protestant Succession in England too restricted. The success of Protestant interests throughout Europe would have entailed the practical embodiment of civil liberty and religious toleration. The only reason to distinguish between English and Continental forms of Protestantism, Toland suggested, would have been to maintain a *political* balance in Europe. In his later years he thus treated the Protestant Succession in England no longer as a *general* principle characterizing his writings but

8. "Mangoneutes," *Tetradymus*, p. 223.
9. Toland to Harley, in *Collection*, 2: 226–27.

rather as a restricted theme. It was a part of English foreign policy included within the concern for universal (European) civil liberty and religious toleration.[10]

Perhaps the closest Toland came to an explicit treatment of political theory was in the first section of *Anglia Libera*, entitled "The true Principles of civil Society."[11] As in the case of his remarks on toleration, his political theory is fundamentally Lockean in tone. Men are born equal and "find their Account" in becoming members of civil society, incorporating with some government according as each has education, choice, and opportunity. They unite and form governments to obtain mutual delights, assistance, and increased security against the fraud of deceitful individuals and the violence of invaders. It is for the good of the community and its individuals that men enter into society and set up laws and rules as measures and standards of their actions.

Toland's interest, however, did not lie in theoretical political philosophy or in the speculative attempt to relate liberty and toleration. Instead, he preferred to treat civil liberty and religious toleration as complementary. "A religious foundation, distinct from a political foundation for TOLERATION, is Non-sense; since true Religion and sound Politicks can never disagree, much less contradict each other. . . . CIVIL LIBERTY, without a RELIGIOUS TOLERATION . . . is inconsistent and absurd."[12] Only those forms of civil liberty that permit religious toleration could thus be consistent with "true religion." In fact, true religion endorses the principle of civil liberty by encouraging religious toleration.

Religion, Toland argued, permeated all human activity; thus it could not be divorced from the question of how to control acts by members of divergent sects in order to insure social harmony. "There never was a Nation which lost their religious Rights that could long maintain their civil ones";[13] "according to the degrees of Religious Liberty we see in any country, we may from thence safely judge of its Civil Liberty."[14] Toland's own move from religious to political circles shows the change in his hope for finding the means to institute toleration as a social policy. A religious education that emphasized the need for tolerating

10. *State Anatomy*, pp. 63–64.
11. P. 106. Cf. *Pantheisticon*, p. 9 (pp. 1–2).
12. *Second Part of State Anatomy*, pp. 67, 79.
13. *Letter to a Member of Parliament*, p. 24.
14. *State Anatomy*, p. 28.

different points of view could promote political toleration as well. However, Toland's disappointment with clerical educators prompted his turn to political leaders (especially to Harley) for civil control and support of the educational system. Only when the Whig ideal of supporting the Protestant Succession, to insure civil liberty and religious toleration, was compromised by Harley and other Whigs, did Toland decide that the attempt to use governmental means to instill popular toleration was as undependable as working through Church structures.

In general, Toland did not present the issue of toleration as an arena for debate between Church and State. The flexibility needed for fruitful polemic involved both Church and State, particularly in cases where individuals depended upon their religious beliefs to justify behavior offensive to other members of society. Of special interest to Toland was the question of how political parties or religious sects incorporated into their *principles* a recognition of and respect for the existence of similar (perhaps equally sincere) groups. If a particular group was committed to the gradual eradication of all other groups holding different opinions, then the very principle upon which it was based and was tolerated would be controverted.

The function of toleration was to insure the possibility of debate, from which truth and reason emerge. Scandalized by the loyalty of Roman Catholics to the pope as a foreign and infallible leader, Toland ruled out the possibility that papists could enter into a genuine civil or religious fellowship with men of other persuasions.[15] As became clear in his relationship with Hohendorf, however, he believed that not all nominal Catholics were to be excluded from the commonwealth of learning—especially not those in political positions who recognized the threat the papacy held for any government and not those interested in writers whose works were banned by the papacy.

Because of his belief that true religion and sound politics could never disagree, Toland only rarely suggested that one should actually dominate the other. For example, in describing the location of the civil and ecclesiastical centers at either end of the village of Epsom, he gave priority to civil government. Epsom, he wrote, had "a Palace for its head, and a Church for its tail."[16] Temporal and ecclesiastical

---

15. *Anglia Libera*, pp. 101–2.
16. *Description of Epsom*, p. 5. Cf. *Vindicius Liberius*, p. 5.

authorities complemented one another, with this difference: more often than not, the clergy lacked civility and decorum in promoting toleration and should yield to those in civil government who had learned toleration as a necessary part of their commerce with other men.

Toland proposed that just as the magistrate, or civil authority in general, should be concerned with *actions* that fall under the regulation of law, so the religious minister should confine himself to preaching and not attempt to judge the sincerity of individuals.[17] The magistrate exceeds his authority when he deals with opinions rather than actions:

> For in matters of Property, Civil disobedience, or moral virtue, which are common to all Mankind, and without which no private faith or Publick Community cou'd Subsist, the Magistrate is to restrain what the Laws prohibit, let a Man alleadge never so much persuasion or conscience for his proceedings; Since Murder, Defamation, and the like, are plainly Evil and Injurious, be the inward motives of the Transgressor what they will. But in Point of Simple Opinions, nothing can be justly punisht by the Magistrates, since he's only to Punish where he can be a Competant Judge: Whereas neither by his own Discretion, nor by the Evidence of others, can he certainly judg of mens sincerity or Hypocrisy, or their Obstinancy or Docility, nor whether they receive Solid Satisfaction, or continue still perplext with Doubts and Scruples, which (according to their various Dispositions, apprehensions, and prepossessions) they may well do, not withstanding the Truth has been never so adequately demonstrated.[18]

Because the morality of actions must be determined using specified criteria, the magistrate must appeal to law in his determination of immoral behavior.

Civil liberty depends upon, and is limited to, what is prescribed by law. "For nothing is more consistent than Law and Liberty; nay, there cannot be any political Liberty without Law."[19] The regulation of actions and the freedom to engage in nondestructive activity cannot be based upon the shifting attitudes of party or sect. Only civil law can

---

17. *State Anatomy*, p. 75; *Memorial of the State of England*, p. 43.

18. See Toland's letter to the Dissenters, Jan. 1706, Gibson MS 933, 8, fol. 2, Lambeth Palace Library, London. Toland quotes this letter in *Second Part of State Anatomy*, pp. 54–55. Also see *Serena*, p. 135; and *Appeal to Honest People*, p. 6.

19. *State Anatomy*, p. 12; *Pantheisticon*, p. 84 (pp. 66–67).

protect the individual and society from the domination of particular groups bent on imposing a uniformity of belief.

Although law deals most immediately with regulating the *actions* of individuals, it also controls groups that would try to restrict our freedom to hold certain opinions or to inform ourselves about matters of "pure speculation." Toland's appeal to law was directed primarily toward protection of beliefs. For, not only is it difficult to determine what is socially harmful action (e.g., in the case of writers who publish pieces like *Christianity Not Mysterious*); but the "liberty of conscience" is itself presupposed in supporting freedom of action. "The Liberty of the Understanding is yet a nobler Principle than that of the Body ... and where there is no Liberty of *Conscience*, there can be no civil liberty."[20] When men are not free to engage in the commerce of ideas with numerous others who may be able to provide novel insights, they are denied the social context necessary for free personal inquiry.

Toland did not hold hard and fast to the distinction, proposed by some philosophers, between *liberty*, as applied to conscience or opinions, and *freedom*, as applied to actions. He used the terms interchangeably to refer to the ability to express opinions publicly (observably) in speech and action. Without the freedom to hold and to defend particular opinions, one would be *unable* to act freely or to aid in the formulation of laws protecting civil liberty. But without the protection of law, insuring free discussion, the conditions under which fruitful and free discussion could occur would not materialize.

Such visible traits as populousness, industry, and commerce are indications, Toland believed, of the civil and intellectual liberty of a country.[21] The more populous, industrious, and commerce-oriented a country is, the better able and more willing are its inhabitants to engage in informed discussion and the easier it is to attract and to support foreign settlers and investors.[22] Toland supported the naturalization of foreigners (even the French) and Jews in England, because of the economic benefits he predicted would follow from allowing them to own and to develop property.[23] Also—and more important in terms of Toland's methodology—populousness, naturalization, industry, and

---

20. *Anglia Libera*, p. 100.
21. *Second Part of State Anatomy*, p. 79.
22. *State Anatomy*, pp. 19, 56, 79. Also see "Life of Harrington," p. iii; *Anglia Libera*, p. 100; and *Art of Restoring*, p. 44.
23. Footnotes to *A Philippick Oration*, pp. 20, 83–84.

commerce would expand the practical contacts of reflective thinkers and promote the European and worldwide character of philosophic inquiry that Toland desired.

Toland considered the topic of toleration so fundamental to his enterprise that he expanded his discussion of it beyond even European or nationalistic contexts to that of humanity at large. Toleration, he argued, is a self-evident duty according to the law of nature and "is the promoting of Humanity, and the doing good to all Mankind."[24] Not only does toleration benefit the tolerated; it also humanizes those who tolerate, making them less dogmatic in their claims of conscientiousness and more open to the possibility that free inquiry does not jeopardize the public peace. "As for the *Publick Peace*, which is pretended to be endanger'd by a TOLERATION, it has been disturb'd or subverted in all Ages and Places of the World, not either by *Conscientious* or *Enquiring* Men, but by those who no less dogmatically than tyrannically *impose* upon their Understandings; and who, in spite of all their Disguises, appear to be much more concern'd for SOVERAIGNTY than REFORMATION."[25] As a methodological demand of promiscuous communication and polemic, toleration thus became, for Toland, a moral principle and imperative.

Objections against Toland's support of civil liberty and religious toleration often characterized civil liberty as freedom to commit immoral and disruptive actions or portrayed religious toleration as indifference to any religious position. Toland's reponse makes clear that he did not support licentiousness, nor did he consider indifference of opinion desirable or even possible. By liberty of conscience

we do not mean Licentiousness in morals (which has no Plea from Conscience) nor Indifference as to all Religions: but a free Toleration but of such actions as are in their own nature allow'd to be indifferent, or in their circumstances unsinful; and of such doctrines or opinions as are not destructive of humane Society and all Religion, but consisting in bare speculation, and solely regarding the conscience or persuasion of men. The equity of this Liberty is grounded upon the use of Reason which is equally the right of all men, upon the nature of things, and upon the difference of Education as well as of Capacities.[26]

24. "Barnabas-Original," *Nazarenus*, p. 40; *Reasons for Naturalizing the Jews*, p. 5. Also see *Second Part of State Anatomy*, p. 66.

25. *Apology*, p. 45.

26. *State Anatomy*, p. 27. Cf. *Second Part of State Anatomy*, p. 54; "Mangoneutes," *Tetradymus*, p. 223.

He pointed repeatedly to the prosperous Dutch as an example of a people who tolerated differing religions while still holding strongly to their own professions.

The man of toleration, Toland maintained, adopts an *indifference of temper* rather than an *indifference of opinion*. If he were indifferent in opinion, he would not be engaged in the polemical enterprise at all. His task is to be able to tolerate (indeed, to expect) opinions contrary to his own, without succumbing to the temptation of those who test a man's sincerity by his intolerance of contrary positions.

Attempting to clarify his position on this point, Toland remarked to one of his "orthodox friends," "for the repose of so good a Friend, I wish you were grown better acquainted with that Indifference of Temper, which in me you seem so much to condemn; for Indifference of Opinion I neither approve, nor believe to be possible. Yet the Opinions of others cannot hurt your Judgment, if you govern it by sound Reason; their Variety will delight your Contemplation, their Opposition will augment your knowledg, and their Difficulty shou'd abate your Censure."[27] Because he believed that the Whigs endorsed his attitude toward toleration, Toland felt that his support of Whig principles did not vitiate his indifference of temper.[28] Rather, such support was the political expression of philosophic toleration.

In a 1706 letter to heads of the major dissenting communions in England (i.e., Presbyterians, Independents, Quakers, and Anabaptists), Toland proposed reducing the "doctrine of toleration" to a "clear and positive system" expressed and contained in three questions. Only the Presbyterians hesitated to endorse the system contained implicitly within these questions:

1st. Whether . . . you hold and approve an impartial Toleration in Religion, both of such actions as are of themselves indifferent, or in their circumstances unsinfull, and of Such Doctrines or Opinions as are not Destructive of human Society and of all Religion, but consisting in bare Speculation, and Solely regarding the Conscience or persuasions of Men?

2dly. Whether you think diverse Religions, or diversitys in the same Religion . . . to be Consistent with good Government; and that, if you had the same Civil Magistracy in your own hands, you wou'd, on these Principles,

---

27. *Socinianism Truly Stated*, p. 7.
28. See *Some Plain Observations*, p. 1.

Tolerate the Worship of those who are now the National Religion, and of all other Protestant Communions?
And

3rdly. Whether you believe, that not only all Compulsion in matters of mere Opinion is improper, useless, and unjust; but that depriving men of their Native advantages, and excluding them on the Score of Such differences from Civil Trusts, is a real Force and Punishment, which you wou'd no more practice upon others, than you approve of them as practiced against your Selves, according to the precept of Our Saviour, who injoyns his followers, to do to others, what they wou'd be done unto?[29]

Conscious that the persecuted often become the persecutors when they come to power, Toland proposed his doctrine of toleration as a definite, practical policy.[30] This was what he understood by a *system* of toleration, whose emphasis was on the practical implementation of principles in a society characterized by de facto sectarian and individual disagreements.

Toland's system of toleration presumes the possibility and desirability of a *union* of men without a *uniformity* of beliefs. Its thrust furthermore assumes that the only practicable and desirable union of men is achieved through an indifference of temper. In matters of religion, for example, this means that all men under the same civil government should tolerate other sects. United by a "mutual good understanding" of the similarities and differences in their doctrines and ceremonies, individuals belonging to different groups within a given country should not expect a more comprehensive or stricter unity. "A stricter unity in the nature of things cannot be obtain'd, as in the effects it is equal to perfect unity, any other *Comprehension* being impracticable.... the *Union* propos'd will serve all the ends and purposes of Government as well as the strictest *Uniformity*, which nothing can procure but an Inquisition."[31] Strict political uniformity undermines the very existence of individuals as individuals. Thus it is

29. *Second Part of State Anatomy*, pp. 47, 59. See Toland to Thomas Tennison, archbishop of Canterbury, 2 May 1707, Gibson MS 930, 229, fol. 1; and Toland's letter to the Dissenters, fol. 3. Also see Thomas Hearnes to Elisha Smith, 23 Jan. 1706, Rawlinson MS C. 146, fol. 47, Bodleian, Oxford.

30. *Art of Governing by Partys*, p. 12.

31. *Second Part of State Anatomy*, pp. v–vi. Also see *CNM*, pp. 72–74; *State Anatomy*, p. 31; and *Nazarenus*, preface, p. v.

misunderstood, because as a goal for *individuals* in society, it is unobtainable even in theory.

Toleration of divergent views was not only a demand of civility and political expediency but also a necessary condition for development of knowledge. Toland refused to limit the toleration issue simply to political theorizing. The liberty to investigate new ideas and to test divergent opinions provided for the growth of knowledge; and, as he noted, "the more knowledge any people have, the more they value Liberty."[32] Liberty of inquiry, or toleration in general, was the "source of science" and the condition for the growth of knowledge through new discoveries.[33] The existence of divergent groups of investigators, whether in a society, a government, or a church, may have contributed to an atmosphere of dispute and polemic. But as far as Toland was concerned, such divergent groups infused *life* into society or a church; "held within due Bounds, they always keep it from stagnation."[34] The communal growth of knowledge was to be insured by the toleration of inquiry. And the greater the growth of knowledge, the greater the appreciation for freedom of inquiry and toleration of dispute.[35]

2. THE DOCTRINE OF THE EXOTERIC-ESOTERIC DISTINCTION

What began for Toland as a relatively straightforward caution against dealing with men as they ought to be (i.e., in hoping for some future state of nonpolemical harmony) quickly became more complex after 1704. In his treatment of toleration he often appeared to be holding

---

32. *Art of Governing by Partys*, p. 149; *Anglia Libera*, p. 185.

33. "Letter Concerning the Roman Education," in *Collection*, 2: 3.

34. *State Anatomy*, pp. ii–iii.

35. For a discussion of how political toleration can be understood, in Toland, as the predominant atmosphere in which thinking occurs, see Anna Seeber, *John Toland als politischer Schriftsteller* (Schramberg-Württenberg: Gatzer and Hahn, 1933), pp. 52–61. A standard work dealing with the history of toleration (especially in seventeenth- and eighteenth-century Europe) is W. E. H. Lecky's *History of the Rise and Influence of the Spirit of Rationalism in Europe*, rev. ed., 2 vols. (New York: D. Appleton and Co., 1925).

Much of Toland's discussion of toleration relies on Locke's famous treatment of it, but I have chosen not to emphasize this theoretical dependence for two reasons. First, Toland's comments appear at first glance only to duplicate many of Locke's ideas. Second, such a comparison could undercut my attempt to show that Toland's focus is not on developing a theory of toleration as much as it is on portraying toleration as a methodological principle in relation to which his other ideas could be developed.

out an *ideal* toward which men should strive in polemic—namely, indifference of temper in disputes. Although he felt that human nature was not to be characterized by considerations of what men ought to be, Toland did suggest that ideal standards, or *rules*, should apply to the acquisition of knowledge. In this way the concept of *ought* appeared (as toleration) in the *method* of investigation but was not incorporated into its *content*. Toland's thinking was based on his belief that reason and meaning were to be defined only in terms that were actually used and understood. Infinite reason, mysteries, and vague notions of human nature could not be tested, because they are unintelligible.

Toland limited his discussion to the attitude and techniques that ought to be employed in describing what human nature *is*. But, as he pointed out, people engaged in rule-governed polemic often exhibit characteristics of human polemics, which themselves violate the rules of *fruitful* polemic. In short, Toland came to see that his emphasis on what men are, rather than on what they ought to be, must take into account the *actual* methods of debate. He was aware that charging de facto governmental and religious intolerance in particular with violating the rules of polemic overlooked the fact that people *are* intolerant in disputes. This recognition was to become the starting point for a new line of thought. Claims about mysteries, he had argued, had to be limited to meaningful and accessible concepts. Similarly, the ideal of toleration, as part of a method of general inquiry, had to be qualified in the face of de facto (obvious and meaningful) methodological intolerance.

Of immediate concern to Toland were the very practical consequences of methodological intolerance. The danger of publicly expressing his views, particularly on religious topics, remained a lifelong concern. That he appears to have been justified in his fears is borne out by his treatment at the hands of the Irish Parliament. Furthermore, in 1696, the year in which *Christianity Not Mysterious* was published, an eighteen-year-old boy was hanged in Edinburgh for blasphemy.[36] Although England proved to be a safer place for Toland than Ireland or Scotland, he recognized that the climate of intolerance was not limited to particular countries. "Such is the deplorable Condition of

36. See Ella Twynam, *John Toland: Freethinker, 1670–1722* (privately printed, 1968), p. 2.

our Age, that a Man dares not openly and directly own what he thinks of Divine Matters, tho it be never so true and beneficial, if it but very slightly differs from what is receiv'd by any Party, or that is establish'd by Law; but he is either forc'd to keep perpetual Silence, or to propose his Sentiments to the World by way of Paradox under a borrow'd or fictitious Name."[37]

Toland's evaluation of this condition did not change appreciably during his lifetime. What did change was his understanding of the more subtle means by which men were forced, through threats to their fame or fortune, to refrain from freely speaking their minds. In 1720, he wrote that

daily experience sufficiently evinces, that there is no discovering, at least no declaring of TRUTH in most places, but at the hazard of a man's reputation, imployment, or life. These circumstances cannot fail to beget the woful effects of insincerity, dissimulation, gross ignorance, and licentious barbarity.... considering how dangerous it is made to tell the truth, tis difficult to know when any man declares his real sentiments of things.... In this state of things ... liberty in its full extent is more to be wish'd than expected, and ... thro human weakness people will preferr their repose, fame, or preferments, before speaking of Truth.[38]

Toland's response to this state of affairs was to offer his complete theory of toleration to those who *expected* liberty in its full extent. To those who felt justified in only *wishing* for such liberty, he suggested adopting the ancient practice of distinguishing external and internal, or public and private, doctrines.

By adopting the distinction between an exoteric and an esoteric doctrine, thinkers could engage discreetly in that polemic essential to growth of knowledge but neither encouraged nor allowed in the "deplorable Condition of our Age." As early as in his *Letters to Serena*, Toland had pointed out that throughout the history of ideas philosophers had adopted the distinction between their exoteric and esoteric doctrines: "the one internal and the other external, or the one private and the other publick; the latter to be indifferently communicated to all the World, and the former only very cautiously to their best Friends,

37. *CNM*, pp. iv–v. On Toland's treatment of anonymous and pseudonymous publication, see above, chap. 2.

38. "Clidophorus," *Tetradymus*, pp. 67, 95–96. Also see *Tetradymus*, preface, p. vii.

or to some few others capable of receiving it, and that wou'd not make ill use of the same."[39] Not only did thinkers like the Pythagoreans protect their teachings from the vulgar by shrouding them in secrecy; most ancient philosophers distinguished between their public doctrines and those that they revealed to select followers.

By the time he wrote the "Clidophorus" section of *Tetradymus*, Toland had decided that the only realistically attainable freedom for any reflective thinker was to be found in *the small group*. After a lifetime of struggling to bring the vanguard of philosophic thinking to the level of popular discussion, he settled for limiting such thinking, "stript of all disguises," to a few "capable and discrete" individuals.[40] This did not mean that the philosopher could not and should not publish his ideas (when he could safely do so), accommodating popular prejudices and the religions established by law. It simply meant that when the philosopher did speak or write publicly, only he, and perhaps his close acquaintances, would know whether he was expressing his true sentiments.

This duplicity—born of the experiences surrounding publication of *Christianity Not Mysterious* and nurtured in the political atmosphere of his work with Harley—was not accepted by Toland without awareness of its disappointing and unfortunate consequences. In the first place, the whole point of engaging in clandestine polemic was to overcome those prejudices in others resulting from their not having been publicly exposed to novel ideas or encouraged to participate in disputational thinking. To speak or to act in a way that implied an endorsement of popular prejudices only reinforced them.[41]

In the second place, where one's actions have an effect on others—for example, in politics and legislation—none of his pronouncements can be trusted if he employs the exoteric-esoteric distinction. "*Tricks are so much practic'd, encourag'd, and authoriz'd by ambitious or corrupt Statesmen, to whom they are habitual; that a Minister, who shou'd regulate his conduct or intrigues by the moral rules of prudence, might pass for an honest man, but wou'd be counted a very sad Politician.*"[42] In fact, Toland's awareness of the duplicity of statesmen—particularly after his political involvement with Harley—

---

39. Pp. 56–57. Also see pp. 114–17.
40. "Clidophorus," *Tetradymus*, p. 61.
41. *Serena*, pp. 9–10.
42. *Grand Mystery Laid Open*, p. 31.

prompted him, on a number of occasions, to warn that a man's principles should always be judged by his actions rather than by what he professed.[43] When making his final break with Harley in *The Art of Restoring*, Toland attacked him as "a man that never spoke a Syllable of direct Truth in his Life, that never made a Promise without a double meaning. Though his Head is naturally muddy, yet the confusion and ambiguity of his expressions proceeds as much from Design as from Nature, that he may be bound by nothing."[44] Particularly in regard to domestic policy, Toland was adamant in his demand that government leaders be honest with their countrymen. This general principle grew out of his personal disappointment with Harley's lack of support as well as out of his philosophic demand that meaningful communication be easily intelligible.

When the question of foreign policy arose, however, it became apparent that Toland's movement to the exoteric-esoteric distinction did not stem solely from having to respond to the intolerance of polemic. From 1705 to 1712, his correspondence took on a note of secrecy and intrigue. In a letter to Shaftesbury, he described how visitors could come to him incognito, using the back door of his residence. In letters to Harley, offering his services as a spy in Hanover ("where you'll find me as secret, as I hope to be successful"), Toland claimed that, knowing Holland so well, he could pass through it without being observed. He developed alibis for himself and indicated that secret means could be used to employ him without public knowledge—all this from a man who later complained bitterly about the secrecy and intrigue of Harley's coalition government.[45]

The ambiguity of Toland's position on political secrecy during these years becomes more understandable when we recognize that his thought was undergoing a transition. His anticipated goal of open, universal polemic was replaced by acceptance of small-group discussion within the larger framework of the exoteric-esoteric distinction.

Toland appealed to the *principles* of political discretion and secrecy in

---

43. *Militia Reform'd*, p. 7. Also see *Some Plain Observations*, p. 2; and *State Anatomy*, p. 18.
44. P. 11. Also see p. 8.
45. See the following letters: Toland to Shaftesbury, 22 Oct. 1705, PRO, Shaftesbury Papers, 30/24/20, fol. 105 (quoted in Heinemann, "Toland and Age of Reason," p. 50); Toland to Harley, 6 June, 3 Dec., 7 Dec., and sometime in 1712, *Portland MSS*, 5: 4, 120, 127–28, and 258; in *Collection*, 2: 219; Dr. William Stratford to Edward, Lord Harley (nephew of Toland's benefactor-adversary), 14 July 1726, *Portland MSS*, 7: 441.

formulating a *response* to political and religious intolerance of open, practical, scholarly debate. His early allusions to the practical scholar's need for toleration in the expression and exploration of new ideas (e.g., in *Socinianism Truly Stated*) pointed to the same conclusion as did the practice of political intrigue learned under Harley from 1705 to 1712. "Secrecy," Toland wrote in 1714, "together with Resolution, are the Life and Soul of great Actions."[46] One who acted with discretion and determination had a greater chance of being effective than one who did not. Not only did Toland harken to the suggestions of his friends that he be more discreet; he went so far as to incorporate discretion into his thinking as a major methodological principle.

As early as *Christianity Not Mysterious*, Toland had pointed out that members of particular groups and professions maintained secrecy by adopting esoteric languages or meanings.[47] But at that time he had objected to the practice, arguing that it undermined the attempt to involve the common man in the development of plural uses of language. In the *Letters to Serena*, he recognized that in some professions of even the vulgar ("les metiers des roturiers") members were sworn to secrecy concerning aspects of their trade.[48] Many groups adopted special (esoteric) forms of communication not in response to intolerance but for the purpose of maintaining the distinctive character of the group.

In the early years of his public life, Toland had insisted on presenting his message as clearly as possible, so that anyone could understand him and perhaps contribute to the same enterprise. By 1714, however, he began to make explicit the exoteric-esoteric distinction in his writing. Noting at one point that he was little concerned with those who addressed themselves to the vulgar and were understood by everyone, he added, "Their language is understood by every body, and therefore minded by no body that I wou'd have mind what I write."[49] In the latter part of his life, Toland felt no compulsion to make the speculative matters he considered important understandable to the vulgar. Communicability and intelligibility were still crucial,

---

46. *A Collection of Letters written by His Excellency General George Monk*, ed. Toland (London: J. Roberts, 1714), introduction, p. vi.

47. P. 108; "Clidophorus," *Tetradymus*, p. 94.

48. P. 11; and Toland's French MS translation of *Serena*, ONB MS 10325, fol. 92.

49. *Art of Restoring*, p. 48.

but he no longer believed that the size of an appreciative audience could be used as a measure of the profoundity or truth of the author's insights.

In *Patheisticon* Toland followed through with the exoteric-esoteric distinction. Not only did he have very few copies printed (many of which he distributed personally), but in the text he only alluded to some topics that he said were dealt with in a lost work, his *Esoterics*. The physical description of the origin of fossils, the motions of the earth, and the incorporeality of ideas were treated esoterically, he said.[50]

Political matters that affected the vulgar (i.e., matters to be dealt with in exoteric philosophy) still deserved to be intelligible to the populace. He wrote in the *Second Part of the State Anatomy* (1717), "it has always been one of my principal rules, *so to express my self, as to make it impossible I shoul'd not be understood.*"[51] General intelligibility remained the cardinal rule in exoteric doctrines. Esoteric philosophizing, however—responding to intolerant popular prejudices—did not attempt to appeal to any others than those who shared in an indifference of temper in disputes.

Toland's gradual disenchantment with the intolerance of the vulgar and of the clergy became complete when he recognized the distinguishing characteristics of the *true philosopher*. Hesitant throughout most of his life to separate *the philosopher* from the generality of men, he finally, in 1720, presented the philosopher as standing almost as an adversary against the vulgar. "I easily conceive the threefold passion of a true Philosopher ... to have been, despising the MOB, detesting the PRIEST, and delighting in his own LIBERTY."[52] Sharing the ancient philosophers' caution about the fury of the vulgar, Toland suggested that reflective thinkers had always disdained those who were prejudiced, challenged those who profit from the credulity of others, and reveled in their passion for freedom of investigation.

Encouraged in their prejudices and superstitions, the vulgar appeared much too enamored of the power of politicians and the mystique of priests to be depended upon by philosophers. In this respect, philosophers could appreciate the plight of the Jews, who had always had three sorts of enemies in all countries. "There are first the *Zealots*, under whom may be listed *Priests* and *Hypocrites*; secondly,

50. Pp. 25, 34, 48, 108 (pp. 14, 22, 33, 87).
51. P. 9.
52. "Clidophorus," *Tetradymus*, p. 94.

Politicians, comprehending corrupt *States-men*, and *drivers of private Interest*; and thirdly the *vulgar*, who under colour of *religion* and the *public good*, are acted, animated, and deluded by the other two, the better to serve their own sinister purposes."[53] The *individual* common man has the ability to see through the devices of priests and politicians. But because the process of reasoning is essentially communal, he cannot be treated as an individual when his thinking becomes polarized by the self-seeking activities of priests and politicians. "Thus at all times have the multitude (that common Prey of Priests and Princes) been easily gull'd; swallowing secrets of natural Philosophy for divine miracles, and ready to do the greatest good or hurt, not under the notions of vice or virtue: but barely as directed by men, who find it their Interest to deceive them."[54] Statements such as this would have been unheard of from the Toland of *Christianity Not Mysterious*. But as Toland refined his understanding of the communal process by which reason is developed, he began to replace his early statements of confidence in "the vulgar" with derisive comments about "the mob" and "the multitude."

Toland recognized that even political leaders had to adapt to the prejudices of the people. In his French translation of *Serena* (sent to Hohendorf for Prince Eugène of Savoy), he observed that a prudent leader is always aware of his ability to direct his people toward increased rationality—often in spite of themselves:

Political men have to treat the people as infants (for their own good), in appearing to yield to all their childishness, so as to be in a better position to guide them insensibly toward more solid reasoning. For, given the world as it is, a wise man will only hope, at the most, to render the superstition of his country less burdensome and mischievous; and to accommodate it, as much as he can, to the principles of honesty and virtue, to compliance with the magistrates, and to the common good of the country.[55]

The world "as it is" should not be confused with the world as it should be: it behooves both the politician and the philosopher to remember this.

---

53. *Reason for Naturalizing the Jews*, p. 49.

54. "Druids," p. 83; "Clidophorus," *Tetradymus*, p. 81.

55. Fol. 94. On Toland's connections with Hohendorf and Eugène of Savoy, see Jacob, *Radical Enlightenment*, pp. 55, 147, 178.

Writers like Bruno, whose works Toland considered a thousand times more obscure than those of the "sectarians" of Thomas Aquinas or Scotus Erigena, should not be "indifferently communicated to every body," especially individuals who lack the good sense and force of reason necessary to detect Bruno's sophisms.[56] Only when surrounded by others who study such writers as Bruno with indifference of temper could one be assured of regulating those passions that in the mob or multitude would impel him into prejudices and superstitions.

That Toland himself was able to find kindred spirits interested in the study of Bruno's philosophy is evident from inquiries he received about the Italian philosopher. It was probably Toland who translated and published Bruno's *Spaccio della Bestia Trionfante, or The Expulsion of the Triumphant Beast* (1713) to satisfy requests from correspondents in England and on the Continent.[57] Like Bruno, Toland believed that moral and political regeneration was to be achieved through the expulsion of the beast of superstition. But Bruno pointed beyond the adoption of the attitude of the "unsuperstitious man" to a description of the metaphysical and epistemological causes of polemic. In Bruno's philosophy Toland discovered how civil liberty (bordering on republic-anism) could be linked to a religion of nature grounded in pantheistic materialism.[58] Toland's acceptance of a materialistic philosophy of individuals engaged in active contest is fashioned, as we shall see in the next chapter, by his belief that philosophical claims must be made *sensible* (i.e., both intelligible and tied to experience).

The threefold passion of the philosopher—much like the heroic frenzy referred to by Bruno—arises, Toland believed, in response to the prejudices of the mob and the superstitions of the priest. In fact, the philosopher tests the force of his reason, polemically (and often esoterically), against these prejudices and superstitions; he learns of his own powers and abilities in the context of challenge. In much the same

56. See Toland to Leibniz, 22 Feb. 1710, concerning Bruno's *Expulsion of the Triumphant Beast*, in Carabelli, "Otto Lettere," p. 425. Also see "Lettre de Mr. Toland, sur le *Spaccio della bestia triomphante*," *Nova Bibliotheca Lubecensis*, 5 (1754): 159. For Toland's remarks about Bruno and the sectarians of Aquinas and Erigena, see ONB MS 10390, fol. 391.

57. See Giovanni Aquilecchia, "Scheda bruniana: la traduzione 'tolandiana' dello *Spaccio*," *Giornale storico della letteratura italiana* 152 (1975): 311–13; and Giuntini, *Panteismo*, pp. 293, 310.

58. See Jacob, *Radical Enlightenment*, pp. 36–37.

way as the metaphysician describes the individual existence and characteristic forces of bodies, Toland examined the forces of reason and prejudice.

Particularly under the influence of Bruno, Toland provided a metaphysics to account for the passion of the philosopher and the general need for polemic. The following chapter examines this turn to metaphysics—a turn in which Toland attempted to justify the foundations of his proposals for toleration and polemic.

VII

The Metaphysics of Polemic

TOLAND'S MOVE INTO METAPHYSICS was occasioned by the convergence of several influences in his life. Late in the 1690s, when he was becoming recognized as one of the chief pamphleteers of the Whigs, some of Newton's supporters (particularly Samuel Clarke) began an attack on his religious doctrines and philosophic techniques. Although Toland had not singled out the Newtonians for any explicit criticism, attacks on the principles of partisans of High Church Anglicanism and of the Tories had been interpreted as an indirect slap at the structured and ordered universe described by Newtonians. Many of those belonging to the High Church faction—emphasizing the divine institution of the order of bishops, the inflexibility of the liturgy, and the prerogative and power of the prince in temporal affairs and of the bishops in ecclesiastical affairs—had found Newtonian descriptions of absolute space-time very much in accord with their ideas of the relations between God and the world, the prince and his people, or the bishops and the laity. When Toland attacked Tories or High Church-men, Newtonians within and outside those groups took offense.

The dispute between Toland and Clarke over natural philosophy appears to stem from their conflicting religious and political views. At least we can say that Newtonians and non-Newtonians alike were conscious of the political and religious implications of physical and cosmological positions being discussed at the time. Even Newton tried to extricate himself from sectarian squabbles generated by his theories, but with little success. And writers like Toland and Clarke seemed more than willing to raise issues about space and time in practical contexts such as political theorizing or religious debate.

In general, Newtonians supported the position that ideals of civic

virtue and public interest were attainable only insofar as men acknowledged the harmony of a mechanical universe. Such a universe was
controlled by some providence that directed the natural and established leaders of society and government. To attack the intransigent
government or religion, as Toland did, was tantamount to discrediting
the Newtonian world view, which was so successful in explaining so
many other aspects of nature.[1]

If one concentrates, on the other hand, on the *Letters to Serena*, he can
conclude that Toland's attacks against the Newtonian emphasis on
absolute space-time were intended to prevent the theologically conservative characteristics of Newtonian mechanics from gaining widespread support.[2] In other words, Toland can be understood as
primarily concerned with raising doubts about the work of Newtonians
in order to undermine its use by High Churchmen. Whether Toland
attacked Newtonians because they applied their positions to religious
matters and politics or whether he attacked religious and political
conservatives because they used Newtonian mechanics to support their
positions—he did take an interest in religious and political implications
of Newtonian metaphysics.

As early as in his studies at Edinburgh (1690), Toland had been
exposed to Newtonian ideology. But it was not until the latter part of
the decade that he began to fall under the influence of a completely
different thinker—Bruno. Not only did Bruno's writings address
many of the same religious topics as Toland's; they also raised
metaphysical questions about the status of *matter* within the discussion
of religion. And when Toland conversed and corresponded with
Leibniz, he appealed to Bruno for insights into metaphysics whenever
Leibniz pushed the discussion in that direction. But in his published
writings on extension and matter-in-motion, Toland turned to the
teachings of Spinoza to dramatize the explicit religious and political
implications of metaphysical speculation.

As indicated in the manuscripts he sent to Hohendorf, Toland was
interested not only in Bruno's writings but also in the accounts of his
life and death. As one who lived the life of philosophic polemic, Bruno

1. See Jacob, *Newtonians and the English Revolution*, pp. 228, 249. Also see her "John
Toland and the Newtonian Ideology," *Journal of the Warburg and Courtauld Institutes* 32
(1969): 307–31.
2. See Paolo Casini, "Toland e l'attività della materia," pp. 41–42; and Giuntini,
Panteismo, p. 225.

had a temperament similar to Toland's. It is almost as if Toland saw him as an itinerant sixteenth-century version of himself. By learning about Bruno's career and fate, he was able to crystallize much of his own thinking about the role and passion of the philosopher.

Because his concept of the philosopher emerged from discussions in coffeehouses and the chambers of politicians, Toland's treatment of the metaphysical foundations of philosophic passion was guided by practical interests and experiences characteristic of the politician or merchant. Restraint and guidance of metaphysical speculation were to be found, accordingly, in the practical, everyday experiences of the individual thinker.

The two focal works by Toland on matter and motion or action were the *Letters to Serena* and *Pantheisticon*. In those works he described the theoretical elements involved in topics that, at first glance, often seem only indirectly associated with metaphysics. By appealing to a metaphysical explanation of the interaction of bodies Toland not only revealed his ties to a tradition of speculative thought but also clarified the role of metaphysical appeals within his general methodology. One of the main concerns of this chapter, therefore, is to indicate how Toland formulated metaphysical positions (often acknowledging his debt to Bruno) using his practical experience of prejudice and polemic. The first section describes how his emphasis on sensible experience and practical activity developed into the position that action is essential to matter. The second reveals how he used this view of matter to explain the nature of change in the world and how such an explanation bears on the question of the relationship of God and nature.

1. PRACTICAL EXPERIENCE AND THE CONTEXTS OF BODIES IN ACTION

Toland at times seemed to imply that there is something more to the frequent disagreements among people than sheer accident. That men have been exposed to different forms of education or have had diverse experiences might, of course, explain why they form divergent views. But Toland wanted to make a stronger claim, namely, that this difference is *essential* to their being individuals. This point has arisen in several contexts thus far. For example, I referred earlier to Toland's remark that "as men have different Capacities, Apprehensions, and Opportunities, so they cannot possibly but have *different Notions* of

Things."[3] Although such differences appear most strikingly in political and religious disputes, they indicate a characteristic of all nature. That is, political and religious distinctions are as natural and as much a metaphysical feature of men as are distinctions in physical appearance. Toland developed the metaphysical explanation of such distinctions in works like the *Letters to Serena* and *Pantheisticon*, but in such works as *The Art of Governing by Partys*, he indicated that the practical experience of political and religious factions and of distinctions among men provides a paradigm for understanding his own position. "'Tis not more common (nor indeed more natural) for Men to vary from one another in the color of their Hair, the air of their Face, or the measure of their Stature, than it is for them to disagree in their opinions (whether relating to Religion or any other subject) by reason of their different opportunities, applications or capacities, and that things are not plac'd in the same degree of light to all sorts of People."[4]

Nature itself appears to stand in the way of attempts to overcome differences in capacities, apprehensions, and opportunities (or experience in general) that would allow a uniformity of belief. Not only did Toland object to such an ideal as undesirable—as contradicting fundamental assumptions of polemical philosophy—but he also argued that, in at least one important sense, the ideal of uniformity is impossible to attain *in principle*. Beginning with the observation that each man is distinct in virtue of his different background and experience, Toland implied that there is something fundamentally unnatural about the attempt to eradicate such distinguishing characteristics. A cardinal virtue of polemic is that polemical discussion clarifies exactly how opinions differ. In fact, without engaging in some such form of communication, an individual has no viable way to test the uniqueness and strength of his opinions.

Toland's observation that indifference of opinion is impossible reverts to his more general belief that there are speculative demands, as well as practical pressures, to develop differing opinions on matters of importance to oneself and to others. In short, insofar as one is an individual, it is theoretically impossible for him to be indifferent in his opinions; for to be indifferent in opinion is to be indistinguishable from all else—that is, to not exist as an individual.

3. *Memorial of the State of England*, p. 44.
4. *Art of Governing by Partys*, p. 11.

Because he believed that experience plays such a major role in determining individual character, Toland placed a great deal of importance on developing the widest possible sphere of acquaintances in as many sects and countries as possible. He applied this principle, for example, when he charged that Harley had betrayed the ideals of the Protestant Succession and had joined the Jacobite faction. The point was not that Harley had Jacobite acquaintances but that he associated exclusively with Jacobite partisans.[5]

Corollary to this was Toland's belief that one should show *publicly* that he had developed a variety of contacts. Appeal to public, observable experience characterizes the practical frame of mind of the merchant and the politician; and it is this frame of mind upon which Toland depended for his explanation of the individuality of the self. He maintained that all questions, even those about immaterial things such as the soul, can be resolved only by appeal to publicly observable and publicly communicable experience.

For example, in response to Leibniz's question whether reasoning could occur without use of the senses, Toland noted that even knowledge of the soul is attained only by means of sensible experience of the body.[6] The method by which the soul is known determines what is known about the soul. And because we can know what the soul is only by means of the body and corporeal things, what we can say about the soul must be limited to a corporeal manner of explanation. In fact, Toland went so far as to say that without sensible things, all reasoning, principles, consequences, and systems would be nothing. Limiting discussion to these empirical techniques, he changed the focus of investigation from the soul, which appeared to him as methodologically inaccessible, to the *self*, which he defined as nothing else than the result of the impression of sensible things upon the brain.

Although he preferred to speak more of the self than of the soul, Toland did point out (in some remarks that Pierre Bayle published in the second edition of his *Dictionary*) that a materialistic, methodologically accessible explanation of the soul is possible. In living bodies, the soul could be understood as the arrangement of different parts of

5. *Art of Restoring*, p. 28. Also see Toland to Sophie Charlotte, no date given (but sometime in 1702), Leibniz, *Schriften*, 6: 511.

6. For the discussion of the points raised in this paragraph, see Toland to Sophie Charlotte, Leibniz, *Schriften*, 6: 509–12.

matter or as a certain disposition of various organs.[7] But Bayle noted that while Toland suggested this explanation as a possible way of arguing materialistically for the existence of the soul, he acknowledged the practical falsity and impiety of the position. He argued that a materialistic explanation of the soul fails to insure immortality and undermines any hope of reward or fear of punishment in an afterlife. The belief in an immortal soul is a universally applicable requirement of proper social behavior; the *function* of such a belief is this-worldly. Toland preferred to downplay any discussion about philosophical justification of an afterlife and of an immortal soul because the only claims about the soul that could be *experientially* verified concern how *belief* in personal immortality affects behavior rather than whether an immortal soul actually exists.

Toland did not later change his mind about the method for defining the self and thought. In *Pantheisticon*, written almost twenty years after his discussions in Hanover, he identified thought as a "peculiar motion of the brain"; and he commented that since the brain cannot produce anything incorporeal, all ideas must be corporeal.[8] By shifting attention away from the theologically laden term "soul" to the philosophically regulated term "self," Toland tried to avoid undermining the practical effectiveness of the religious belief in immortality without claiming that the existence of an immortal soul is methodologically justifiable in a philosophic sense.

Toland also remarked in *Pantheisticon* that his description of the pantheist sodalities and their beliefs was philosophical, not theological. It is one thing, he noted, to explicate nature and to treat it in terms of philosophically justifiable arguments; but it is quite another to discourse on religion.[9] The religious function of belief in the immortality of the soul is important for social intercourse. But philosophically, there seems to be little justification for the belief in *personal* immortality. If after his death he was a soul, Toland observed, then he would no longer be the same person, because while alive he was a body-soul

---

7. See note "L" of the article "Dicearchus," in *The Dictionary Historical and Critical of Mr. Peter Bayle*, ed., P. Des Maizeaux, 2nd ed. London: J. J. and P. Knapton et al., 1735), 2: 660. Cf. Bayle, *Dictionnaire historique et critique*, 2nd ed. (Rotterdam: Reinier Leers, 1702), 1: 1046. Also see Leibniz to Bayle, 5 Dec. (?) 1702, *Schriften*, 3: 68.

8. Pp. 22, 24 (pp. 12, 14).

9. P. 7 (p. vi).

conjoint.[10] In one sense, then, something about the individual would survive death, but it could not be identified as the self. "Death is in effect the very same thing with our Birth; for as to die is only to cease to be what we formerly were, so to be born is to begin to be something which we were not before."[11] Birth and death are transition points by means of which the philosopher can distinguish methodically between individuals. But such a description has a third-person, observer character about it: it is the philosopher's description of individuals seen "from the outside." Seen from the inside, from the perspective of the self, birth and death are not only the beginning and end of existence but also the beginning and end of the meaningfully observable and experientially accessible existence of all. "As our birth brought us the beginning of all things, so shall our death bring the end."[12] From the personal, self-oriented perspective, nothing at all in the universe survives when the self dies.

My purpose in bringing up Toland's discussion of the *method* for treating the question of the soul, here in a study of the metaphysics of polemic, is to note his fundamentally *materialistic* method of dealing not only with the question of the soul but also with that of the importance of personal, practical experiences in the formation of the self. Matter itself became a topic of major philosophic importance for Toland because of its central role in his treatment of knowledge. In addition, the seemingly unphilosophic themes of travel and experience, which recur in his writing and activities, became topics of speculative concern for him under the rubrics of motion (or action) and intelligence. The convergence of Toland's adoption of a *materialistic epistemological method* with his practical concerns for *promiscuous communication* resulted in his proposal that *action is essential to matter*. In other words, seen as part of the general movement of his thought, Toland's proposal about the essential activity of matter was an attempt to formalize his epistemological and practical tendencies and was intended to have certain recognizable political implications for his contemporaries. Toland's practical, observable activity, in the form of promiscuous communication, thus had its metaphysical parallel in his belief that matter—the basis upon which all sensible experience is founded—is essentially active.

10. Toland to Sophie Charlotte, sometime in 1702, Leibniz, *Schriften*, 6: 514.
11. *Serena*, p. 191.
12. *Pantheisticon*, p. 88 (p. 71).

Probably resulting in part from his discussions with Leibniz, Toland's treatment of the activity of matter appeared originally in the *Letters to Serena*. Pointing out that "Matter is never conceiv'd but under some Notion of Action,"[13] he objected to the attempt to understand matter as something passive or inert. Because matter is *always known* in the context of some action, he argued, definitions of matter that fail to respect this fact can only prejudice and mislead. "*Action is essential to Matter* ... Matter cannot be rightly conceiv'd nor consequently be rightly defin'd without it ... [and] nothing can be accounted for in Matter without this essential Action."[14] Because cognitive activity itself is nothing more than the impressions of sensible objects on the brain, nothing that contradicts the constant experience of material things in action can be legitimately incorporated into a definition of matter.

To clarify what he meant by the *action* of material things—particularly those that often do not appear to be engaged in any action—Toland distinguished between the *general motion* (or "action") of all that exists and *local motions*. As long as such a distinction was kept in mind, he felt free to claim that *motion* is essential to matter:

I hold then that *Motion is essential to Matter*, that is to say, as inseparable from its Nature as Impenetrability or Extension, and that it ought to make a part of its Definition.... the better to be understood, I wou'd have this Motion of the Whole be call'd *Action*, and all local Motions, as direct or circular, fast or slow, simple or compounded, be still call'd *Motion*, being only the several changeable *Determinations* of the *Action* which is always in the Whole, and in every Part of the same, and without which it cou'd not receive any Modifications. I deny that Matter is or ever was an inactive dead Lump in absolute Repose, a lazy and unweildy thing.[15]

The action that is essential to matter, and thus present in all material things, need not be observed in actual local motion. Borrowing an idea from those he referred to as "the mathematicians," Toland indicated that this intrinsic action of matter is what is often referred to as the *conatus ad motum*,[16] the inclination, tendency, or impulse toward local motion.

Leibniz had discussed the entire question of bodies and matter with

13. P. 170.
14. Ibid., p. 160.
15. Ibid., pp. 158–59.
16. Ibid., p. 237.

Toland on Toland's second visit to Berlin, in 1702. Writing to a correspondent the following year, Leibniz suggested that there is nothing objectionable in the claim that movement is essential to matter. "I maintain that a body without action and movement is as little acceptable to nature as a space without matter."[17] Toland agreed, claiming that the mistaken Newtonian notion of a really existent space apart from matter had its origin in the purely mathematical treatment of space, time, and mathematical points.[18] Philosophers, he charged, had misunderstood the nature of matter and had characterized it as inactive because they adopted the mathematical paradigm and then tried to explain the movement of bodies within the container of absolute space.

Leibniz had also pointed out that all bodies have an essential and primitive force, a *vis motrix* or *conatus ad motum*, which causes all local movement.[19] But because the essential tendency to movement has an indefinite direction, a body is limited in its actual and determinate movement by its concourse with other bodies. When Toland said that the *conatus-ad-motum* concept could be used to support his position, he did so cautiously; for when Leibniz employed the concept, he still claimed that matter could be conceived as having no character of action without the presence of an entelechy or substantial form. Without the addition of this nonmaterial entelechy, matter could not be determined as a specific and individual body, Leibniz argued.

The introduction of the spiritualistic and nonexperiential entelechies was precisely what Toland had tried to avoid. But Leibniz claimed that there is no way to avoid it because, without such an appeal, determinate and individual bodies-in-motion could never have become individuated within matter in general. Ironically, this is exactly the complaint Toland raised against Spinoza—that he had failed to explain how individual bodies become individuated within the infinite attribute of extension.

Toland seemed to say that in placing the source of vitality and motion outside of bodies, Spinoza separated the principle of life (God) from all bodies, including social, political, and religious bodies, as well as individual physical bodies and individual men. By locating the

---

17. Leibniz to Jacquelot, 22 Mar. 1703, *Schriften*, 3: 457–58.
18. *Serena*, p. 181.
19. Cf. Heinemann, "Toland and Leibniz," *Philosophical Review* 54 (1945): 455.

source of motion and life in matter itself, Toland is much closer to Hobbes than to Spinoza—a fact that Leibniz pointed out in a letter to the Electress Sophia.[20] It is nevertheless interesting to note that Toland criticized Spinoza—that God-intoxicated man—for alienating God from men—this, at a time when many of Spinoza's critics were claiming that his god was not transcendent enough.

Linking Toland to Hobbes and to Spinoza, Samuel Clarke interpreted Toland's concept of conatus as a limitation or an exclusion of divine activity in an autonomous material world. But Clarke went further than either Toland or Leibniz in attacking the very concept of conatus. He argued that the inclination of a body to move is an inclination to move either in some determinate way (in which case the inclination to action is not essential to all matter) or in every direction at once (in which case there would never be any movement).[21]

Although Clarke identified Toland as the object of these remarks, his real adversary was Leibniz. Both Toland and Leibniz agreed that Clarke failed to recognize that a *part* of matter is determined as an individual, with a determinate conatus, by external, surrounding bodies. Toland argued that essentially, and as matter itself, a body has a universal, multidirectional conatus. It is not part of the *essence* of material objects (or "bodies") that they be experienced in *actual* local motion, because *inclination* or *tendency* does not entail actuality. Local motion is the change of situation of a body in respect to others; and laws of motion are simply based on the observations of modifications of matter due to some force or action either within the body or outside.[22] Local motions and other distinguishing characteristics of bodies can be understood either as the result of "peculiar internal dispositions" or in terms of their relations with other bodies.[23] Toland insisted, contrary to Leibniz, that just as the laws of motion applying to bodies as they are related to each other must be based on that which is observable, so also must be the description of the peculiar internal dispositions of bodies.

20. Sometime between 13 and 16 Sept. 1702, *Schriften*, 6: 519. Cf. Jacob, *Radical Enlightenment*, pp. 57–59.

21. *A Demonstration of the Being and Attributes of God* (London: William Botham, 1705), pp. 46–47. See Giuntini, *Pantheismo*, p. 347; Hélène Metzger, *Attraction universelle et religion naturelle chez quelques commentateurs anglais de Newton* (Paris: Hermann and Cie, 1938), pp. 109–10; and Sabetti, *John Toland*, pp. 198–219.

22. *Serena*, pp. 140–41.

23. Ibid., p. 184.

In other words, not only must the laws of motion be based on observations, but explanations of the *causes* of local motion must also be limited to what is, in principle, observable—namely, matter. To say that the moving force or action responsible for local motion is not essential to matter is to place that force or action beyond human grasp. Knowledge is limited, in practice and in principle, to sensible experience or to assumptions about sensible experience based on its strictly materialistic characteristics.

The above points might be summarized in the following way. What makes sense to the merchant, to the politician—to anyone in general—is that which he can sensibly observe. Starting with this concentration on the practical man's experience, Toland structured his epistemology to allow for concepts that are meaningful only to the extent that they incorporate ordinary (i.e., sensible) experience. A practical concern for meaningfulness and sensibleness (i.e., for what is said *to make sense*) conditioned Toland's description of how we know anything; and the conditions establishing the knowability of objects themselves are limited to how we can know them. As far as Toland was concerned, it is absurd to speak about the metaphysical principles underlying the existence of things without first addressing how human knowing must fashion such principles.

Unlike Leibniz, Toland would not admit explanations of the individuation of bodies without explaining the source of such individuation as essential to matter itself. And in this regard, he felt that he corrected a basic weakness in Spinoza's account, because the distinction of bodies should have been interpreted solely in terms of matter. Spinoza had been correct in identifying matter as extension; he had erred in not identifying extension as one perspective, or "attribute," of matter. Locke had made the same mistake about matter in regard to solidity; and Leibniz failed to recognize action as an essential property of matter. Extension, solidity, and action, according to Toland, are the three essential properties of matter. They are three distinct ways of conceiving matter, the principle upon which all sensible knowledge is based.[24]

Toland's concern for limiting the discussion of bodies to what is observable had implications for—and, indeed, may have been grounded upon an awareness of—the status of political, religious, and social

24. Ibid., pp. 166, 178, 229–30.

bodies. His definition of bodies, emphasizing their material unity and the epistemological means by which they are distinguished from one another, was intended to be flexible enough to account for differences among religious sects and political entities. "By Bodys I understand certain Modifications of Matter, conceiv'd by the Mind as so many limited Systems, or particular Quantitys mentally abstracted, but not actually separated from the Extension of the Universe."[25] To see why Toland felt justified in claiming that bodies are not *actually* separated in the universe, we must recall that he viewed thought itself as something material, a motion of the brain that employs the "ethereal fire" surrounding and permeating all things.[26] The mind's activity of conceiving modifications of matter as limited systems is itself an activity of matter-in-motion. The way that the mind distinguishes bodies is determined by the history of sensible impressions that characterizes the self, or in materialistic terms, by its own background and its practical experiences in travel, business, and communication.

Toland's own shifts in attitude toward the various dissenting religious sects, for example, exemplified how the perception of bodies as limited systems changes as a function of the experience of the mind. It was only after "greater Experience and more Years had a little ripen'd his Judgment," and after his "Travels increas'd, and the study of Ecclesiastical History perfected this Disposition," that Toland recognized the essential unity of all Protestant sects.[27] The differences among Protestants or the differences in their "private notions" were not so great, he argued, as to raise doubts about the essentially identical universe of discourse in which all operated. Similarly, the limited systems of matter ("bodies") were essentially united to one another in sharing in the same universe or "world" of discourse. Sects that could communicate with one another by means of mutually understandable terms, that "made sense" to one another, did so only by means of their experience with and study of one another.

Curiously, as the self becomes individuated through its practical experience, all things that the self comes to understand (including differences among bodies) become united through inclusion within the extension of the meaningful universe of the self. Although Toland

25. Ibid., p. 173.
26. *Pantheisticon*, p. 22 (p. 12).
27. *Apology*, pp. 16–17.

described the self as the product of a history of sensible experiences, he did not believe it to be essentially passive. As with all matter, its essential activity is indeterminate until it begins to define itself in contrast to (i.e., in polemical confrontation with) other things or selves. Essentially, the self is active, even though its specific determination as this or that self is the result of sensible impressions of things that become "other" only as it develops its own autonomy. The entire world becomes determinate and meaningful only as the self becomes determinate and reflective. Methodic forms of reflection and polemic—that is, systems of philosophy in general—create *new worlds*, not simply new interpretations of the same, already-meaningful world.[28] And the process of developing such world views is fundamentally that of developing an autonomous self. This is why birth of the self is the beginning of the meaning of all things (including doctrines of the Christian mysteries and immortality); and death of the self brings the end of all meaning.[29]

Toland underscored the nonmetaphysical implications of his discussion of matter and bodies by following the first three letters to Serena, explicitly on the issue of action and matter, by two letters dealing with superstition, prejudice, and the formative process by which individuals come to hold their opinions. The analysis of motion, in the fifth letter, has a retroactive impact on the first letter, which is concerned with the origin and force of prejudices. If all local motion of bodies is relative, then all opinion based upon experience, without which there is no thought or opinion, is relative as well.[30] The explanation of the origin and force of prejudices is to be found by examining the origin and strength of opinions. In like manner, the explanation of the origin and force of local motion in bodies is to be found by understanding the essential action of matter and the way in which bodies affect one another.

Toland's treatment of the interaction of bodies serves as a model for the interaction of individuals who hold different positions based on their different beliefs or notions. Those notions are recognized as different in the same way that bodies are distinguished, namely, in terms of their relative movements or forces. Because the force of a notion or opinion is discerned only in its interaction with other notions

28. *Serena*, p. 137.
29. *Pantheisticon*, p. 88 (p. 71).
30. See Casini, "Toland e l'attività della materia," p. 48.

or opinions, all distinctions of opinion will be recognized and characterized by means of *polemic*. Toland's discussion of bodies—religious, political, as well as physical—is the application of his principles of polemic to the domains of religion, politics, natural philosophy, and metaphysics.

Toland believed that a body can be at rest in respect to those bodies around it and still not be in "absolute repose." Although the bodies around it may prevent its actual movement locally, the body exists as an individual as long as it is conceived as expressive of the tendency of all matter to move. All particular motions mutually restrain or accelerate themselves according to the manner and strength of every resistance or impulse. Everything that exists is in motion and is identifiable as an individual in virtue of its motion. A body at rest is essentially in a "motion of resistance," an affirmation of existence in the context of other bodies.[31] "Since Rest therefore is but a certain Determination of the Motion of Bodys, a real Action of Resistance between equal Motions, 'tis plain that this is no absolute Inactivity among Bodys, but only a relative Repose with respect to other Bodys that sensibly change their place."[32] A body at rest exerts a real force against other bodies with equal though opposite motions. All rest, determined by the tension of forces established between two or more bodies, is essentially social and interactive (perhaps even combative) in nature.

This observation recalls Toland's abhorence of *solitude* and his delight in *retirement*. A solitude in which the individual (or body) is not confronting others—challenging their opinions (or strengths, forces) and testing his own abilities—sooner or later is fatal. The body that is not engaged in *striving* (conatus) to make a place for itself in the context of other bodies quickly perishes. That is, the very existence of a body depends upon its activity and motion.[33] Absolute rest is impossible, just as is a solitude out of touch with surrounding events. In retirement the individual, like the body at rest, is engaged in a holding situation, neither thrusting himself into the public view nor yielding to the attempts of others to dominate the development of meaning and reason.

The absolute negation of all polemic, like the triumph of absolute

31. *Pantheisticon*, pp. 20–21 (pp. 10–11).
32. *Serena*, p. 199.
33. Cf. Cecilia Motzo Dentice di Accadia, *Preilluminismo e deismo in inghilterra* (Naples: Libraria Scientifica Editrice, 1970), p. 200.

rest among bodies (physical, political, or religious), would result in a uniformity and a *peace* in which individuality is absent. In addressing the question of motion and rest, Toland gave a metaphysical argument for the necessity of including considerations of travel, retirement, and polemic in his overall enterprise. Thus his analysis was not limited solely to speculative issues of interest only to metaphysicians and natural scientists.

2. POLITICAL AND THEOLOGICAL COSMOLOGY

In proposing that matter is essentially active, Toland avoided a number of the cosmological and cosmogonical problems that plagued Descartes and the Newtonians. For example, if matter is essentially active, then there is no need to postulate space as distinct from matter in order to explain how matter can move from its supposedly inert state into action. In fact, there is no need for any *generation* of motion in matter at all, for everything material is in motion because the essence of matter is action (even though some bodies may appear to be in a state of rest relative to other bodies).[34]

Furthermore, because local motion applies only to bodies (which are modifications of matter), and because matter itself cannot *move* locally, the universe (comprising all the modifications of matter) must be infinite in action and unlimited in extension. In language highly reminiscent of Bruno's *On the Infinite Universe and Worlds* and *Concerning the Cause, Principle, and One*, Toland pointed out that if there is no place or space into which the universe can move, then its lack of local motion is due to infinite extension. And because it is extended infinitely, the action by which all of its parts move locally must be infinite as well.[35]

Toland shared with Bruno a fascination for this infinite power and activity of the universe. In 1698 Toland obtained the volume of Bruno's dialogues that had belonged to Queen Elizabeth. It included the *Della causa, De l'Infinito, Spaccio della Bestia Trionfonte*, and *La Cena de la Ceneri*.[36] Throughout the *Letters to Serena* and *Pantheisticon*, Toland's arguments about the activity of matter and the infinite extension of the

---

34. *Serena*, pp. 181–82.
35. *Pantheisticon*, pp. 15, 20 (pp. 6, 10).
36. See Aquilecchia, "Nota su John Toland," pp. 83–86.

universe touched on themes Bruno had raised. But whereas Bruno had preferred to formulate much of his discussion in scholastic terminology, Toland adopted the language of the Hermetic tradition. Bruno himself provided Toland with much of the spirit and enthusiasm of Hermetic themes; and Toland appears to have broadened his acquaintance with such sources by obtaining copies of works like the opera of Hermes Trismegistus.[37] But Toland revitalized the Hermetic description of matter by incorporating it into his own methodology and by relating it to treatments of nature by Leibniz and the Newtonians.

The essentially active character of matter accounts for the almost overwhelming variety and vivacity of the universe, Toland believed. An infinity of figures and forms, mixtures and qualities, continually appears in the universe. All these traits are modifications of matter through which every individual shares in the existence and eternality of all else.[38] Nature embodies all the change and bustle of the marketplace and the exchange. Everything is in motion; and the essential activity of *matter* is the unifying theme:

No Parts of Matter are ty'd to any one Figure or Form, losing and changing their Figures and Forms continually, that is, being in perpetual Motion, clipt, or worn, or ground to pieces, or disolv'd by other Parts, acquiring their Figures, and these theirs, and so on incessantly; Earth, Air, Fire, and Water, Iron, Wood, and Marble, Plants and Animals, being rarefy'd or condens'd, or liquify'd or congeal'd or dissolv'd or coagulated, or any other way resolv'd into one another.... But the Changes in the Parts make no Change in the Universe: for it is manifest that the continual Alterations, Successions, Revolutions, and Transmutations of Matter, cause no Accession or Diminution therein.[39]

There is no real innovation in the world except change of place.[40] The exchange of particles of matter continues incessantly in the "flowing and transpiration of matter" among the bodies of animals and plants.[41]

---

37. See the list of works in Toland's possession, Oct. 1720, BM Add. MS 4295, fols. 41–43. On the appearance of elements of Bruno's metaphysics in the writings of English writers in the early part of the seventeenth century, see Daniel Massa, "Giordano Bruno's Ideas in Seventeenth Century England," *Journal of the History of Ideas* 38 (1977): 227–42.

38. *Serena*, p. 140.

39. Ibid., p. 189–90.

40. *Pantheisticon*, p. 21 (p. 11).

41. *Serena*, p. 192. Cf. Toland's translation of the prefatory dedication of Bruno's *Of the Infinite Universe and Innumerable Worlds*, in *Collection*, 1: 334, 343.

In this sense, "nothing is more certain than that every material Thing is all Things, and that all Things are but one."[42] This theme of eternally changing material forms had been pointed out by Ralph Cudworth as part of the esoteric doctrine of the Egyptians; and Toland claimed that even the Druids held such a position. As part of the Hermetic tradition of Bruno's philosophy, this doctrine reinforced the biblical dictum that what was, will be again, and that there is nothing new under the sun.[43]

All things, Toland claimed, contain the seeds for becoming all other things. Because matter is active and all bodies have a conatus to movement, all bodies can be said to contain a generative principle. That is, not only do plants and animals grow, but also minerals and crystals share in the universal organic development of bodies. As early as 1695, even before he published *Christianity Not Mysterious*, Toland appropriated a favorite expression of Cudworth and suggested, in his *Two Essays Sent in a Letter from Oxford*, that fossils can be explained as results of the activity of the "Plastick Power" of the Earth. He argued that because matter everywhere contains the seeds of all forms it should not be surprising that the seeds of some marinelike animals, given the proper environment, could grow within the earth itself.[44] Although limestone or shale might be an inhospitable environment for fish, it might be quite suitable for the growth of limestone or shale in shapes of fish skeletons. Is it so strange, Toland asked twenty-five years later, to think of metals or minerals as having their own seeds and growing in certain determinate shapes? After all, "veins" of ore appear to grow like branches or roots and to flow through the earth like blood.[45]

This explanation avoided the difficulties encountered by those who attempted to explain the presence of fossils with a universal-deluge theory. Toland agreed with writers like John Woodward (author of *An Essay towards a Natural History of the Earth*, 1695), who argued that fossils

42. *Serena*, p. 192.

43. *Ecclesiastes* 1: 9. See Toland's "De Genere, Loco, et Tempore Mortis Jordanis Bruni Nolani," sent as a letter to Hohendorf in 1709, in *Collection*, 1: 313; and "Druids," p. 46. Cf. Chiara Giuntini, "Toland e Bruno: ermetismo 'rivoluzionario'?," *Rivista di filosofia* 66 (1975): 214–16. Also see Ralph Cudworth, *The True Intellectual System of the Universe*, ed. John Harrison, 3 vols. (London: Thomas Tegg, 1845), 1: 531ff.

44. Pp. 41, 47.

45. *Pantheisticon*, pp. 28–33 (pp. 17–21). Also see *Serena*, p. 200; and Manlio Iofrida, "Il 'Pantheisticon' di John Toland," *Rivista critica di storia della filosofia* 36 (1981): 21–26.

found deep in the earth were those of real creatures like fish.[46] But contrary to Woodward, Toland maintained that these fish were never in the ocean or in a universal deluge. Rather, the seeds of the fish, trapped within rocks, affected the growth of such rocks so as to give them a fishlike shape.

Toland's description of the origin of fossils might appear strained to a modern reader; and in all fairness to Toland, it should be pointed out that he claimed that the design of the *Pantheisticon* in particular was to address the question of fossils from a historical, not a physical, perspective. The physics of fossil formation and geology in general were not handled in *Pantheisticon*; they were taken up in his (now lost) *Esoterics*.[47] His *Pantheisticon* remarks were intended to undermine the fanciful or mysterious explanations of fossils, such as those that appealed to events like Noah's flood.

Any historical description of the development of minerals or the formation of fossils must include, Toland maintained, parallels between (*a*) the ways in which men come to hold *opinions* and develop their own *ways of thinking*, (*b*) the ways of describing *geological* processes, and (*c*) the ways of characterizing the *metaphysical and cosmological principles* upon which all change is based. The diverse topics with which Toland concerned himself, from 1695 to 1700 alone, included fossils, Christianity, money, and Milton. But it was his increasing clarification of the *methods* by which such topics were to be treated that allowed them to be tied to one another and hence unified his interests.

In 1700, at least two years after his initial exposure to the Italian dialogues of Bruno, Toland composed a poem that outlined his project of describing all of nature. The themes and imagery were essentially Bruno's but with one twist at the end characteristic of Toland, namely, the comprehension of this variety of themes in the activity of *naming*:

> Who form'd the Universe, and when and why,
> Or if all things were from Eternity;
> What Laws to Nature were prescrib'd by JOVE;
> Where lys his chiefest residence above;
> Or if he's only but the World's great Soul;

46. For general treatments of the origins of geology, see Sir Archibald Geikie, *The Founders of Geology* (London: Macmillan and Co., 1897); and C. Schneer, "The Rise of Historical Geology in the Seventeenth Century," *Isis* 45 (1954), pp. 256–68.

47. *Pantheisticon*, p. 48 (p. 33).

Or parts the Creatures are and God the whole
From whence all beings their Existence have,
And into which resolv'd they find a Grave;
How nothing's lost, tho all things change their Form,
As that's a Fly which was but now a Worm;
And Death is only to begin to be
Som other thing, which endless change shall see;
(Then why should men to dy have so great fear?
Tho nought's Immortal, all Eternal are.)
Whether the Stars be numerous Suns, or no,
And what's their use above, or Pow'r below;
What Planets are inhabited, what not;
How many new emerg'd, what forgot;
If the dull Earth dos turn about the Sun,
Or that bright PHEBUS round this Globe does run;
Whence the magnetic Force; how Winds can blow;
What makes the Ocean duly ebb and flow;
How com th'alternat Seasons of the Year,
And why the Weather's warm, cold, dull, or clear;
How Animals and Plants increase their kind,
And what's the source of Life, of Soul or Mind;
How Stones and Metals, Sands or Shells are fram'd,
Shall only after me be rightly nam'd.[48]

Despite its myriad diversity and infinite power, the universe is tamed and becomes manageable (i.e., meaningful) in being "rightly" named —that is, named in terms of those ways of thinking as familiar to the politician and merchant as to the metaphysician or philosopher of nature.

The notion that all things are in perpetual flux had a special appeal for Toland, particularly because he saw the implications for political bodies of such a notion. "The revolutions of empires, kingdoms, and republicks" was paralleled by the revolutions of material forms throughout the universe. "All things are in a perpetual Flux, nothing permanent or in every Regard the same for one Moment. But none of them is so visibly subject to such Variations, as Kingdoms, States, and (in a word) all sorts of *Government*."[49] The fluctuations of civil and ecclesiastical governments, the changes of ministries, and the rise and

48. *Clito*, pp. 8–9.
49. *Destiny of Rome*, pp. 4–5, 7.

fall of political factions and parties serve as exemplars from which the metaphysician and cosmologist learn and to which they appeal for practical regulation and justification of their proposals.

The political domain, in which much of Toland's activity centered and in which he learned the importance of action, toleration, and discretion, contained situations offering him insights even into the role of *God in this universe of flux*. Unwilling to avoid raising theological questions in the context of political theory and cosmology—or perhaps unable to refrain from doing so, due to the pressure of friends and enemies—Toland discussed the question of the role of God as one feature in the larger metaphysical account of change in observable nature. Appealing to a political example, Toland noted that God appears to the world in much the same way as a leader appears to the ignorant. Just as the prince must embody seemingly contradictory characteristics (moderation and exactness, severity and mildness) and often confounds the ignorant, so God himself preserves the world "by the Opposition of Heat and Cold, of Gravity and Levity, of hard and fluid Bodys, whence proceeds the admirable Harmony of all things."[50] The metaphysical characteristics of change in nature become united to the discussion of God's existence and attributes through the understanding of *political* relationships. A diversified and yet harmonized society is nature writ small; and just as fundamental opposition (e.g., heat and cold, gravity and levity) characterize nature and provide the bases upon which the existence of all things is to be explained, so polemical opposition in social discourse must be recognized as the source upon which social harmony is to be based. When the question of the nature of God is understood in this context, Toland believed, it should have a uniting rather than dividing effect in discussions of various forms of religion.

As much as Toland was concerned in his early public life with questions about Christianity, the Scriptures, and disputes among religious sects, he did not really ever address the question of the nature of God in those contexts. The question of *religion* was of much more interest and importance to him than the question of *theology*. How men justify their actions by appeal to religious belief is of more pressing

---

50. *An Account of the Courts of Prussia and Hanover* (London: John Darby, 1705), p. 10. Cf. Bruno, *On the Infinite Universe and Innumerable Worlds*, trans. Dorothea Waley Singer, in her *Giordano Bruno: His Life and Thought* (New York: Henry Schuman, 1950), p. 328.

importance to the polemicist concerned with the origin and force of opinions than are the speculative justifications given for the opinions.

For Toland, the existence and attributes of God, surprisingly enough, are not issues to be raised in the context of religion. The character of religion remains closely tied to that of politics, commerce, economics—to all human endeavors—because the promiscuous communication of polemic is found within it. Matters treated in theological discussion seldom are restricted by the practical demand of the merchant or politician for observability. The effect of such a practical demand in formulating a method for dealing with questions of metaphysics delayed Toland's introduction of the question of God's nature, or activity, until it could be incorporated into a cosmological doctrine.

Toland's route to God as an object of philosophical speculation was not through religion. Characterized methodologically by a concentration on matter as the principle underlying observability, it was instead through a materialistic cosmology.

Toland's description of God concentrated on power and intelligence in the universe. God is the *force* or *energy* of the infinite *whole* and the essential *action* within all matter. Because innumerable individuals arise within matter, they express particular aspects of the universe and are distinguished from all other individuals in the universe and harmonized with them. The order and design of the never-ceasing changes in the universe indicate the presence of an infinitely wise intellect directing all change toward the communion and conservation of the whole.[51] God is not only the process that distinguishes and harmonizes all parts of matter in the universe; he is also the energy or force of matter. Using language consistent with the neo-Platonic tradition, Toland referred to God as the soul (*anima*) and mind (*mens*) of the universe, although he indicated that he preferred to use his own terms, such as action and intellect. The universe can be distinguished from the force of the whole by reason, but this does not mean that this force (God) is really distinct from the universe. "The Force and energy of the Whole, the creator and ruler of all, and always tending to the best end, is GOD; whom you may call the *Mind*, if you please, and *Soul* of the UNIVERSE.... this force ... is not separated from the UNIVERSE itself, but by a distinction of reason."[52] Because matter is considered in terms of

51. *Pantheisticon*, pp. 16–17 (pp. 7–8); *Serena*, p. 235.
52. *Pantheisticon*, pp. 17–18 (p. 8).

the complex of all *individuals* in the universe, there is need to identify the principles upon which individuation is based. *Intellect*, as the principle by which bodies are distinguished and describable in terms of form and purpose, and *motion or action*, as the principle by which bodies are distinguished and described in terms of mechanical or physical laws of interaction, constitute what is *meaningful* about the concept of God in the context of a cosmology.

In a more schematic form, we might understand Toland in this way. The whole—that is, matter—is the principle upon which all knowledge and meaningful discourse is based. It is the principle that results from Toland's concern with the practical, observable, and communicable character of knowledge. It is what the merchant and the politician understand and that upon which they base practical activity. Raised to the level of a metaphysical principle, that which makes practical sense in the world logically antecedes all principles by which the distinction of individuals is explained.

Because God is thought of as different from other beings, he cannot be identified as the whole. And because the universe is understood as comprising a realizable infinity of individuals, it cannot be identified as the whole either. The whole encompasses God and universe. Or, to put this in other terms, the principle of matter (as the methodologically determined foundation for the consideration of questions of God and universe) really includes the principles of intellect and action.

Intellect and action are principles contained within the *cosmological* meaning of God: they describe the universe in terms of its order and power. The relationship of intellect and action in Toland's description of actual cosmology is parallel to that of God and the universe in his description of the metaphysics of such a cosmology.

The universe could be understood either as the infinity of individuals *realizable* because of the essential action of matter or as the totality of individuals actually *realized* due to physical (local) motion. Toland's attempt to avoid confusion on this point can be seen in his decision to use "action" instead of "motion" when discussing the essential character of matter. The universe can be considered either as an expression of action (i.e., as comprising the infinity of realizable individuals) or as the result of local motions of bodies (i.e., as comprising the totality of realized individuals).

Perhaps an approximate parallel to this distinction of the two meanings for "universe" in Toland's writings might be found in Spinoza's distinction between *Natura naturans* and *Natura naturata*. Both are included within the Spinozan *natura tota*. The parallel should not be pressed too far, however. Otherwise, the originality of Toland's concentration on the methodological basis of meaningful discourse can be overlooked. If similarities are to be noticed at all, then certainly Toland's treatment of the principles of matter, action, and intelligence shows a great deal of similarity to Bruno's principles of matter, world soul, and intellect.[53]

Because Toland's discussion of intellect and action is introduced to account for the diversity, harmony, and local movement of bodies, its inclusion of the discussion of the nature, or activity, of God within a cosmological context has a double effect. First, it indicates how the discussion of God is to be understood and regulated in the language and ideas meaningful to all men of practical sensibility. Second, even the *metaphysical* discussion of God in terms of intellect and action becomes readily applicable to contexts in which promiscuous conversation and commerce (i.e., polemic in general) predominate. More than once Toland used the metaphysically laden combination of intelligence and action to refer to the realm of the merchant and politician.[54] For example, at the beginning of *Some Plain Observations*, when speaking of the difficulty of electing good representatives to Parliament due to misinformation in newspapers and pamphlets, he says that he especially pities those who live at a distance from London, "the place of Action, and of Intelligence."[55] London was a special place for Toland because it embodied the diversity, harmony, and activity of all nature, recognizable by the promiscuous communication and commerce found there. In identifying the place of publication of *Pantheisticon* as Cosmopoli—city of the cosmos—he indirectly indicated his attitude toward London.

Always aware of the tendency of metaphysical discussions to lose touch with ordinary experience, Toland emphasized the importance of tying speculative thought to practical experience by using the same terms (e.g., "intelligence" and "action") in each order. In fact, he believed it important that terms be used with an awareness of their import throughout a unified—indeed, cosmic—domain of human interest and activity.

---

53. See Bruno, *Concerning the Cause, Principle, and One*, trans. D. W. Singer, in Sidney Greenberg, *The Infinite in Giordano Bruno* (New York: King's Crown Press, 1950), p. 135.
54. See, for example, *Nazarenus*, preface, p. xiv.
55. P. 1.

Toland shifted his treatment of such metaphysical notions between writing the *Letters to Serena* and *Pantheisticon*. While many of the same ideas were addressed in both works, the manner of presentation differed. The *Letters to Serena* referred to the exoteric-esoteric distinction, but, published openly and intended for wide distribution, it did not *employ* the distinction. By the time he wrote *Pantheisticon*, which was published secretly, Toland had become firmly convinced of the need for discretion in communicating his metaphysical and cosmological ideas. The way in which metaphysical discussion is pursued, he seemed to say, will affect the character of the notions themselves.

The consideration of bodies is a case in point. In the *Letters to Serena*, Toland referred to bodies as modifications of matter conceived by the mind as so many limited systems. Within public and widespread polemic the mind of the individual should be the point of final appeal in the characterization of political-partisan or religious-sectarian bodies. But the whole point of the exoteric-esoteric distinction was that "the conceiving by the mind" of bodies is a communal and for the most part nonprivate endeavor. Although the metaphysical discussion of bodies in *Pantheisticon* appeared to reiterate earlier treatments of the same topic, the context reflected Toland's contention that an understanding of the character of bodies—including political, social, and religious bodies—is gained in small-group communication.

Here again, just as in his use of "intelligence" and "action" in both metaphysical and nonmetaphysical contexts, Toland's metaphysical discussion of "soul" and "action" had a reflexive connotation for their nonmetaphysical context. What appears as a straightforward comment about the need for political discretion or military secrecy takes on a world of new meanings when understood from the perspective of the metaphysician. "Secrecy, together with Resolution, are the Life and Soul of great Actions."[56] Starting from such observations as this— observations easily accessible to and understood by politicians, military men, and merchants alike—Toland drew metaphysical implications: only those actions characterized by and "ensouled with" secrecy and resolution achieve greatness. The secrecy of esoteric communication not only can be justified as the only possible response of thinkers resolved to engage in free and unrestrained inquiry; it can also be supported and explained in terms of a metaphysic of polemic.

---

56. *Collection of Letters by Monk*, introduction, p. vi.

Toland's doctrine of esoteric communication, together with his concern for treating the discussion of the nature of God within the context of a cosmology, occasioned his return to the theme of religion (as distinguished from cosmological theology) as a small-group endeavor. That does not mean that he had lost interest in religion between *Christianity Not Mysterious* and *Pantheisticon*. Much of his work on biblical criticism and toleration in the intervening years was concerned with or occasioned by his work in religion. But *Pantheisticon* returned to the *direct* treatment of religion, a modification of Toland's earlier decision not to address the question of religion again after the turmoil generated by his publication of *Christianity Not Mysterious*. When he wrote *Pantheisticon*, though, he was not writing for the wide audience addressed in *Christianity Not Mysterious*. This narrow focus reflected the size of the small groups of true religious believers.

As Toland described them, religious believers were characterized primarily by their tolerance of open discussion and by their indifference of temper. They constituted small groups of reflective thinkers who appreciated the character of religious experience within the small group. Forced into small-group discussion by the intolerance of polemic in society at large and in the institutionalized religions, these *pantheists* focused their attention on enjoying the fellowship and liturgical structures of formalized religions without giving up their methodologically determined cosmological theology.

Toland's view of the pantheist societies in a sense united a number of themes in his thought. What the pantheists meant to him and how they functioned within the general framework of his philosophy are topics that now deserve explicit treatment.

VIII

Pantheist Philosophy

SELDOM DO EXTENDED TREATMENTS of Toland's thought fail to point out that he appears to have been the first author to use the word "pantheist." The term first occurred in a letter entitled "Indifference in Disputes: Recommended by a Pantheist to an Orthodox Friend," which served as a preface to *Socinianism Truly Stated*.[1] In *Origines Judaicae* (1709) and in *Pantheisticon* the term reappeared; but in these later works it referred not only to the attitudes or methods of some groups of reflective thinkers (as in *Socinianism Truly Stated*) but also to the religious character of the pantheists' beliefs.

Although in *Socinianism Truly Stated* Toland did refer to a "System of Philosophy" held by pantheists, he did not describe what this system contained. A reference in *Origines Judaicae* alluded to the similarity of the beliefs of pantheists and Spinozists. But only in the *Pantheisticon* did Toland go into any detail about pantheist doctrines—doctrines emphasizing toleration of promiscuous communication and a practical, observation-based concern for materiality.

Toland refused to allow his treatment of pantheist doctrines to be divorced from their methodological principles. He ignored attempts by critics to reduce his statements into a set of doctrines that could be identified as "pantheism." In fact, in none of his published works, nor in his surviving manuscripts and correspondence, did Toland ever use the word "pantheism." This might seem a minor point, but it underscores Toland's insistence that the philosophy of the pantheist not be understood in terms of an *-ism*, or a body of beliefs that can be

---

1. Also see *Socinianism Truly Stated*, p. 7.

understood apart from the methods and attitudes of those who profess them.[2] The pantheist adopted a methodic stance that permeated and directed his investigations and resulted in his proposals about the relationship of God and the universe from which the designation "pantheist" follows.

The theme of *the pantheist* pulls together a number of topics raised in the preceding three chapters. The need for promiscuous communication, the demand for discretion and secrecy in the face of intolerance, and the appeal to metaphysics and cosmology—all set the stage for a return to considering the possibility and nature of a religion for the philosopher. Toland never lost his early interest in religion, and his discussion of the pantheists served to reintroduce the question of religious activity within a new context. The difference between his treatments of priestcraft and of the religion of the pantheist demonstrates his gradual recognition of the need for discretion in examining sensitive topics such as religion.

This chapter is divided into two sections. The first describes Toland's characterization of pantheist sodalities as groups which combined the needs for free and open discourse and for fellowship and ritual. The function of cosmological theology in the life of the pantheist is discussed in the second part.

1. PANTHEIST SODALITIES

In the years immediately following the publication of *Christianity Not Mysterious*—when Toland was still arguing for toleration of public polemic—he began to associate increasingly with other thinkers in roughly structured small groups or clubs. He did not refer explicitly to such groups until at least 1705, but he was charged with participation in secret group activity as early as the end of 1701.

Not long after Toland became recognized as a spokesman for Whig interests, Tory adversaries began to cite his participation in the Calves-Head Club, a secret club founded by Milton and others to honor the regicide of Charles I. Every January 30, it was said, the club would

2. For an example of how Toland has been misread on this point, see Hassan El Nouty, "Le panthéisme dans les lettres françaises au XVIIe siècle: Aperçus sur la fortune du mot et de la notion," *Revue des sciences humaines* 100 (1960): 435, 456.

gather, drinking wine from a calf's head, toasting those who had executed Charles I.[3]

Perhaps either because of his association with the republican ideas of Milton and Harrington or because of his contact with several radical Whigs of his own day, Toland seemed a likely candidate for such company. There is some weak circumstantial evidence that Toland might have belonged to a Whig coterie called the College, a coalition of Commonwealthmen and freethinkers who met at one of Toland's haunts, the Grecian Coffee House, on Devereaux Court in the Strand. It has been suggested that the College probably included Locke, his friends John Freke and Edward Clarke (a member of Parliament from Somerset), John Methuen (Lord Chancellor of Ireland), William Simpson (a baron of the Exchequer), Toland's friend and Irish benefactor Robert Molesworth, the Whig propagandists Thomas Rawlins and William Stephens, London merchant Sir Robert Clayton, John Darby and James Roberts (publishers of Whig propaganda), and the freethinker Matthew Tindal.[4] However, there is no strong evidence linking all these men, including Toland, to the College. Nowhere in Toland's writings does he refer to the Calves-head Club or the College. That he was publicly identified as a member of some such club—a charge he never denied—gives credence to the observation, though, that he had moved away from the indiscreet setting of the coffeehouse and tavern to the more secretive small group.[5]

To describe Toland's contact with small-group philosophic exchange, however, we must go back to the early 1690s and his meetings with members of the Lantern at Furly's house, in Rotterdam. Algernon Sidney, the republican theorist, had bequeathed to Furly a large silver goblet that was used as a loving cup "for drinking all round" at the meetings of this society.[6] Many of the members also frequented

---

3. See the anonymously written *Modesty Mistaken: or, a Letter to Mr. Toland, upon his declining to appear in the Ensuing Parliament* (London: J. Nutt, 1702), p. 8; and Jonathan Swift's *T-l-nd's Invitation to Dismal, to Dine with the Calves-Head Club* (broadside; London: Morphew, 1712). Also see Edward Ward, *The Secret History of the Calves-Head Clubb, or the Republican Unmasqu'd* (London: Booksellers of London and Westminster, 1703), pp. 6–9. (*The Secret History*'s author is also sometimes called Ned Ward.)

4. See Jacob, *Radical Enlightenment*, pp. 118, 151–52.

5. For more on the movement away from drawing rooms and taverns into clubs, see Franco Venturi, *Utopia and Reform*, p. 52; and Ashton, *Social Life*, pp. 179–84.

6. See Hull, *Furly and Quakerism*, pp. 77, 87.

gatherings of the Literary Society in Amsterdam, which had been founded by Locke, Limborch, and Le Clerc in 1686. Although these appear not to have been the societies Toland described as those of the pantheists, they had many of the same characteristics. The Lantern, the Literary Society in Amsterdam, the Calves-Head Club, the College, and the sodalities of the pantheists all shared the following: the free exchange of philosophic and literary ideas, political liberalism (even republicanism), secrecy, and even a communal drinking cup or feasting format. Whether Toland modeled the pantheist sodalities on these other small-group gatherings is a matter of conjecture. Similarly, circumstantial evidence and that found in *Pantheisticon* does not conclusively support the claim that the sodalities of the pantheists were forerunners of Freemason gatherings. The abundance of non-Masonic clubs with characteristics very similar to the sodalities of the pantheists, including semisecret groups that supported the work of the Royal Society, presents a problem for any claim that the pantheists were Freemasons.

The pantheist sodalities Toland described differ not only from the older, mid-seventeenth-century form of Masonry (e.g., by minimizing millenarian themes) but also from the new forms found in the Grand Masonic Lodge, established in London in 1717. For example, Toland described the pantheist sodalities as limited in size to the number of the Graces or the Muses; and unlike the Masons, they had no degrees of initiation and no substantially different internal positions or levels. The themes addressed by the pantheist sodalities were characteristic of Toland's republican ideals; of his identification of felicity with virtue; and of his beliefs in the vital universe described by Bruno, in the relationship between liberty and prejudice, and in the serenity of wisdom and vanity of fear of death. In short, to conclude that Toland's pantheists were Freemasons is to confuse *Freemasons* with *freethinkers*.[7]

Whether Toland was really a member of the Calves-Head Club or was simply accused of belonging to it in an attempt to discredit him also appears to be unanswerable at this time. Some allusions to the club imply that it had a rather mysterious character. Perhaps the reason for this is that members of such a secretive group might also have had occasion to discuss unusual and unorthodox doctrines (such as the Hermetic positions of Bruno). Toland expressed sympathy for the

7. See Giuntini, *Panteismo*, pp. 475–82, 489.

positions of Milton, told many of his interest in Bruno, referred on a number of occasions to the secrecy of the mechanic (or Masonic) trades, and professed to belong to a group of pantheists who held secrecy as a part of their doctrine. It is thus understandable that some of his readers would choose the economical interpretation that all these characteristics point to a single small group. But all that can legitimately be said is that Toland did appear to see great value in the freethinking discussions of the small groups of those he refers to as pantheists and that these discussions were not limited to particular topics and were thus open to political as well as cosmological or religious debates.

Throughout his life, Toland argued that men are sociable and have a natural tendency to unite in various societies "for their mutual Peace and Security against the Violence or Fraud of others."[8] This is a Hobbesian position: the prime motivation for social intercourse at large is mutual protection from the oppression of others. On this level, Toland maintained, good education and wholesome laws are the universal means for avoiding civil disruption.[9] On the small-scale level of the family or the small group, the formation of friendships or sodalities is more voluntary, particularly when they provide for the pleasure and instruction of the mind beyond the minimal education necessary for civil concord.[10] The sodalities of the pantheists provided a peaceful and secure setting for free and open discourse not available in the larger society.

Because of the restrictions placed upon promiscuous communication by prejudiced and intolerant elements in society, philosophically inclined thinkers like the pantheists had to resort to the formation of sodalities similar to those of ancient Greeks, characterized by free disputation, feasting, and fellowship.

Our age likewise has produced not a few, who, while feasting, desirous to dispute freely, and with less restraint, upon any topic whatsoever, instituted banquets, not unlike those of the SOCRATICS, and even called them, not improperly, SOCRATIC SODALITIES. Most of these are Philosophers, or, at least, very close to being Philosophers: bigotted to no one's position, nor led aside by education or custom, nor subservient to the religion and laws of their country;

8. *Apology*, pp. 13–14. Also see *Reasons for Naturalizing the Jews*, pp. 2–3.
9. "A Memorial to a Present Minister of State," in *Collection*, 2: 246.
10. *Pantheisticon*, pp. 9–10 (pp. 1–2).

they freely and impartially, in the silence of all prejudices, and with the greatest sedateness of mind, discuss and bring to a scrutiny all things, sacred (as the saying is) as well as prophane. They are called, for the most part, PANTHEISTS, on account of an opinion concerning GOD and the UNIVERSE, peculiar to themselves.[11]

In *Socinianism Truly Stated*, Toland indicated that the *system* of philosophy held by the pantheists reinforced their belief in the need for indifference in disputes.[12] Any philosophical thinker who freely and impartially discusses all things may well become a pantheist, in Toland's view, because of the methodological requirements inherent in nonprejudicial discourse. These requirements include the limitation of discussion to that which can be observed, at least in principle. Given such requirements, philosophic thinkers tend to develop a pantheistic system of cosmology. And because pantheistic cosmology describes all change in terms of the motions of bodies, there is no need for apprehension about death nor any reason to become disconcerted about disputes surrounding the events of one's life. "For your part, Reader, if you choose to follow REASON rather than CUSTOM, for your guide, you shall repute all human casualties to be placed on a level far beneath you; you shall patiently take up your lot, whatever it is; you shall keep at a distance from your foolish ambition and gnawing envy; you shall despise perishable honors, being to perish yourself in a short time; you shall lead a peaceable and pleasant life, neither admiring nor dreading anything."[13] A tranquil temperament and peace of mind follow from the adoption of a pantheistic attitude toward life, the universe, and God.[14]

When Toland suffered a major financial loss in the South Sea Bubble, he appealed to the tranquillity afforded him by his pantheistic beliefs. "I enjoy as profound a tranquillity, as if living in Arabia. And after all I think it the wisest course, at least the most becoming a Pantheist (who ought to be prepar'd for every caprice and reverse of fortune)."[15] Considering Toland's financial status throughout much of

---

11. Ibid., pp. 13–14 (p. 5).

12. P. 7.

13. *Pantheisticon*, p. 6 (p. iii).

14. Cf. Toland's translation of the prefatory dedication of Bruno's *Of the Infinite Universe and Innumerable Worlds*, in *Collection*, 2: 343–44. Also see *Socinianism Truly Stated*, p. 5.

15. Toland to Barnham Goode, 30 Oct. 1720, BM Add. MS 4295, fol. 39.

his life, it appears that his pantheistic beliefs must have provided him with solace on more than one occasion. In addition, these beliefs served the religious and social needs many freethinkers still had after giving up their confidence in some of the institutional forms of religion and social commerce.

One of the reasons sometimes given by modern scholars to explain why purely rational religions failed to become popular during and after Toland's lifetime is that they did not take into account human needs for the fellowship, the mysterious character, and the liturgical trappings of orthodox religions.[16] In the *Pantheisticon*, however, Toland described how pantheists united the use of reason with (*a*) feasting, from which fellowship followed, (*b*) secrecy, which followed from the doctrine of the exoteric-esoteric distinction, and (*c*) a philosophic canon, which served as part of a liturgy in pantheist sodalities. Each of these points contributed to the formation of pantheist sodalities as groups in which unrestricted philosophic discourse was encouraged and the appeal of elements of religious experience taken into account. In the *Pantheisticon* Toland recognized that even though reflective thinkers could attain an indifferent philosophic stance in dispute, they did not give up their basic human needs.

Toland's discussion of the pantheists often included references to their combining feasting and philosophy. In the tradition of the Platonic symposium, and as an essential part of forming a spirit of fellowship (often unattained in institutional religions), the sharing of a meal and sympathetic companionship became characteristics in the philosophic format of the pantheists. "It is a known observation, that there can never be any hearty fellowship, where people do'nt eat and drink together."[17] Pantheists came together in their sodalities "where they feast together, partaking of the sweetest kind of sauce, viz., philosophizing over the meal."[18] Philosophy complemented, rather than supplemented, the human need of fellowship and shared rejoicing embodied to some extent in all societies. The forms of interaction that hold men together in the most fundamental social groups became explicitly incorporated as part of the activities of pantheistic thinkers.

---

16. See, for example, Cragg, *From Puritanism to Age of Reason*, p. 154.
17. "Barnabas-Original," *Nazarenus*, p. 43.
18. *Pantheisticon*, p. 110 (p. 89).

Toland's manuscripts contain perhaps the earliest piece of information describing a proposed meeting of pantheists.[19] It is a record of a meeting, held on 24 September 1710, of the Knights of Jubilation (Chevaliers des Jubilations). The record neither includes Toland's name among those present nor is in his handwriting, but its description of the secrecy, fellowship, and feasting is similar to Toland's account of pantheist meetings.

Margaret Jacob's description of this record as referring to an early Masonic lodge appears to be very difficult to justify, given the possibility that pantheist sodalities may not have been the same as Masonic lodges.[20] Because the account is found among Toland's papers, Jacob assumes that he inaugurated a private Masonic lodge at The Hague sometime between 1708 and 1710. Admittedly, he was interested in establishing a social network for the clandestine exchange of ideas. That such contacts could properly be identified as Masonic, or even that Toland could be included among the Knights of Jubilation, would be conjecture. Jacob finds it odd that Pierre Desmaizeaux chose not to publish the manuscript among Toland's posthumous works (1726); but Desmaizeaux's action is understandable considering that Toland could have borrowed or even pirated this "extraordinary historical document" from its author, Prosper Marchand (bibliophile, manuscript collector, and French Huguenot refugee like Desmaizeaux). Jacob's attempt to draw ties between Toland and Freemasonry —even to the extent of attributing to him the *Letter From an Arabian Physician* (probably by Anthony Collins)—misses an important point made by Giuntini, namely, that the document appears to be a caricature or burlesque of a Masonic meeting rather than an authentic account.[21]

Rough parallels do appear between the development of Freemasonry and Toland's references to societies of pantheists. For example, in

19. BM Add. MS 4295, fols. 18–19.

20. See Jacob, "An Unpublished Record of a Masonic Lodge in England: 1710," *Zeitschrift für Religions- und Geistesgeschichte* 22 (1970): 168–71. Also see Jacob, "A *Magus* in the Scientific Age: An Interpretive Study of the Life and Thought of John Toland" (M.A. thesis, Cornell University, 1966), passim; and *Newtonians and the English Revolution*, p. 222. Cf. Lantoine, *Un précurseur de la franc-maçonnerie*, passim.

21. See Jacob, *Radical Enlightenment*, pp. 156–57, 193, 197, 267; and Giuntini, *Panteismo*, pp. 484–86. For some reason, Jacob pretends that she had not published the "Knights of Jubilation" document in 1970 and claims that it is first published in her 1981 work (which excludes the earlier article from the bibliography).

the *Letters to Serena* he noted that in most professions, "especially in those they repute Mechanick," members were sworn to secrecy.[22] But more often than not, their secrecy concerned only "very trivial matters"—unlike those issues with which pantheists dealt. Furthermore, pantheist sodalities were modeled on those societies of the Greeks and Romans established for the pleasure and instruction of the mind. Toland explicitly noted that these ancient sodalities were not corporations of merchants or artisans; nor were they the religious sodalities or political assemblies prohibited by law.[23] Toland seems to have implied that pantheist sodalities were also not groups of merchants or artisans, nor outlawed religious or political factions.

Toland did say that the pantheist sodalities had placed their See in London, which was also the location of the founding of the Grand Masonic Lodge, in 1717.[24] But the reference could also have been another of his portrayals of London as the "capital of the world" or as Cosmopolis. And even though he claimed that groups of pantheists could be found in London and Paris and throughout Holland, he did not explicitly state that *Pantheisticon* actually described a real group.[25] The work was intended, he said, to describe a mentality and a regimen that characterized the pantheists.

Pantheists engaged in friendly commerce with others and always sought to benefit from contact with virtuous and perceptive men with different views; however, they refused to become involved in the factious squabbles of political and religious partisans.[26] As partisans of the free and impartial development of knowledge, pantheists attempted to maintain an attitudinal distance from most people. For "the generality of mankind is averse to knowledge, and vents invectives against its partisans."[27] In this, Toland claimed to follow the advice of Seneca and Cicero: avoid the multitude, shun the vulgar; think with the philosophers, but talk like the people.[28] The pantheists' embrace of the exoteric-esoteric distinction might have been objectionable to some, prudence and discretion demanded it. By limiting his discussion of his secret philosophy to those "of consummate probity and

22. P. 11.
23. *Pantheisticon*, pp. 10–11 (p. 2).
24. Ibid., p. 58 (p. 42).
25. Ibid., pp. 108–10 (pp. 88–89).
26. Ibid., pp. 100–101 (p. 81).
27. Ibid., p. 4 (p. ii).
28. Seneca, *De Vita Beata*, chap. 2; Cicero, *Tusculan Disputations*, 2, chap. 1.

prudence," the pantheist not only protected himself from reprisals by the mob but also strengthened his fellowship with other learned men by openly sharing with them the secrets of esoteric philosophy. Until pantheists had complete liberty "to think as they please, and to speak as they think," none could risk his well-being by announcing that received theology swerved from truth in philosophic matters.[29]

A major section of *Pantheisticon* was devoted to describing the *liturgy* of the pantheists. The format of the pantheist symposium included formalized exchanges between the moderator of the sodality and other members, recitations from classical writers, hymns (e.g., to the universe), and a litany of ancient thinkers, including such philosophers as Thales, Anaximander, Democritus, Parmenides, and Confucius.[30] In the *Pantheisticon* Toland missed no opportunity to note that pantheist liturgy parodied the liturgies of institutional religions, even going so far as to print the exchanges of the moderator and respondents, found within the philosophical canon, in the form of alternating red and black lines as in the Anglican missal and the Book of Common Prayer.

Toland's purpose was not solely parodic, however. Indeed, to view the *Pantheisticon* as a parody is to overlook the seriousness with which its topics are treated and the selective distribution of the work after its printing. That he took the writing of a philosophic liturgy seriously is evidenced by the fact that he was at work on it as early as 1712.[31] In its final form, the pantheist liturgy indicated how even truly philosophic inquiry and discussion could occur within the structure of ritual.

As much as he objected early in his public life to the stifling effects of the ritualistic trappings of religion, Toland was never able to convince many of his contemporaries that ritualistic religion should be replaced by individualistic, totally reasonable forms of religion. Culminating in the liturgy found in the *Pantheisticon*, Toland's writings gradually revealed his recognition of the need for structure and ritual in religion. His early attacks against the attempts of divines and authoritarian church leaders to convince people of the mysteriousness of their beliefs were sustained in the *Pantheisticon*. But no longer was the burden of fault placed on the ritualistic structures used to promote superstition and prejudice; for by this time Toland realized that some types of

---

29. *Pantheisticon*, pp. 107–8 (pp. 86–87).
30. Ibid., pp. 64ff. (pp. 47ff). See Jacob, *Radical Enlightenment*, p. 153.
31. See Toland to Hohendorf, 7 Mar. 1712, BM Add. MS 4295, fol. 20.

ritual, such as found in pantheist liturgy, could actually promote fruitful philosophic thinking and discussion.

This shift in attitude toward liturgical and religious structures in general appeared in an almost startling way in Toland's *Destiny of Rome* (1718). Portraying himself as a "Divine of the Church of the First-born," Toland characterized this church as emphasizing the same elements of personal friendship, confidential communication, and open discourse found in the pantheist sodalities.[32] Here, though, the sodalities of the pantheists were raised to the status of a church. Writing in the form of a letter much like Saint Paul or Saint Peter,[33] Toland held himself up as an example of how an elder of the Church of the First-born should facilitate the projects of the church.

Why Toland called this group of pantheist sodalities "Church of the First-born" is somewhat unclear. Nothing in *The Destiny of Rome* gives any real indication of the first-born character of its members. But when understood in the context of the pantheist philosophy described in the *Pantheisticon*, the meaning of "first-born" becomes clearer.

Toland noted that the members of pantheist sodalities were philosophers "or those coming very near to being philosophers"—pantheists who had become wise "or at least very nearly possess wisdom."[34] Remembering that in pantheist metaphysics intelligence, as a metaphysical principle, is one step lower (so to speak) than the whole, or *Matter*, we realize that no thinker could hope to attain anything greater than the philosophic wisdom metaphysically characterized as the first-born of the whole, namely, intelligence. As long as we keep in mind that action, or motion, and intelligence complement one another as metaphysical principles, for Toland, we should not be tempted to try to determine which of the two precedes the other (as we would be if we pressed a neo-Platonic interpretation on him). If the philosopher is understood as having access to intelligence and wisdom, in their metaphysical sense, then he participates in the first-born status of the whole. If actually being a philosopher or attaining wisdom is beyond anyone's grasp, then those who at least come near to being philosophers or wise men might thus be considered the first-born.

---

32. *Destiny of Rome*, p. 4.

33. He ends with the typically apostolic remark, "All the First-born at Pella salute you" (ibid., p. 47).

34. *Pantheisticon*, pp. 14, 107 (pp. 5, 86).

2. THE RELIGIOUS CHARACTER OF PANTHEIST BELIEFS

The issue of the Church of the First-born drew Toland's attention away from the disputational, convivial, and liturgical characteristics of pantheist sodalities to the particularly religious character of their beliefs. His description of their emphasis on open and understandable communication portrayed their religion as simple, easy, and free of fables and superstition. Pantheists engaged in intellectual activity religiously, strenuously studying the very abstruse doctrines of others like themselves (e.g., the Druids).[35] They pursued certain intellectual disciplines, always with the purpose of applying their studies to practical activity.[36] The same applied to their consideration of "the divine" or of the transcendent in their lives. For the pantheist, religion united open philosophic discourse with metaphysical and cosmological speculation about the relationship of God and universe. The presence of men—discoursing, feasting, engaging in liturgical forms—more than any explicit thematic treatment, embodied Toland's approach to the explanation of how *man* fits into the relationship of God and universe. Their religion, in short, was fundamentally man-centered rather than God-centered.

Often in reading commentators on Toland—and indeed, sometimes in reading Toland himself—one gets the impression that there are really two Tolands: one, the author of *Christianity Not Mysterious*, firebrand of the deists, volatile spokesman for a natural religion based solely on reason; the other, the author of *Pantheisticon*, proponent of esoteric, pantheistic philosophy, sectarian supporter of a religion of nature.

For the most part, interpreters prefer to explain this difference by positing a development in Toland's thinking or a change in emphasis. Eugene Dyche, however, suggests a way in which the two pictures can be united. Toland's original purpose, according to Dyche, was to show that true religion must necessarily be reasonable. Any religion that is not reasonable must be based upon sectarian interests and prejudices; and criticism of those sectarian forms of religion in effect associates the

35. Ibid., pp. 94–95 (pp. 76–77). For more on the belief of English revolutionaries that a Druid republic highlighting indigenous paganism would restore freeborn Anglo-Saxons to self-governance, see Jacob, *Radical Enlightenment*, p. 154.

36. *Pantheisticon*, p. 106 (p. 86). Cf. *Nazarenus*, preface, p. xiv.

critic with yet another sect. A sect of philosophers—or partisans of knowledge—was thus established unintentionally, in the course of raising objections against the errant character of religious sects. The sect of philosophers professes an *exoteric* religion (deism) emphasizing restraint of ecclesiastical authority, need for religious toleration, and allowance for revealed and naturalistic religion. And it tends to support a materialistic and atomistic explanation of the universe while recognizing the need for a creator-god (i.e., the god of deism). However, the need to appeal to a creator-god is eliminated as the universal substance and force of matter come to be understood by this sect. It is this move beyond needing a creator-god that Dyche sees as the *esoteric* doctrine of the sect of philosophers.[37]

An interpretation like Dyche's seems to imply that this progression of thought almost has its own momentum, which sweeps up Toland and carries him along. But apart from its subordination of the individual, such an interpretation does provide a framework in which Toland's treatments of religion can be understood. With such an ideal in mind, we can note how Toland's early insistence upon the reasonableness of a religion already filled with natural and supernatural elements (Christianity) became supplanted in his later works by his demand that religion be based upon the practical interests of men living within nature.[38]

Instead of assuming the meaningfulness of that which transcends human existence, pantheist religion began by addressing the human need for considering the possibility of the transcendent. Pantheistic *worship* emphasizes discourse, feasting, and liturgy because it is based on the assumption that the focus of *religion* is not God but man. Religion is man's response to the need for addressing the transcendent in his life. But only to the extent that the transcendent is accessible and meaningful—a contradiction in terms, argued some of Toland's critics—can men engage in true religion.

As the pantheist emphasis on promiscuous communication made clear, religion is not an activity of a solitary individual. By placing importance on the meaningfully communicable character of religious beliefs, Toland restrained the attempts of some to undermine the

37. "Life and Works of Toland," pp. 290–95.
38. Cf. J. F. Nourrisson, *Philosophies de la nature: Bacon, Boyle, Toland, Buffon* (Paris: Perrin, 1887), p. 176.

essentially social character of religion. Through his description of the pantheist sodalities, Toland implied that unless religious philosophizing incorporated characteristics of ritual, conviviality, and communication, it would result in promoting atheism. The key to the religion of the pantheists, then, lay not in their theology but rather in their methodology.

Such a methodological concentration can present problems for the attempt to understand exactly what is meant by a *pantheist's* religion. If Toland's use of "pantheist" is taken to refer to someone who maintains that God and the universe are metaphysically distinct but cosmologically identical, then it seems that he was referring not to a religion at all but rather to a metaphysics or a cosmology. Indeed, in the *Pantheisticon* he cautioned against identifying his discussion of the pantheist sodalities with one about theology or theology-based religion: "it is a Philosophical, and not a Theological, description that is here given of the SODALITY (for it is one thing to explicate NATURE, and another to discourse on RELIGION)."[39] Underlying such a remark, though, was Toland's insistence that a philosophically accessible, man-centered, and humanly regulated religion was *natural*; whereas, a God-centered, theological religion was *supernatural*. God's actual transcendence of the universe made him inaccessible to any communal, publicly observable, and linguistically regulated religion. Theology could not replace natural, man-centered religion without forcing God outside all meaningful discourse. Toland intended to restrain the tendency of traditional theology and religion to emphasize God's transcendence. For if God were truly transcendent, he would have little concern for human affairs (as the common understanding of deism points out), and, more importantly for Toland, he would be inaccessible to man. The liturgical-religious format of *Pantheisticon*, combined with his references to the Church of the First-born, indicates that Toland did not reject religion or religious forms. He simply demanded that religion, and any god of religion, remain as accessible to men as anything else in nature.

Toland generally attempted to avoid using the word "pantheist" as a strictly methodological term to mean one who indifferently considers all theisms. In *Socinianism Truly Stated*, for example, he distinguished between the pantheists and those who were indifferent in disputes

---

39. P. 7 (p. iv).

(most of whom happen, however, to have been pantheists). As he noted in *Origines Judaicae* and in *Pantheisticon*, the pantheists not only adopted methods of promiscuous communication employed by indifferent disputants but also believed that nature, or the universe of things, and God were distinguished only by reason.[40]

The cosmological identification of God and universe was the only means of making God accessible to men. Using the testimony of the historian Strabo, Toland argued (reaffirming a claim by Bruno) that Moses himself was a pantheist in this regard. He noted that in more contemporary terms, Moses would be called a Spinozist, because of his description of the relationship of God and universe.[41] Furthermore, the Mosaic view had received endorsements from Ockham, Aquinas, and Cajetan.[42] Supported by the company of such respected thinkers, the pantheists, Toland believed, felt that they had ties with many of the ancients, with whom they shared a "Pantheistic world of philosophers and poets."[43]

Such a world united men of different times and places who shared in the ideals of promiscuous communication, serenity in disputes, and tranquillity in the face of adversity. Closely tied to one another and to their god, the pantheists Toland described no longer felt bound to a particular place and time. They were citizens of the cosmos, unrestricted by petty religious squabbles or political partisanship. The pantheistic ideal thus provided a point of convergence for Toland's interest in maintaining ties with the ancients while enjoying conversation and commerce with his contemporaries.

40. *Origines Judaicae*, p. 117; *Pantheisticon*, p. 18 (p. 8).

41. *Origines Judaicae*, p. 117.

42. *Pantheisticon*, p. 18 (p. 8). A possible source for Toland's point is Claudio Berigard's *Circulus Pisanus* (1661) (see Iofrida, "Il 'Pantheisticon'," p. 7).

43. *Origines Judaicae*, p. 109.

IX

Structure in Toland's Thought

IT MIGHT BE true that the ideal of the pantheist sodality served as a point of convergence for some of Toland's interests, but one could indeed be on shaky ground to claim that it was the *culmination* of his philosophic thinking. In the two years of his life remaining after the appearance of *Pantheisticon*, Toland continued to address many of the topics that had interested him throughout his life. But although engaged for the most part in research for his projected history of the Druids, the scheme of which was completed in 1718, he did not live long enough to produce another major work.

As did his earliest biographer, Edmond Curll, perhaps Toland recognized the need to allow more time to pass before commenting further on the 1720 publications (*Tetradymus* and *Pantheisticon*). He appears to have been little concerned to pull together the themes he had treated throughout his life into a magnum opus. His magnum opus was his life itself, because philosophy could not be limited to printed works: for him, philosophy is reflective living. Thus any treatment of Toland's philosophizing has to take into account his activities as well as his writings.

Because Toland treated certain topics intermittently and sometimes did not reveal any continuity in his thought, interpreters often have doubted whether his writing can really be said to have unity or direction. Many of his works appear to be products of a temporary interest, unrelated topically to his other works produced at or about the same time. Even his remark that civil liberty and religious toleration are the two major topics in all his writings appears, when applied in certain instances, to be a somewhat strained attempt to find unity in a multiplicity of topics and treatments.

If there is any indication of an overall unity in Toland's writings, it might be found at the end of *Pantheisticon,* where he included a translation of the first section of Cicero's first book of the *De Legibus.* The selection from Cicero serves as a guide to the movement within Toland's philosophy—if we can be so bold as to call it a philosophy. In the selection, Cicero describes the ideal man, the man unequaled in virtue and splendid in all his abilities. But instead of describing him as a finished product, Cicero gives the steps by which he attains the stature of *vir optimus et ornatissimus*; and it is this process that characterizes the development of Toland's thought.

Following the guidance of Cicero, Toland indicated that the topics that served as focal points for his writings were those the best or ideal man would address, and in roughly the same order. Themes in Toland's work were thus united by the idea of the man who excels in virtue and who is exceedingly well equipped to address both practical and speculative issues.

Toland appears to have valued this selection from Cicero, for he treated it uniquely. At twelve locations in the selection, he inserted words or phrases in the margin as keys for the student of Cicero and Toland alike. These remarks (italicized below) serve as the strongest indication that Toland saw his own life and thought as that of a philosopher, a searcher after wisdom. They also reveal how a representative thinker of the early eighteenth century attempted to implement the classical ideal of man.

Cicero begins the selection by noting that (*a*) *the knowledge of one's self* as a part of divine nature makes the *vir optimus* realize that his genius is consecrated. The mind of the individual, Toland similarly would have said, has an essential value and integrity that no deception or priestcraft could ever totally undermine. (*b*) When the individual thus knows himself, he will consider the *faculties of the mind* with which nature has provided him as the means by which he can attain wisdom. Correspondingly, Toland had claimed that his own ability to reason prompted him to the investigations of *Christianity Not Mysterious* in which he first described the acts of reason. (*c*) By means of his *ideas and notions,* one sees how he is to attain practical wisdom and thus happiness. And from an investigation of ideas and notions, Toland concluded that meaningful discourse is discourse accessible to the practical man, the politician, the merchant. (*d*) In attaining virtue, the best man seeks the companionship of others. The practice of *ethics,* for Toland, is the "practice of the world" in promiscuous communication.

(*e*) The best man piously worships the gods by means of true *religion* without yielding to superstition. The *prudentia* of the religious man, in Toland's view, rests in his foresight and prophetic abilities (*providentia*). (*f*) The best man examines the universe—*physics*—seeking to discover the origin and destiny of things both eternal and perishable—coming in the end (as Toland did in *Pantheisticon*) to a comprehension of the Being who guides and regulates all. (*g*) Eventually the best man realizes that he is a citizen of the whole world, not the citizen of one country or one city. The pantheist, according to Toland, is just such a practitioner of *cosmopolity*. (*h*) As he reaches this stage, Cicero continues, the best man will scorn the approbation of the mob, protecting his beliefs by means of *dialectic*, the ability to distinguish truth and falsity through the "art of understanding." Polemic—Toland's equivalent for this—tests whether beliefs can be meaningfully understood. (*i*) *Politics and Eloquence*: If equipped for public life, the best man will employ not only subtle persuasion but a broad and enduring kind of oratory by which he may sway the populace and establish laws, punish the wicked (for Toland: Harley), defend the good, and sing the praises of famous men (for Toland: Milton, Harrington). (*j*) In the *administration of the republic*, the ideal man will lay down rules of conduct that persuade his fellow citizens to aspire to glory and turn from disgrace—just as Toland had recommended rules for promiscuous communication among religious and political writers. (*k*) Through his accounts of *history*, the best man will comfort the afflicted (e.g., Dissenters, Jews) and record for everlasting recollection not only the deeds and counsels of the wise and brave (e.g., Bruno) but also the infamy of the wicked (e.g., Sacheverell or the priest-incited mobs who killed Hypatia of Alexandria). (*l*) Finally, this ideal man will recognize that wisdom is the mother of all of these powers in man—powers that can be developed by those who wish to know themselves. This *greatest wisdom* is thus the source and terminus of Toland's striving for philosophic wholeness. Together, these twelve points outline a program for mapping the development of wisdom in Toland's life.

The primary concern of my own presentation of Toland's philosophy has been to demonstrate how an attempt to understand his thought in a unified way might yield productive results if the concentration is on the methodological strains running throughout his writings rather than on particular topics such as liberty or toleration. Admittedly, individual subjects—such as biography, toleration, metaphysics, or the pantheist sodalities—arise from a wealth of material often spread widely throughout Toland's writings. And each of these topics contains its own peculiar methodological characteristics.

In each chapter, I have attempted to point out the special methodological characteristics of Toland's treatment of a particular topic. In doing so, I have not intended to give the impression that the techniques which he employs for one subject are applicable to others. In addition, my ordering of the chapters is meant to indicate how topics as disparate as metaphysics, polemic, and biography can be understood as parts of an overarching methodological pattern implicit in Toland's thought emphasizing the individual's capacity to think for himself.

Two types of methodological patterns emerge from such an approach: first, those addressing specific themes (as treated in individual chapters), and second, that pattern characterizing the overall thrust of the individual themes. With an awareness of these different patterns in Toland, readers interested in other seventeenth- and eighteenth-century thinkers might be able to obtain fresh insights without feeling impelled to carry over Toland's general philosophic methodology en masse.

One final word: To deny Toland recognition as a foremost philosopher is understandable; but to deny him recognition as an active, exhuberant, philosophic, and even systematic thinker is not. If Toland lacked originality in some areas of his thought, he surely made up for it in his comprehensiveness and in his attempt to weave together intricate political, religious, and philosophic themes.

Bibliography

PRIMARY SOURCES

Published Works by John Toland

An Account of the Courts of Prussia and Hanover. London: John Darby, 1705.
Adeisidaemon, sive Titus Livius a superstitione vindicatus. To which is added,"Origines Judaicae." The Hague: Thomas Johnson, 1709.
Amyntor; or a Defence of Milton's Life. London: Booksellers of London and Westminster, 1699.
Anglia Libera: or the Limitation and Succession of the Crown of England explain'd and asserted. London: Bernard Lintott, 1701.
An Apology for Mr. Toland. London, 1697.
An Appeal to Honest People Against Wicked Priests: or, The very Heathen Laity's Declarations for Civil Disobedience and Liberty of Conscience, contrary to the Rebellious and Persecuting Principles of some of the Old Christian Clergy; with an Application to the Corrupt Part of the Priests of this Present Time, publish'd on Occasion of Dr. Sacheverell's last Sermon. London: Booksellers of London and Westminster [1713].
The Art of Governing by Partys: particularly, in Religion, in Politicks, in Parliament, on the Bench, and in the Ministry. London: Bernard Lintott, 1701.
The Art of Restoring. 3rd ed. London: J. Roberts, 1714.
Christianity Not Mysterious: or, a Treatise Shewing that there is nothing in the Gospel Contrary to Reason, nor above it: and that no Christian Doctrine can be properly call'd a Mystery. 1st ed. (1696), with notes on the 2nd ed. corrections and additions. Edited by Günther Gawlick. Stuttgart–Bad Cannstatt: Friedrich Frommann, 1964.
Clito: A Poem on the Force of Eloquence. London: Booksellers of London and Westminster, 1700.
A Collection of Several Pieces of Mr. John Toland. Edited by Pierre Desmaizeaux. 2 vols. London: J. Peele, 1726.

The Declaration Lately Publish'd, In Favour of his Protestant Subjects, by the Elector Palatine. London: A. Baldwin, 1707.

A Defence of Mr. Toland in a Letter to Himself. London: E. Whitlock, 1697.

The Description of Epsom. London: A. Baldwin, 1711.

The Destiny of Rome: or, the Probability of the Speedy and Final Destruction of the Pope. Concluded partly, from natural reasons, and political Observations; and partly, on Occasion of the famous Prophesy of St. Malachy, Archbishop of Armagh, in the XIIIth Century. . . . In a Letter to a Divine of the Church of England, From a Divine of the Church of the First-Born. London: J. Roberts, 1718.

Dunkirk or Dover. London: A. Baldwin, 1713.

The Grand Mystery Laid Open: Namely, By dividing of the Protestants to weaken the Hanover Succession to extirpate the Protestant Religion. London: J. Roberts, 1714.

Her Majesty's Reasons for Creating the Electoral Prince of Hanover a Peer. London: A. Baldwin, 1712.

High-Church Display'd: Being a Compleat History of the Affair of Dr. Sacheverel. London, 1711.

The Jacobitism, Perjury, and Popery of High-Church Priests. London: J. Baker, 1710.

The Judgment of K. James the First, and King Charles the First, Against Non-Resistance. London: J. Baker, 1710.

A Letter to a Member of Parliament, Shewing that a restraint On the Press is inconsistent with the Protestant Religion. London: J. Darby, 1698.

Letter from Toland to Jean LeClerc on Daniel Williams's *Gospel Truth Stated and Vindicated. Bibliothèque universelle et historique,* 23 (1692): 504–9.

Letters to Serena. Edited, with an introduction to the 1704 original, by Günther Gawlick. Stuttgart–Bad Cannstatt: Friedrich Frommann, 1964.

"Lettre de Mr. Toland, sur le *Spaccio della bestia triomphante.*" *Nova Bibliotheca Lubecencis,* 5 (1754): 158–62.

"The Life of James Harrington." In *"The Oceana" of James Harrington, and his other works; som whereof are now first publish'd from his own manuscripts. The whole collected, methodiz'd, and review'd, with an exact account of his life prefix'd, by John Toland.* London: Booksellers of London and Westminster, 1700.

"The Life of John Milton." In *A Complete Collection of the Historical, Political, and Miscellaneous Works of John Milton.* Vol. 1. Amsterdam, 1698. Reprinted in *The Early Lives of Milton.* Edited by Helen Darbishire. London: Constable, 1932.

Memoirs of Denzil, Lord Holles. London: Tim. Goodwin, 1699.

Memoirs of Lieutenant General Ludlow, The Third and Last Part. [London: John Darby] 1699.

The Memorial of the State of England. London: Booksellers of London and Westminster, 1705.

The Militia Reform'd. London: John Darby, 1698.

Mr. Toland's Reflections on Dr. Sacheverelle's Sermon. London: J. Baker, 1710.

Nazarenus: or Jewish, Gentile, and Mahometan Christianity. Containing The History of the Antient Gospel of Barnabas . . . also The Original Plan of Christianity . . . with the Relation of an Irish Manuscript of the Four Gospels. London: J. Brown, 1718.

A New Edition of Toland's History of the Druids. Edited, with notes, by Robert Huddleston. Montrose: James Watt, 1814.

Pantheisticon: or, the Form of Celebrating the Socratic Society. Anonymous translation of Toland's Latin original. London: Sam Paterson, 1751.

Pantheisticon; sive Formula Celebrandae Sodalitatis Socraticae. Cosmopoli [London], 1720.

Propositions for Uniting the Two East India Companies; in a Letter to a Man of Quality, who desir'd the Opinion of a Gentleman not concern'd in either Company. London: Bernard Lintott, 1701.

Reasons for Addressing His Majesty to invite into England their Highnesses, the Electress Dowager and the Electoral Prince of Hanover. And Likewise, Reasons for Attainting and abjuring the pretended Prince of Wales. London: John Nutt, 1702.

Reasons for Naturalizing the Jews in Great Britain and Ireland, on the same foot with all other nations. Containing also, A Defence of the Jews against All vulgar Prejudices in all Countries. London: J. Roberts, 1714.

Reasons . . . Why . . . An Act for the better Securing the Dependency of the Kingdom of Ireland upon the Crown of Great-Britain, Shou'd not Pass into a Law. London: R. Franklin, 1720.

The Second Part of the State Anatomy of Great Britain. London: John Philips et al., 1717.

A Short Essay upon Lying. London: A. Moore, 1720.

Socinianism truly Stated, Being An Example of fair Dealing in all Theological Controversys. London, 1705.

Some Plain Observations Recommended to the Consideration of every Honest Englishman. N.p. 1705.

The State Anatomy of Great Britain. 4th ed. London: John Philips et al., 1717.

Tetradymus. Containing I. "Hodegus"; or the Pillar of Cloud and Fire, that Guided the Israelites in the Wilderness, not Miraculous. II. "Clidophorus"; or of the Exoteric and Esoteric Philosophy. III. "Hypatia"; or the history of a most beautiful . . . Lady, who was torn to pieces by the Clergy of Alexandria. . . . IV. "Mangoneutes"; being a defence of Nazarenus. London: J. Brotherton and W. Meadows, 1720.

Two Essays Sent in a Letter from Oxford to a Nobleman in London. The First Concerning some errors about the Creation, General Flood, and the Peopling of the World. In Two Parts. The Second concerning the Rise, Progress, and Destruction of Fables and Romances. London: R. Baldwin, 1695.

Vindicius Liberius: or M. Toland's Defence of Himself Against the Lower House of Convocation, and Others. London: Bernard Lintott, 1702.

Works Toland Translated, Edited, and Introduced

Boissat, Pierre de. *The Fables of Aesop.* Translated, with a preface, by Toland. London: Tho. Leigh and Dan. Midwinter, 1704.

Cicero, Quintus Tullius. *The Art of Canvassing at Elections.* Translated, with a preface, by Toland. London: J. Roberts, 1714.

Davanzati [Bostici], Bernardo. A Discourse upon Coins. Translated, with a preface, by Toland. London: Awnsham and John Churchill, 1696.

A Lady's Religion. Prefatory epistle by Toland. London: T. Warren, 1697.

LeClerc, Jean. *A Treatise on the Causes of Incredulity.* Translated, with a preface, by Toland. London: Awnsham and John Churchill, 1697.

Monk, George. *A Collection of Letters Written by His Excellency General George Monk.* Edited, with an introduction, by Toland. London: J. Roberts, 1714.

The Ordinances, Statutes, and Privileges of the Royal Academy, Erected by his Majesty the King of Prussia. Translated by Toland. London: John Darby, 1705.

Schiner, Matthew Cardinal. *A Phillipick Oration to Incite the English against the French.* Translated by Toland. London: Egbert Sanger and John Chantry, 1707.

Shaftesbury, third earl of (Anthony Ashley Cooper). *Letters from the Right Honourable The Late Earl of Shaftesbury to Robert Molesworth.* Edited, with an introduction, by Toland. London: J. Peele, 1721.

Sophie Charlotte of Prussia. *A Letter Against Popery.* Dedicatory letter by Toland. London: A. Baldwin, 1712.

Manuscripts by Toland

Bodleian Library (Oxford). "Livius Vindicatus." Rawlinson Coll., Cod. D. 377, fols. 132–39.

British Museum (now referred to as the British Library). (*a*) "A Collection of Miscellaneous Papers by John Toland." BM Add. MS 4465 (*b*) "Miscellaneous Letters and Papers by John Toland." BM Add. MS 4295. (*c*) Marginal and prefatory notes by John Toland in his copy of Martin Martin's *A Description of the Western Islands of Scotland.* 2nd ed. London: A. Bell, 1716. B.M. copy shelfmark, C. 45. c. 1.

Lambeth Palace Library (London). Letters concerning the Dissenters and toleration. Cod. Gibsoniani 930, fol. 229; and 933, fol. 8.

Public Record Office (London). Shaftesbury Papers, bundles 30/24/20, fols. 68 and 105; and 30/24/21, fols. 231, 237, 329–30.

Österreichische Nationalbibliothek (Vienna). (*a*) Autographen XLV. 83. (*b*) "Dissertations Diverses de Monsieur Tolandus," MS 10325. (*c*) "Varia Doctorum Vivorum de Jordano Bruno," MS 10390, fols. 374–99.

SECONDARY WORKS

Books

Ashton, John. *Social Life in the Reign of Queen Anne.* London: Chatto and Windus, 1919.

Bayle, Pierre. *Dictionnaire historique et critique*. 2nd ed. Rotterdam: Reinier Leers, 1702.
– *The Dictionary Historical and Critical of Mr. Peter Bayle*. 2nd ed. Edited by Pierre Des Maizeaux. Vol. 2. London: J. J. and P. Knapton et al., 1735.
– *Miscellaneous Reflections Occasion'd by the Comet*. Anonymous translation. 2 vols. London: J. Morphew, 1708.
Berthold, Gerhard. *John Toland und der Monismus der Gegenwart*. Heidelberg: Carl Winter, 1876.
Biddle, Sheila. *Bolingbroke and Harley*. New York: Alfred A. Knopf, 1974.
Brett, Thomas. *Tradition necessary to explain and interpret the Holy Scriptures ... with a Preface containing some remarks on Mr. Toland's "Nazarenus."* London: James Bettenham, 1718.
Browne, Peter. *A Letter in Answer to ... "Christianity Not Mysterious."* London: Robert Clavell, 1697.
Bruno, Giordano. *Concerning the Cause, Principle, and One*. Translated by Dorothea W. Singer. In *The Infinite in Giordano Bruno*, by S. Thomas Greenberg. New York: King's Crown Press, 1950.
– *On the Infinite Universe and Innumerable Worlds*. Translated by Dorothea W. Singer. In *Giordano Bruno: His Life and Thought*, by Dorothea W. Singer. New York: Henry Schuman, 1950.
Carabelli, Giancarlo. *Tolandiana: materiali bibliografici per lo studio dell'opera e della fortuna di John Toland*. Firenze: La Nuova Italia, 1975.
– *Tolandiana ... Errata, addenda e indici*. Ferrara: Universita de Ferrara, 1978.
Clarke, Samuel. *A Demonstration of the Being and Attributes of God*. London: William Botham, 1705.
– *Some Reflections on ... "Amyntor."* London: James Knapton, 1702.
Coward, William. *Second Thoughts concerning the Human Soul*. London: Richard Bassett, 1702.
Cragg, Gerald R. *From Puritanism to the Age of Reason*. Cambridge: Cambridge University Press, 1950.
Cudworth, Ralph. *The True Intellectual System of the Universe*. Edited by John Harrison. 3 vols. London: Thomas Tagg, 1845.
Curll, Edmond. *An Historical Account of the Life of Mr. Toland*. Bound as part of *The Theological and Philological Works of the late Mr. John Toland*. (This latter is a reprint of Toland's *Nazarenus*.) London: J. Mears, 1732 (first published in 1722).
Defoe, Daniel. *An Argument Proving that the Design of Employing and Enobling Foreigners, Is a Treasonable Conspiracy ... With an Appendix; wherein an insolent Pamphlet, Entitled, "The Anatomy of Great Britain," is* Anatomiz'd; *and it's Design and Authors detected and exposed*. London: Booksellers of London and Westminster, 1717.
Ellis, Frank H. Introduction to *A Discourse of the Contests and Dissentions Between the Nobles and the Commons in Athens and Rome*, by Jonathan Swift. Oxford: Clarendon Press, 1967.

–, ed. *Jonathan Swift: A Discourse on Contests and Dissentions*. Oxford: Clarendon Press, 1967.

– ed. *Poems of Affairs of State*. Vol. 6. New Haven: Yale University Press, 1970.

Erman, J.-P. *Mémoires pour servir à l'histoire de Sophie Charlotte, Reine de Prusse*. Berlin: G. F. Starke, 1801.

Fiddes, Richard. *Remarks on the "State Anatomy of Great Britain."* London: J. Morphew, 1717.

Frantz, R. W. *The English Traveller and the Movement of Ideas, 1660–1732*. Lincoln, Neb.: University of Nebraska Press, 1967.

Garin, Eugenio. *L'Illuminismo Inglese: I Moralisti*. Milan: Fratelli Bocca, 1942.

Geikie, Sir Archibald. *The Founders of Geology*. London: Macmillan and Co., 1897.

Giuntini, Chiara. *Panteismo e ideologia repubblicana: John Toland (1670–1722)*. Bologna: Il Mulino, 1979.

Hanson, Laurence. *Government and the Press 1695–1763*. London: Oxford University Press, 1936.

Hefelbower, S. G. *The Relation of John Locke to English Deism*. Chicago: University of Chicago Press, 1918.

Historical Manuscripts Commission. *The Manuscripts of His Grace, the Duke of Portland*. Vols. 2, 4, 5, 7, and 8. London: Her Majesty's Stationery Office, 1893–1907.

Holmes, Geoffrey. *Religion and Party in Late Stuart England*. Historical Association General Series Pamphlet no. 86. London: The Historical Association, 1975.

Hull, William I. *Benjamin Furly and Quakerism in Rotterdam*. Swarthmore College Monographs on Quaker History, no. 5. Lancaster, Pa.: Lancaster Press, 1941.

Hume, David. *The Natural History of Religion*. Edited by H. E. Root. London: Adam and Charles Black, 1956.

Hunt, John. *Religious Thought in England from the Reformation to the End of the Last Century*. Vol. 2. London: Strahan and Co., 1871.

Jacob, Margaret C. *The Newtonians and the English Revolution, 1689–1720*. Ithica, N.Y.: Cornell University Press, 1976.

– *The Radical Enlightenment: Pantheists, Freemasons, and Republicans*. London: George Allen and Unwin, 1981.

Kemble, John M., ed. *State Papers and Correspondence Illustrative of the Social and Political State of Europe from the Revolution to the Accession of the House of Hanover*. London: John W. Parker and Son, 1857.

Kümmel, Werner Georg. *The New Testament: The History of the Investigation of Its Problems*. Translated by S. McLean Gilmour and Howard C. Kee. Nashville, Tenn.: Abington Press, 1972.

Lantoine, Albert. *Un précurseur de la franc-maçonnerie: John Toland, 1670–1722*. Paris: Librairie Critique Émile Nourry, 1927.

Lechler, Gotthard Victor. *Geschichte des Englischen Deismus.* Forward and bibliography by Günther Gawlick. Hildesheim: Georg Olms, 1965.

Lecky, W. E. H. *History of the Rise and Influence of the Spirit of Rationalism in Europe.* 2 vols. Rev. ed. New York: D. Appleton and Co., 1925.

Leibniz, Gottfried Wilhelm. *Opera Omnia.* Vols. 5 and 6. Edited by Ludovici Dutens. Geneva: Fratres de Tournes, 1768.

– *Die Philosophischen Schriften von Gottfried Wilhelm Leibniz.* Vols. 3 and 6. Edited by C. I. Gerhardt. Reprint of the 1875–90 edition. Hildesheim: Georg Olms, 1960.

– *Die Werke von Leibniz.* Series 1, vols. 8, 9, 10. Edited by Onno Klopp. Hanover: Klindworth, 1873–77.

Leroy, André. *La Critique et la religion chez David Hume.* Paris: Félix Alcan, 1930.

Lillywhite, Bryant. *London Coffee Houses.* London: George Allen and Unwin, 1963.

Locke, John. *The Correspondence of John Locke.* Edited by E. S. De Beer. Oxford: Clarendon Press, 1976–.

– *The Correspondence of John Locke and Edward Clarke.* Edited by Benjamin Rand. Cambridge, Mass.: Harvard University Press, 1927.

– *Epistola de Tolerantia; A Letter on Toleration.* Edited and translated by Raymond Klibansky and J. W. Gough. Oxford: Clarendon Press, 1968.

– *Essay concerning Human Understanding.* Edited by Peter H. Nidditch. Oxford: Clarendon Press, 1975.

– *Original Letters of Locke; Algernon Sidney; and Anthony Lord Shaftesbury.* Edited by Thomas I. M. Forster. London: J. B. Nichols and Son, 1830.

– *The Reasonableness of Christianity.* Edited by George W. Ewing. Chicago: Henry Regnery Co., 1965.

– *Several Papers relating to Money, Interest, and Trade.* New York: Augustus M. Kelly, 1968.

– *The Works of John Locke.* Vols. 9 and 10. London: Thomas Tegg et al., 1823.

McInnes, Angus. *Robert Harley, Puritan Politician.* London: Gollancz, 1970.

McLachlan, H. J. *Socinianism in Seventeenth Century England.* Oxford: Oxford University Press, 1951.

Mangey, Thomas. *Remarks Upon Nazarenus.* London: William and John Innys, 1718.

Metzger, Hélène. *Attraction universelle et religion naturelle chez quelques commentateurs anglais de Newton.* Paris: Hermann et Cie, 1938.

Modesty Mistaken: or, a Letter to Mr. Toland, upon his declining to appear in the Ensuing Parliament. London: J. Nutt, 1702.

Mosheim, J. L. *De Vita, fatis, et scriptis Joannis Tolandi Commentatio.* Added to the 2nd ed. of Mosheim's *Vindiciae antiquae Christianorum disciplinae, adversus celeberrimi viri Jo. Tolandi, Hiberni, Nazarenum.* Hamburg: Benjamin Schiller, 1722.

Mossner, Ernest C. *Bishop Butler and the Age of Reason.* New York: Macmillan, 1936.

Motzo Dentice de Accadia, Cecilia. *Preilluminismo e deismo in inghilterra*. Naples: Libreria Scientifica Editrice, 1970.

Muff, Margrit. *Leibnizens Kritik der Religions-philosophie von John Toland*. Affoltern am Albis: Buchdruckerei Dr. J. Weiss, 1940.

Newcombe, Thomas, ed. *The Life of John Sharp*. Vol. 1. London: C. and J. Rivington, 1825.

Noack, Ludwig. *Die Freidenker in der Religion*. First part, *Die Englische Deisten*. Bern: Jent and Reinhert, 1853.

Norris, John. *An Account of Reason and Faith*. London: S. Manship, 1697.

Nourrisson, J. F. *Philosophies de la Nature: Bacon, Boyle, Toland, Buffon*. Paris: Perrin, 1887.

O'Higgins, James, S. J. *Anthony Collins: The Man and His Works*. The Hague: Martinus Nijhoff, 1970.

Piggott, Stuart. *William Stukeley: An Eighteenth-Century Antiquary*. Oxford: Clarendon Press, 1950.

Pocock, J. G. A. Introduction to *The Political Works of James Harrington*. Cambridge: Cambridge University Press, 1977.

Redwood, John. *Reason, Ridicule and Religion: The Age of Enlightenment in England 1660–1750*. Cambridge, Mass.: Harvard University Press, 1976.

Sabetti, Alfredo. *John Toland, un irregolare della societá e della cultura Inglese tra seicento e settecento*. Naples: Liguori, 1976.

Sayous, Edouard. *Les déistes anglais et le christianisme principalement depuis Toland jusqu'à Chubb (1696–1738)*. Paris: G. Fischbacher, 1882.

Seeber, Anna. *John Toland als politischer Schriftsteller*. Schramberg-Württenberg: Gatzer and Hahn, 1933.

Shaftesbury, third earl of (Anthony Ashley Cooper). *Characteristicks of Men, Manners, Opinions, Times*. 3 vols. London: [John Darby], 1711. Without authorization, Toland published part of an earlier version of this work as *An Inquiry Concerning Virtue*. London: A. Bell, 1699.

Sophie Charlotte, Queen of Prussia. *Briefe der Königin Sophie Charlotte von Preussen und der Kurfürstin Sophie von Hannover an Hannoversche Diplomaten*. Edited by Richard Doebner. Publication aus den k. Pruessischen Staatsarchiven, vol. 79. Leipzig: S. Hirzel, 1805.

Stephen, Leslie. *History of English Thought in the Eighteenth Century*. 3rd ed. 2 vols. 1902 Reprint. New York: Peter Smith, 1949.

Sullivan, Robert E. *John Toland and the Deist Controversy*. Cambridge, Mass.: Harvard University Press, 1982.

Swift, Jonathan. *Toland's Invitation to Dismal to Dine with the Calves-Head Club*. Broadsheet. Signed December 1711.

Thorschmid, Urban Gottlob. *Vollständige Engländische FreydenkerBibliothek*. Vols. 3 and 4. Cassel: Johann Friedrich Hemmerde, 1766–67.

Twynam, Ella. *John Toland: Freethinker, 1670–1722*. Privately published by David Low Emmington, 1968.

Venturi, Franco. *Utopia and Reform in the Enlightenment*. Cambridge: Cambridge University Press, 1971.

Ward, Edward. *The Secret History of the Calves-Head Clubb, or the Republican Unmasqu'd*. London: Booksellers of London and Westminster, 1703.

Willis, Richard. *Reflexions upon Mr. Toland's Book, Called "Christianity Not Mysterious."* The Occasional Paper, no. 3. London: M. Wotton, 1697.

Winnett, Arthur R. *Peter Browne: Provost, Bishop, Metaphysician*. London: Camelot Press, 1974.

Wodrow, Robert. *The History of the Sufferings of the Church of Scotland from the Restoration to the Revolution*. Vol. 4. Glasgow: Blackie, 1835.

Wotton, William. *A Letter to Eusebia*. London: Tim. Goodwin, 1704.

Yolton, John W. *John Locke and the Way of Ideas*. Oxford: Clarendon Press, 1968.

Articles

Aquilecchia, Giovanni, "Nota su John Toland traduttore di Giordano Bruno." *English Miscellany* 9 (1958): 77–86.

— "Scheda bruniana: la traduzione 'tolandiana' dello *Spaccio*." *Giornale storico della letteratura italiana* 152 (1975): 311–13.

Barzilay, Isaac E. "John Toland's Borrowings from Simone Luzzato." *Jewish Social Studies* 31 (1969): 75–81.

Biddle, John, C. "Locke's Critique of Innate Principles and Toland's Deism." *Journal of the History of Ideas* 37 (1976): 411–22.

Carabelli, Giancarlo. "Un inedito di John Toland: Il *Livius Vindicatus*, orvero la prima edizione (mancata) dell'*Adeisidaemon* (1709)." *Rivista critica di storia della filosofia* 31 (1976): 309–18.

— "John Toland e G. W. Leibniz: Otto Lettere." *Revista critica di storia della filosofia* 29 (1974): 412–31.

Casini, Paolo. "Toland e l'attività della materia." *Rivista critica di storia della filosofia* 22 (1967): 24–53.

Colie, Rosalie L. "Spinoza and the Early English Deists." *Journal of the History of Ideas* 20 (1959): 23–46.

Crocker, Lester G. "John Toland et le matérialisme de Diderot." *Revue d'histoire littéraire de la France* 53 (1953): 289–95.

Daniel, Stephen H. "Political and Philosophical Uses of Fables in Eighteenth-Century England." *The Eighteenth Century: Theory and Interpretation* 23 (1982): 151–71.

Dudon, Paul. "John Toland fût-il un précurseur de la franc-maçonnerie?" *Etudes* 204 (1930): 51–61.

Dussinger, John A. "'The Lovely System of Lord Shaftesbury': An Answer to Locke in the Aftermath of 1688?" *Journal of the History of Ideas* 42 (1981): 151–58.

Dyche, Eugene I. "The Life and Works and Philosophical Relations of John (Janus Junius) Toland, 1670–1722." *Abstracts of Dissertations, the University of Southern California* (1944), 64–69.

Emerson, R. L. "Heresy, the Social Order, and English Deism." *Church History* 37 (1968): 389–403.

El Nouty, Hassan. "Le panthéisme dans les lettres françaises au XVIIe siècle: Aperçus sur la fortune du mot et de la notion." *Revue des sciences humaines* 100 (1960): 435–57.

Firpo, Massimo. "Il rapporto tra socinianismo e primo deismo inglese negli studi di uno storico polacco." *Critica storica* 10 (1973): 243–98.

Flam, L. "De Toland à d'Holbach." *Tijdschrift voor de studie van Verlichting* 1 (1973): 33–54.

Gawlick, Günther. "Cicero and the Enlightenment." *Studies on Voltaire and the Eighteenth Century* 25 (1963): 657–82.

Giuntini, Chiara. "Toland e Bruno: ermetismo 'rivoluzionario'?" *Rivista di filosofia* 66 (1975): 199–235.

Heinemann, F. H. "John Toland and the Age of Enlightenment." *Review of English Studies* 20 (1944): 125–46.

– "John Toland and the Age of Reason." *Archiv für Philosophie* 4 (1950): 35–66.

– "John Toland, France, Holland, and Dr. Williams." *Review of English Studies* 25 (1949): 346–49.

– "Prolegomena to a Toland Bibliography." *Notes and Queries* 185 (1943): 182–86.

– "Toland and Leibniz." *Philosophical Review* 54 (1945): 437–57.

Hunt, John. "John Toland." *Contemporary Review* 8 (1868): 178–98.

Iofrida, Manlio. "Il 'Pantheisticon' di John Toland." *Rivista critica di storia della filosofia* 36 (1981): 3–28.

Jacob, Margaret Candee. "John Toland and the Newtonian Ideology." *Journal of the Warburg and Courtauld Institutes* 32 (1969): 307–31.

– "An Unpublished Record of a Masonic Lodge in England: 1710." *Zeitschrift für Religions- und Geistesgeschichte* 22 (1970): 168–71.

Kuhn, Albert J. "English Deism and the Development of Romantic Mythological Syncretism." *PMLA* 71 (1956): 1094–1116.

Maitland, S. R. "Toland." *Notes and Queries*, ser. 3, 1 (1862): 6–7.

Massa, Daniel. "Giordano Bruno's Ideas in Seventeenth Century England." *Journal of the History of Ideas* 38 (1977): 227–42.

Mautner, Franz H. "Noch ein Wort zu 'Amintor'." *Deutsche Vierteljahrsschrift für Literaturwissenschaft und Geistesgeschichte* 32 (1958): 111–12.

Meyer, H. F.. "Reply to William C. Wright's 'Pierre Desmaizeaux, John Toland and a Pirated Publication of Shaftesbury's *A Letter Concerning Design*'." *Notes and Queries* 219 (1974): 471.

Nicholl, H. F. "John Toland: Religion without Mystery." *Hermathena* 100 (Summer 1965): 54–65.

Ognowski, Zbigniew. "Le 'Christianisme sans mystères' selon John Toland et les sociniens." *Archiwum Historii Filozofii i Myśli Spolecznej* 12 (1966): 205–23.

Patrick, David. "Two English Forerunners of the Tübingen School: Thomas Morgan and John Toland." *Theological Review* 14 (1877): 562–603.

Reedy, Gerard, S.J. "Socinians, John Toland, and the Anglican Rationalists." *Harvard Theological Review* 70 (1977): 285–304.

Ricuperati, Giuseppi. "Libertinismo e Deismo a Vienna: Spinoza, Toland e il 'Triregno'." *Rivista storica italiana* 79 (1967): 628–95.

Schneer, C. "The Rise of Historical Geology in the Seventeenth Century." *Isis* 45 (1954): 256–68.

Simms, J. G. "John Toland (1670–1722), a Donegal Heretic." *Irish Historical Studies* 16 (1969): 304–20.

Weiner, Max. "John Toland and Judaism." *Hebrew Union College Annual* 16 (1941): 215–42.

Worden, Blair. "Edmund Ludlow: The Puritan and the Whig." *Times Literary Supplement*, 7 January 1977, pp. 15–16.

Wright, William C. "Pierre Desmaizeaux, John Toland and a Pirated Publication of Shaftesbury's *A Letter Concerning Design*." *Notes and Queries* 219 (1974): 49–51.

Other Materials

Bodleian Library Oxford. Assorted MS letters by Edmund Gibson, Thomas Hearnes, Edward Llwyd, and Elisha Smith, relating to Toland. (*a*) Ballard 5, fols. 27, 46–58. (*b*) Lister 36, fol. 90. (*c*) Rawlinson C. 146; Rawlinson D. 401 (fol. 30) and D. 923.

Burnett, Gail Allen. "The Reputation of Cicero Among the English Deists (1696–1776)." Ph.D. diss., University of Southern California, 1947.

Candee (Jacob), Margaret Catherine. "A *Magus* in the Scientific Age: An Interpretive Study of the Life and Thought of John Toland." M.A. thesis, Cornell University, 1966.

Dienemann, Wolfgang. "A Bibliography of John Toland (1670–1722)." Thesis in librarianship, University of London, 1953.

Dyche, Eugene I. "The Life and Works and Philosophical Relations of John (Janus Junius) Toland (1670–1722)," Ph.D. diss., University of Southern California, 1944.

Evans, Robert R. "John Toland's Pantheism: A Revolutionary Ideology and Enlightenment Philosophy." Ph.D. diss., Brandeis University, 1965.

Glasgow, University of. Archives Office, Principal's Memorandum Book, 1684–1702 (Archives no. 26630).

Lambeth Palace Library, London. MS letters from Arthur Charlett, Stephen Nye, Will Simpson, and Thomas Tennison, relating to Toland. (*a*) Misc. Coll. MSS 933, 6; 942, 110; 953, fols. 64, 79. (*b*) Codex Gibsoniani MS 933, 74.

National Library of Scotland, Edinburgh. Letter by James Fall, Principal of the College of Glasgow, MS 9251, fols. 150–51.

Nicholl, H. F. "The Life and Work of John Toland." Ph.D. diss., Trinity College, University of Dublin, 1962.

Rechtien, John G. "Thought Patterns: The Commonplace Book as Literary Form in Theological Controversy during the English Renaissance." Ph.D. diss., St. Louis University, 1975.

Williams, James. "An Edition of the Correspondence of John Aubrey with Anthony à Wood and Edward Llwyd, 1667–1696, with Introduction and Notes." Ph.D. diss., University of London, 1969.

Index